# A KNIGHT OF ANOTHER SORT

Shawnee Classics: A Series of Classic Regional Reprints for the Midwest

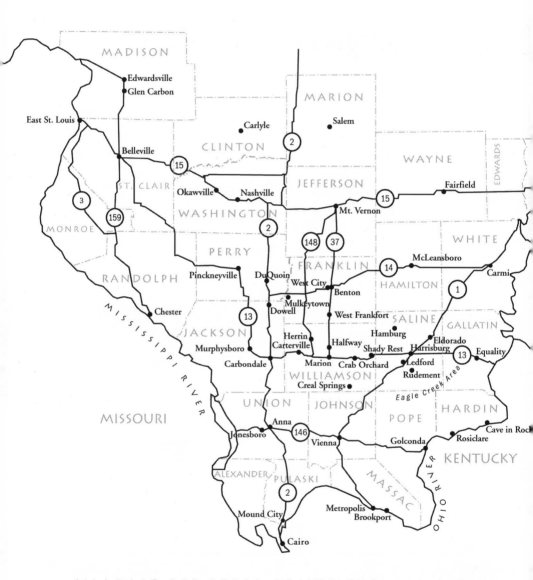

CHARLIE BIRGER'S SOUTHERN ILLINOIS

# A Knight of
# Another Sort:
# Prohibition Days
# and
# CHARLIE BIRGER

## GARY DeNEAL
### With a Foreword by Jim Ballowe

SECOND EDITION

Southern Illinois University Press
Carbondale and Edwardsville

Library of Congress Cataloging-in-Publication Data
DeNeal, Gary, 1944–
    A knight of another sort : prohibition days and Charlie Birger / Gary DeNeal ;
       with a foreword by Jim Ballowe. — 2nd ed.
       p.   cm.
    Originally published: Danville, Ill. : Interstate Printers & Publishers,
       c1981.
    Includes bibliographical references and index.
    1. Birger, Charlie, 1880–1928. 2. Murder—Illinois—Case studies.
       3. Murderers—Illinois—Biography. 4. Prohibition—Illinois.
       I. Title.
    HV6248.B56D46   1998
    364.15′23′092—dc21
    [b]
    ISBN 0-8093-2216-1 (cloth : alk. paper)           98-12837
    ISBN 0-8093-2217-X (pbk. : alk. paper)           CIP

To Judy who urged me to write it

IN A JEWISH CEMETERY IN UNIVERSITY CITY, MISsouri, a small stone bears the name of Shachna Itzik Birger. To motorists on the street nearby, the name means nothing. That "Shachna Itzik" made headlines in the days when getting high meant sipping bathtub gin in the back seats of Model T's might be of passing interest to some of them, especially if they were also told that "back then" he was better known as Charlie Birger. Even so, to most Missourians, this Charlie Birger is a shadowy someone mentioned by grandparents.

Far across the river in southern Illinois counties of Williamson, Franklin, and especially, Saline, Birger is anything but a dim figure from the past. He is as nearly a legend as that region has produced. While smarter and better men "made good" only to be forgotten by their grandchildren's generation, this gangster is remembered and will be remembered for a long time to come. Blame that on his good looks, his charm, and his violent career that inevitably ended in tragedy. But save some blame for the general "cussedness" of human nature. Despite our protests to the contrary, we cherish our misfits, seeing in them mirror images of the selves we dare not reveal.

# Contents

CONTENTS

CONTENTS

# Illustrations

# Foreword

Well, there he stood on the sanded floor, a medium-sized wiry man in his early forties, but not looking a day over thirty. He was dressed, as always, in a soft brown leather coat and riding breeches. These latter were made for him by one of Chicago's best tailors, and did credit to both cutter and wearer. A leather hunting-cap perched on his thick black hair. Brightly polished yellow army boots and jingling, sparkling spurs completed his romantic make-up.

W HEN BALTIMORE SUN REPORTER W. A. S. DOUGLAS DREW this portrait of a jaunty Charlie Birger for an obituary essay in the *American Mercury* in August of 1928, his subject had been dead for some four months and Douglas was remembering Charlie's improbable presence of over a year before when he had seen him in a roadhouse deep in southern Illinois.[1] A veteran reporter of international events, Douglas was not given to useless superlatives. Still, Charlie's looks and character required broad strokes to contain the exotic posturings of the man. Douglas thought Charlie to be a "dead ringer for Tom Mix" in those post–World War I silent movies. Charlie apparently believed this, too. But while Douglas found Charlie to be charismatic, he also knew that he was unsettlingly sinister.

A significant part of Charlie wanted adulation and rewards for what he did, but what he did better than anything else was to rob and kill people. It seems the more he wished to be known as a solid citizen, the more gruesome his actions became. Like many of his ilk who were virtually created by the Eighteenth Amendment and the Volstead Act that implemented it, Charlie Birger was a servant of the public's thirst for both liquor and drama in an otherwise dry and colorless era. Douglas and many successors have contributed to the legend, which today has taken on a life of its own with multiple interpretations.[2] As with other successful mobsters of the twenties who were empowered by their willingness to exert brutality but were made weak by their own psychical fragility, Charlie was a cynosure in one instant and a predator the next. Gary DeNeal tells us in this biography that doing good was but a thin cover for Charlie's dominant nature, which was to prey on others. Toward the end of his life, he fixated on protecting himself from his enemies, both real and imagined, and thus he brought about his own destruction.

The person described in Douglas's essay is a consummate actor, a man who more than others around him had developed a persona, believed in it, and perfected it. Even so, the outrageous invention that was Charlie Birger was not his doing alone. The communal reputation of those who lived in deep southern Illinois had been scarred by the horrific events of the Herrin Massacre that took place on June 22, 1922, in which twenty strikebreakers were complicitously murdered by a crowd of miners and no case could be made to convict any of the perpetrators or conspirators. Then an ignorant and clumsy attempt to show the world that the region (in particular Williamson County, where Charlie Birger set up his operations) could become culturally sanitized of immigrants and liquor resulted in the demagoguery of the Ku Klux Klan. The plan was demented from the outset, but competing criminals found in the Klan a common foe, and Charlie Birger, whose career had been in stasis within the poor mining communities of southern Illinois, discovered his professional niche. In the next five years, he would help engineer the death of the Klan's leader, spend six months in jail for bootlegging, become a partner and then an antagonist of the notorious Shelton brothers in a slot machine enterprise, lend his gang to help in the decisive defeat of the Klan in a noon-day gun battle on the streets of Herrin, Illinois, be responsible directly or indirectly for the murders of at least a dozen people, many of whom had been his loyal followers, and, finally, spend the last year of his life in a turn-of-the-century county jail awaiting his execution for the murder of one of his most inconsequential but most hated enemies, Joe Adams, the mayor of West City, car salesman and colleague of the Sheltons with whom Birger had gone to war.

Even as his heinous crimes were recounted at his trial and while he languished in jail, Charlie's reputation grew. Likely, the citizenry of southern Illinois found in him the ultimate example of independence from the law that some of them had practiced for nearly a decade. The fine spring morning Charlie Birger died, uttering "It is a beautiful world," may have been the first time many citizens of the area were persuaded that operating outside of law and order is not always rewarded. A little over a year later, the crash signaling the Great Depression was heard from afar by these same citizens, for their economy had already been decimated and their collective morality severely damaged by the Massacre, the Klan, and the gang wars, a feast of evil large enough to have engorged the nation's passion for blood, but for which the nation, once satiated, had proscribed the region and its inhabitants.

Upon this stage of recurring horror lived many innocent people whose lives were not only affected economically and physically but also intruded upon in more subtle and lasting ways. A case in point is the final Klan and gang encounter, which took place on the streets of Herrin, the central location for some of the most horrendous events of this period. On a balmy spring election day, April 13, 1926—four years after the Herrin Massacre and two years preceding his execution—Charlie Birger gave notice that he had the gun power and the willingness to use it to eradicate any force that threatened his operation. In the process, he and his henchmen demonstrated how heedless they were of accidental bystanders. Just thirteen months earlier, Seth Glenn Young, the hypocritical goad of the Klan, had been killed in a shoot-out in Herrin, along with his own killer and two other men. Some Klansmen thought that showing their resolve on Election Day would be a way to prove to the town that they were still in charge. But Charlie and his confederates among the Shelton gang decided that this would be the opportunity to rid their territory once and for all of Klan influence.

The main polling place in this town of ten thousand was located at a prominent intersection at which stood three iconographic institutions: to the southwest, the hospital that had been shot up by the Klan some months earlier; to the northwest, the Masonic Temple that harbored the poll; and to the northeast, the southern Baptist church whose minister had been one of the town's leaders who welcomed the Klan as a godsend. On this day, women and men and a few children came and went under the watchful eye of the Klan. Known Catholics (principally of Italian descent) were intimidated as they passed by Klan members. My mother, then twenty, had just delivered lunch to my grandmother, a poll clerk.[3] As she stood inside the temple, she heard the staccato of machine-gun fire. There was brief panic before all the women inside rushed toward a back room. A Klansman, mortally wounded, crawled toward the hall, leaving a trail of blood. In minutes the church and the Masonic Temple lawns, facing one another, were transformed into gardens of carnage. Six men, three gangsters and three Klansmen, lay dead or dying.

Moments later, three blocks away, a fourteen-year-old girl (who later became my aunt) stood on her family's front lawn. A car carrying several young men drove around the corner with no apparent urgency. My aunt, a portrait and landscape painter and teacher with an eidetic memory even now into her mid-eighties, recalls how the doors of the four-door car were open on her side. On each seat a man sat facing the curb, feet on the running board, white socks flashing. Both wore a dark suit and hat, dressed for business. One held a rifle, the other a Thompson submachine gun. They were laughing boisterously as if having just shared in a good joke.

Such are the memories of childhood given to those into whose lives the errant and aberrant knight Charlie Birger came. The life that Charlie Birger lived—immigrant child, newspaper boy, soldier, broncobuster, miner, father, sometime husband, ice cream store owner, profligate, savage murderer—was repeated with modifications by hoodlum role models throughout the country, most notably, of course, by Al Capone. And like many of them his life keeps nudging toward legend, suffering along the way accounts that distort it. Some writers, such as Donald Bain in *War in Illinois* (1978), a book issued under the novelistic guise of a "true story," would perpetrate the belief that Charlie suffered schizophrenia and drug addiction.[4] Others, such as those responsible for the movie *Bad Charleston Charlie* (1973) would have it that Charlie lived the life attributed in folklore to twenties gangsters, full of comedy and chic.[5] There is scant evidence that Charlie did either.

Uneducated as to who he was or where he came from or how he might live productively, he pursued a path that he thought would bring him the power and respect that he understood accrued to movie stars, successful businessmen, and community leaders. For this, Charlie eschewed the legacy of his traditions. He was born into a peasant Jewish family in western Russia and at about the age of four was brought by his parents to New York City and then to St. Louis. He learned to survive first on city streets among toughs and bullies and later among broncobusters and miners. His gravitation to southern Illinois in his thirties was a descent into a region well suited to be transformed by him into his own netherworld. The description of his hidden retreat, Shady Rest, the culmination of a lifelong dream, supports this image with its bestial dogfights and cockfights, its incessant carousing and drunkenness, and its use for plotting executions that he alone decreed. All seem to have taken place under cover of nights lit garishly by the flickering flames of Shady Rest's two large fireplaces. A final irony is that his cheerful good-bye on the scaffold was made as if he had just escaped the suffocation of a dark and dreary region and were breathing fresh air for the first time. Of course, he had carefully steeled himself to make a brave impression.

As Gary DeNeal's book undergoes this revised edition, the legend of Charlie Birger is taking on a new dimension. Old Route 13 has been relocated. The foundation of Shady Rest—located just across the Williamson County line to the west of his protectorate Harrisburg—deteriorates within a scraggly wood, and the barbecue stand that served as its front is no more. But in Benton, Illinois, where he spent the last year of his life awaiting execution in the old Franklin County jail, Charlie is a prominent presence. The jail has become a museum and is undergoing a face-lift.[6] On the east side, but a story below the cell blocks, stands a solid, red-stained pine scaffold, a replica of the oak structure on which the last man to be hanged in the State of Illinois walked up his final thirteen steps.[7] The jail proper has a Birgeresque quality about it. Charlie's cell is set off a little from the others, and it is comparatively large. He shared it with no one. The cell door opens onto a secluded three-foot by eleven-foot hall where he could exercise and look through a single east window and hold court with passersby and curious school children standing on the lawn below. On the west side of this cell block is a longer corridor where—according to locals—several incarcerated prostitutes once took their fun and exercise by sliding nude down its length on soap-slicked cement.

The sheriff's quarters of this multifaceted jail-museum are being renovated. The rooms below the cell block house Birger artifacts, including what is said to be the actual noose from which he dangled. The noose has been preserved by the children of Jim Pritchard, the indomitable sheriff who purportedly tricked Charlie into surrendering. Incongruously, in one room the visitor finds visual reminders of John A. Logan, the revered Union general from southern Illinois who lived in Benton for a decade. Charlie craved such company in life and now has it in death. In the museum store, a visitor can buy *The Last Public Hanging in Illinois*, a video produced by WSIL-TV, located in the heart of Bloody Williamson County where Charlie's enterprises flourished in the twenties. Its cost is $13, a figure reflecting the entrepreneurship of the founders of the museum, mirroring as it does the thirteen steps up the gallows and Birger's cell key number 3313. In the background of the tape can be heard the popular country singer Vernon Dalhart's plaintive rendition of "The Hanging of Charlie Birger," a song Dalhart performed in the year of Charlie's death.[8]

The restored Franklin County jail is intended to attract tourists, of course. But of coincidental interest—and one that must have occasionally been on Charlie's mind as he languished for a year in captivity—is that it sits just a half mile from West City, the Benton suburb where Charlie sent two teenage brothers to murder Mayor Joe Adams and for whose assassination he paid with his own life. Now this tiny Benton suburb is riven by I-57, and the house of Joe Adams has long been demolished. The absence of evidence of Fat Joe's existence is in itself a reminder of how thoroughly Charlie succeeded in extirpating his enemies.

It is necessary after all to remember that Charlie Birger's end was vainglorious, the actor found out finally by his audience. The anomaly of his final moments is too rare for fiction. That is why

Gary DeNeal's book is so important. DeNeal surrounds Charlie with the facts of the gangster's own duplicitous life. These facts reveal that Charlie was a sinister Samaritan, a quixotic psyche at every turn, resisting opportunities to be honest with others or with himself. DeNeal shows him embracing all the vices from which he boasted of protecting Harrisburg and the little daughters he professed to cherish. But in the end, this middle-aged man walked up the gallows, guilty of much more than just the killing for which he was sentenced. Followed closely by a rabbi, a representative of the ancient moral traditions that he forsook in early life, and tended to almost lovingly by the hangman and those crowded around him, Charlie postured before his public until the last. Charlie Birger left behind a legacy of lawlessness and a story that could be told only as Gary DeNeal has told it, factually from the records of justice, from scraps of personal documents, and from the memories of fellow henchmen, hangers-on, and lucky survivors of his disaffection.

James Ballowe
Bradley University

# NOTES

1. Douglas's essay entitled "Robin Hood Is Hanged" is, in fact, based on three trips he made to report on Charlie Birger, the first trip prompted by the ineffectual bombing from the air by the rival Shelton gang of Shady Rest, Charlie's headquarters and pleasure resort. The air raid brought national attention to Charlie, always quick to court the media. Pointing out ironic incongruities, Douglas speaks of "the Baron" showing him a cache of high-powered rifles and packaged bullets and adds, "He was most affable and kind. The drinks had mellowed him, he was bursting with grievances, and we had found a common ground, being both ex-cavalrymen." On the second visit, Birger accused Douglas of having perpetrated the story that he was a dope fiend. Douglas convinced Charlie otherwise, and Charlie remained "affable." His third visit was occasioned by Charlie's trial for murder, and after writing the account of that event, he concluded, "I am writing no brief for Charley [sic] but if it had not been for the Anti-Saloon League, which first opened up for him the opportunities which he took, he would in all probability be today an excellent and highly prized top-sergeant of cavalry."
2. The most reliable history of Charlie Birger, other than that in the

present volume, remains Paul M. Angle's *Bloody Williamson: A Chapter in American Lawlessness* (Alfred A. Knopf, New York, 1952). Kept in print by Knopf for a generation, *Bloody Williamson* was revised with illustrations and an introduction by John Y. Simon (University of Illinois Press, Urbana and Chicago, 1992). This comprehensive and dependable treatment of Charlie Birger places him at the apex of some half century of lawlessness in southern Illinois.

Another credible account of Charlie Birger is found in "The Shelton Boys," a chapter in John Bartlow Martin's *Butcher's Dozen and Other Murders* (Harper Brothers, New York, 1950). While it has some obvious errors (e.g., "Birger, born in 1882 of Russian-Jewish immigrant parents in St. Louis, had grown up on a farm near Harrisburg, Illinois. . . . ), Martin's account is valuable in detailing the volatile interaction between Charlie and the Sheltons. Also, in a section called "Final Exhibits," Martin gives a lengthy excerpt of the testimony of Art Newman (once Charlie's trusted lieutenant) of the bizarre murders of Lory and Ethel Price (pp. 244–248).

3. My mother provided me with her account of the shooting two years before she died, at the age of eighty-five. Vigorous and clear-minded until her death, she had begun almost reluctantly to tell me of what she knew of the Herrin Massacre, the Klan, and the gang wars, although, like many others, she remained protective of her friends and relatives who had taken part in one or the other of these activities. Records indicated, for example, that my maternal grandfather had a hand in the Massacre and had Klan sympathies. Like so many, his role remains shadowy.

The family of my Aunt Opal Dillard Maynard was not linked to the troubles. But my aunt's remembrance of the maniacal behavior of the gangsters on their way from murder is compelling.

4. *War in Illinois* was first published in 1978 (Prentice-Hall, New York) and then republished as *Charlie and the Shawneetown Dame* (Donald Bain, A.E.R.P. Publisher, PO Box E, Johnston City, IL 62951) in the early eighties. Bain declares that his tale is true, but it leans more to the novelesque than to historical fact. The book's imagined dialogue and concocted events stretch the facts of Charlie's life, and Bain uses Charlie's resemblance to Tom Mix for a motif in helping flesh out his character.

5. The movie *Bad Charleston Charlie* was mercifully pulled from theatres shortly after it was released. Produced by Ivan Nagy, a still photographer, it was a slapstick comedy that completely distorted the facts of Birger's brutal if bumbling career and of the consequences to the culture of the region in which he practiced. One reviewer called it "rancid." Its only name actor was John Carradine.

6. In the spring of 1997, I went to Benton to interview Robert Rea,

the owner of a local insurance firm, who has been the principal champion of the museum. To help raise funds for the cause, Rea often dresses in period costume, sports a mock submachine gun, and visits clubs and marches in parades throughout the region. In his promotional enthusiasm, he once offered to suffer a mock hanging on the reconstructed scaffold if his fellow citizens would come up with $10,000 to help support the museum. When they raised $7,700, he spent the night in Birger's cell to commemorate the sixty-ninth anniversary of the hanging. Rea is devoted to making the museum work both because he believes that Charlie Birger should be an object lesson in southern Illinois history to present and future generations and because he sees the jail itself as an attractive historical site that will lure travelers passing by on I-57.

Rea has missed nothing. Besides the considerable Birger memorabilia and the General Logan room, a bedroom of the sheriff's quarters has been designated as a National Basketball Association shrine. This is the bedroom in which Doug Collins, star player with the Philadelphia 76ers and later coach of the Chicago Bulls and Detroit Pistons, lived when his father was sheriff of Franklin County.

7. When *A Knight of Another Sort* was first published, it was widely believed that Charlie Birger had been the last person to be hanged in the State. Certainly his hanging was accompanied by wide media coverage, and his behavior made the event memorable to the hundreds in attendance. But on Tuesday, October 18, 1928, the *Marion Leader* reported the hanging death of Charles Shader on October 10 at the Will County jail in Joliet, Illinois. Shader's hanging seems to have been tightly controlled, with "fewer than forty persons" in attendance. Unlike Birger's, it was not a "public" affair. Shader had been sentenced to die for the slaying of Peter M. Klein, a deputy warden.

8. This song was written by Carson Robison, the "granddaddy of the hillbillies," who specialized in "event songs." See Melvin Shestak's *The Country Music Encyclopedia* (Thomas Y. Crowell Co., New York, 1974).

# Preface

IN LESS TIME THAN IT TOOK TO WRITE THIS BOOK, EMPIRES BLOS-
somed, flourished, and fell, toddlers grew into school lads, and
saplings matured into sizable trees. As the clacking of the type-
writer drifted down the years, resulting in a wealth of notes and
at least four drafts, I wondered more than once which would be
finished first, this book or the one who wrote it.

After a staggering series of setbacks, here at last is the finished
product. That is not to say that further revisions may not be un-
dertaken when new information becomes available, nor does it
mean that I consider the work at hand to be grammatically or
structurally perfect. After all, the fellow who wrote it is the same
who managed to daydream his way through high school English
courses, thereby missing out on such handy items as sentence dia-
gramming and the proper use of pronouns. As a matter of fact,
nothing I have ever written is final in the sense that every word is
fitted jigsaw fashion into its appointed niche, every phrase touched
with just the right nuance. An admission of failure, you say?
Hardly! It's more a celebration of the infinite possibilities of language.

Exploring those possibilities might result in prose of a bell-like
quality, but only at the expense of such necessities as mowing the
lawn, celebrating loved ones' birthdays, studying the stars for
hours on end, and best of all, reading. In other words, everyday
living, despite the derogatory press it receives, isn't so bad. (In

fact, with each passing year and each new gray hair, it's beginning to look better and better.)

The Birger story, I felt, was not merely a transposed Western full of "shoot-'em-ups" and dead bodies—although it is true that the shootings were numerous and the resultant bodies frequently littered the scene. Quite simply, I saw it as a character study set against the backdrop of the gin-soaked, money-mad twenties. Should anyone wish to deduce my character and mentality from this interest in a gangster's misspent life, I would have him or her know that my passions are literature and art. Now try to figure that out!

And another thing! For too long we southern Illinoisans lived under a cloud. I am referring not only to the Herrin Massacre and the Klan wars and the gang wars and the coal mine wars, terrible though they all were, but also to this business of folks up north believing we didn't wear shoes. For a lengthy period following the twenties and early thirties, to be from our area, and Williamson County in particular, was to face the attitude that all our people were either dangerous gangsters and thugs from whom respectable people should beware or hayseeds blind to life's amenities. And we, in turn, felt folks up north were so bedazzled by dollar signs that they had no time for the good things in life, such as listening to the sounds of nature or fishing for bluegill in some sleepy farm pond. The best you can say for stereotypes is that they are worthless.

During all the labor troubles, during all the gang wars, and yes, even during the Klan raids, there were people—in fact, a majority of the people in southern Illinois—who lived quiet, law-abiding lives far divorced from the stories that titillated the interest of the readers of the daily press. Perhaps our recent past included more—many more good people to whom the acts and crimes of the Birger gang were as unfamiliar as they were to the people who read of such escapades in their big-city newspapers.

Therefore, I suggest to my readers that just as Missouri had its Jesse James and Chicago its Al Capone and New York its Mafia, our local "bad men" were not a part and parcel of the lives of most of our people. And perhaps the appellation "Bloody Williamson" was a disservice to those good citizens who themselves never had a connection with any of these events or even, for the most part, knew about them except by reading their newspapers.

I worked on this book long and hard. I prowled the darkest recesses of courthouse files where the air was bad and the dust was worse. I interviewed a lot of people, most of them sterling folk. Along the way, I possibly picked up an enemy or two, but if so, they were quickly lost in the crowd of new friends. A joy and a burden, this book was mine alone for almost five years.

Now I'm sharing it with you.

# Acknowledgments

Despite the interval of nearly twenty years, I have chosen to keep the acknowledgments essentially as they appeared in the first edition.

So many people have helped with this project that it is pointless to list them all, but a baker's dozen merit special recognition.

*Ethel Ashby.* Her enthusiasm for the Birger story helped keep my spirits high. Being in her company was like a spring tonic.

*Beatrice Bainbridge.* (This was her maiden name.) In the course of a dozenplus interviews, we became close. For my sake, she tried to recall her past life with Birger, some of which was painful. Despite my incessant questioning, I was always made to feel like one of the family in her home, and for that I am grateful to her and her husband.

*"The Blonde Bombshell."* (This nickname was given her more than fifty years ago and was used by her in lieu of her real name.) She was there. Because many of the gangsters were her pals, her memories provided me with good background information and a real "feel" for the era. She proved herself my friend as well.

*Arlie O. Boswell.* What Boswell was or was not in the twenties is now a matter of history and continuing debate. But in the 1980s (and incidentally, his own eighties), he was a grand old gentleman. He was one of the most remarkable men I have ever met.

*Rosalie DeNeal.* She helped in so many ways. Mothers are like that.

*Charles Hammond.* One of my closest friends, Charles is a dedicated musician and an accomplished photographer. The many photographs in this book are evidence of his patience and dedication.

*Noel Hurford.* The fearless newspaper editor of decades past lives on in this unassuming Hardin countian. Over the years, he has helped me in many ways. Twice he read the manuscript, the second time with an editing eye.

*Dan Malkovich.* There is no way I can say what the late Dan Malkovich meant to me without using the kind of gushing prose Dan himself abhorred. (Note: Once he outdid himself by striking out the best line of prose I ever wrote, but I kept my peace—until now—and thought no less of him for it. After all, we were from different generations.) I always saw him as a knight in shining armor, a hero from another age. Shortly before his untimely death, Dan read and corrected the manuscript.

*Bernard Moore.* Gentle, thoughtful, wise, and tolerant are attributes of a gentleman; and "gentleman" best describes "Bernie" Moore. Along with the Old Stone Face and Womble Mountain, he is one of Saline County's treasures. (Incidentally, he taught me everything I know about historical research.)

*Melba Patton.* An ally in my researching efforts, Melba Patton is a top-notch librarian with an astonishing knowledge of books, both rare and not so rare. The many years we go back—as they say—are, for me, rewarding.

*Ronald Reed.* In addition to being a librarian, Ronald Reed is a writer, a scholar, a storyteller of rare ability, a one-man encyclopedia of Indian lore and southern Illinois history, and a noted authority on General John A. Logan. What a delight it is to be in his company.

*Pearl Roberts.* Fine writer, meticulous historian, Pearl Roberts read the manuscript at my request but edited it and retyped it out of the goodness of her heart. To say I valued her judgment is an understatement.

*Rev. George Wright.* I did not know Rev. Wright quite as well as the others listed above, but the one time I was in his company, I was impressed not only with his knowledge but also with his youthful outlook and quickness of step. If we could all be Rev. Wrights in our eighties, the terror of old age would vanish like mist in the morning sun.

Among the others to whom I am indebted are several who insist upon anonymity—just why I can't quite say. That ex-gangsters would wish to remain far, far in the background is understandable, but why others, whose records are relatively unblemished, would insist that their names be omitted is a mystery. I thank them anyway.

That leaves the following, some of whom are no longer with us: John Adams, John Alexander, Isadore Alvis, Delbert Balabas, James Ballowe, Billy Beal, John Belt, Rhoda Bey, Dimple Black, Marie Blackard, Helen Brookbank, Garland Brown, Bill Bunch, Amos Butler, Homer Butler, Mrs. Walter Choate, Jesse Cremer, George Cummins, H. A. Cummins, Earl Dabney, Mrs. Harry Deck, Flora Decker, Opal Dietz, Gerald DeNeal, Guy A. DeNeal, Robert DeNeal, Hazel Durant, Mr. and Mrs. Jess Evans, John Robert Fenoli, Betty Furlow, Charles Gidcumb, Edith Gulley, Mr. and Mrs. Glenn Gurley, Julian Harper, Charlie Harris, Ernest Hawkins, George Hermann, Tim Hopson, Barbara Burr Hubbs, Dick Hunter, Carl Hutson, Mary Kinser, Stephanie Lane, Murray Lawyer, Wilbur Leitch, Dr. J. C. Lightner, Mr. and Mrs. Otis McBride, Hugh McDole, Mary Alice McGill, Kuma McNabb, Dan Minner, Charles Mitchell, Homer Mitchell, Robert Mitchell, T. Mills Moore, Rollie Moore, Ted Moore, Leo Morris, Virgil "Copper" Motsinger, Harry Moyer, Orval Nelson, Rev. Ron Nelson, Carolyn Norris, Elbert Norris, Jay Norris, Mr. and Mrs. Gerald Page, Oldham Paisley, Ralph Pallister, Howard Pearcy, Brose Phillips, Claude Piersall, Eugenia Plater, Lois Quint, Leo Richmond, Joe Schafer, Joe Scroggins, Leo Simmons, Mr. and Mrs. Harvey Slaton, Curtis Small, Leonard Stearns, Willard St. John, Frank Thomas, Ralph Thomas, Evelyn Todd, John Utter, Dawn Vandenboom, Rudy Walker, Rev. Cloid Wesley, Kenneth Wiley, Grover Wise, Harold E. Wolfe, M. Cody Wright, Mavis Wright, Bill Yarbrough, and Dovie Younger.

And a special word of thanks to Mike Novotnak of the Chicago Crime Commission.

# Introduction

AS A CHILD VISITING IN THE HOME OF MY GRANDPARENTS, GUY A. and Lula DeNeal, I heard Grandpa and his older sister, Mary Parks, talking about "Old Birger." Hearing the name of "Birger" made me think of the boogerman of bad dreamland and the ground beef patties we often had for dinner. I was confused.

My grandfather and his sister had their reasons for mentioning the name of a man who had been hanged more than two decades earlier. His memory still troubled them, perhaps even marked them. It certainly affected Grandma, who would all but shudder when, years later, Grandpa told me about Charlie Birger and the old days in southeastern Illinois.

I would learn in time that my dad's family was only one of many in Saline County that were adversely affected by the gangster. In a way, my relatives were lucky; they suffered, at worst, a few sleepless nights and some stolen property.

Still, listening to Aunt Mary and Grandpa reminisce gave me a "feel" for local history that even the best books could not deliver. Perhaps that had something to do with the way the old folks had of recalling their past, and besides, Grandpa was a noted story-teller in the area.

The year they remembered was 1926. Local gambler Dan Lockwood got word to Aunt Mary's husband, Hosea Parks, that Birger was planning to kill him during Steve George's trial, which was soon to be held at Harrisburg. The gangster planned to use the machine gun he kept hidden beneath his heavy overcoat, or so the story went. For his own protection during the trial, Parks borrowed a pistol from one of Sheriff John Small's deputies. Of course, it is unlikely that Birger really carried a machine gun into the courtroom, but Parks's belief that such brazenness was possible tells us much about that lawless time. That incident, along with events leading up to it, can be found in the first edition of *A Knight of Another Sort*. What is not included concerns something that happened after Steve George's conviction for robbing Parks's store at Rudement. Written up as a hero on page one of the *Daily Register*, my schoolteacher grandfather suddenly had more acclaim than he had ever known, this despite his assertion that it was his brother-in-law who deserved most of the credit for capturing Birger's henchman, the notorious Steve George. That small matter notwithstanding, the Saline County sheriff decided on his own that Guy A. DeNeal was just the fellow to track down and arrest other local desperadoes. In fact, Small knew of one such fugitive who was thought to be hiding out with a bootlegger relative in a ramshackle shack located between Rudement and Williams Hill.

Late one night a car drove up to my grandparents' home near Rudement. Believing some of Steve George's gangster friends were paying an unfriendly visit, Grandpa slipped behind the door; in his hand was a loaded shotgun. Then came the knock. There was no response from within the house. My terrified grandmother held close her two young sons and expected the worst. A voice called out Grandpa's name. Sheriff John Small had arrived at an ungodly hour to ask Grandpa a favor: Would he consider apprehending a certain party known to be in hiding just north of Williams Hill? Grandpa thought a moment before declining the honor. After all, Sheriff Small was getting paid to risk his life making arrests while Guy A. DeNeal was only an underpaid schoolteacher who had inadvertently helped bring to justice a notorious gunman. Rightly or wrongly, Grandpa never quite forgave Sheriff Small for terrorizing his family that night and for making what he believed to be an unreasonable request.

Grandpa also recalled having been followed on the sidewalks of Harrisburg by Steve George's brother, and he told the sheriff about it. John Small dismissed the incident, saying the brother probably wanted Steve's pistol, which was known to be in his possession.

(Thinking one of his sons might get careless with the weapon, he later gave the gun to Uncle Hosea when the latter lived in New Mexico. Parks traded the pistol for another gun, thus losing in the southwest a bit of southern Illinois history.)

So, due to special circumstances when growing up, I heard much about Birger's dark side and little if anything about his charitable activities in and around Harrisburg. Reading Paul M. Angle's *Bloody Williamson* reinforced first impressions of a local gangster. In 1953, on the third floor of Hart's Department Store, which was located on the northwest corner of Harrisburg Square, I bought my copy of the first edition of this classic work. Remember that I was nine years old and that my family did not yet own a television set. As dark on the inside as its cloth cover was on the outside, *Bloody Williamson* found this young reader eager to turn the next page, only to be appalled by what was there. No wonder Grandma DeNeal preferred not to talk about the "good old days."

I read Paul M. Angle's book with a mingling of fascination and horror. The several chapters devoted to the Herrin Massacre were scenes from hell; Edgar Allan Poe might have written the section devoted to Charlie Birger and the Sheltons. As with *Jim Bridger* and *Geronimo*, books I read over and over at Rudement's one-room school because the other books in our school "library" were boring, I read *Bloody Williamson* many times, learning by heart its darkest passages.

Strangest of all, one of the leading characters in the book was still practicing law in Harrisburg. Not until late 1975, while researching a three-part article on Charlie Birger for *Outdoor Illinois*, did I meet this man, Arlie O. Boswell, in his law office on the fifth floor of the Harrisburg National Bank Building. In 1983, the year of his death, I was still interviewing the elderly attorney from time to time and was still learning that the deeper one peered into the story of Boswell's remarkable life, the more puzzled one became. Was it possible this wise and kindly old gentleman could have once been associated with one of Illinois's most violent gangsters, himself a study in contradictions?

Between 1975 and 1983, others were interviewed who had known Birger, including ex-gang members, Birger's former wife, and a prominent ex-member of the Shelton Gang. Listening to the old men who had spent behind prison bars what should have been their best years, one could feel the glamour of the Roaring Twenties slipping away, to be replaced by the sad realization that here was a tale of senseless mayhem and sordid intrigue. More than once in my presence Arlie O. Boswell referred to his years as state's attorney in Williamson County during the 1920s as "that crazy time." No man epitomized that craziness better than Charlie Birger did.

Lives were destroyed as if they were moths before a flame. Often the giddy refrain of the Charleston could not be heard above the deadly monotone of the machine-gun chatter. The shadow of the hangman's noose served to chill the laughter spilling from the many roadhouses. Even the affable Arlie O. Boswell, who seemed to view almost whimsically the various twists and turns his own life had taken, had much to regret from ever having known a certain gang leader of dark complexion who walked with a distinctive swagger.

The only surviving member of the Birger Gang to retain an aura of menace was Riley "Alabama" Simmons. Simmons insisted that Birger was no more colorful or interesting than the other bootleggers and criminals he had known both in and out of prison.

"Did he talk about his days out west?" I asked, hoping the question would trigger a striking response.

"No," came his terse reply, "though he did mention selling newspapers as a boy."

A one-time member of the Shelton Gang, Charles "Blackie" Harris found most of the characters in my book to be essentially worthless, the exception being Mrs. Lory Price. Harris was a realist and had no illusion that his own role as counterfeiter, bootlegger, and killer would earn him even a murmur of honorable mention from future historians.

Charlie Harris was hard to figure. On the one hand, he was personable, grandfatherly in appearance and demeanor. At the Vienna Minimum Security Prison where he was serving time for murder, he attended church regularly, though more to make the minister feel appreciated than for spiritual nourishment. He was forever dispensing advice to fellow prisoners, many of them young enough to be his great-grandchildren. During his long lifetime, he had been blamed for many killings, including those of former pals

Carl and Bernie Shelton, and at one time, he had suffered the dubious distinction of being the oldest man on the FBI's Most Wanted list. Yet, in person he seemed almost delicate, as if he were an artist at heart. He also seemed obsessed with the idea of being a good neighbor to others when he finally got out of the penitentiary. To better appreciate my dilemma, try picturing an elderly Mr. Rogers of a hit man serving time in the slammer.

Birger's ex-wife Beatrice viewed her former husband as a man of limited ability who had unlimited ambition. His long talks with Harrisburg's leading businessmen seemed pointless to her and unbearably boring. Imagine that! The most talked about, most written about individual ever to call Harrisburg home often bored his wife to distraction.

Other, more dramatic surprises were still to come—one so unlikely that a writer of realistic fiction would have immediately discarded it. In 1929, former Williamson County State's Attorney Arlie O. Boswell was unlucky enough to find himself in Leavenworth alongside men he had prosecuted in the past, including Monroe "Blackie" Armes of the Shelton Gang and Riley "Alabama" Simmons of the Birger Gang. Three years earlier Armes and Simmons would have been gunning for each other; now they were the closest of friends, according to their fellow prisoner Charles "Blackie" Harris, who chuckled when recalling this amazing turnaround. Together they plotted to slide a knife blade into the innards of fellow prisoner Boswell. Seeing his opportunity at last, Simmons made the plunge, though not to fatal effect.

Sixty-four years after that knifing attack, Arlie O. Boswell found himself in the Marion Memorial Hospital with a roommate who kept begging the nurses for a knife. The account given here is based on a June 1, 1983, entry in my journal and refers to an incident that occurred a few days earlier. I recorded it immediately after getting a telephone call from Boswell.

His roommate heard that his name was Boswell and said he used to know a man by that name who was the prosecuting attorney of Williamson County. When Boswell asked his name, the fellow said Riley Simmons.

After much cross-examination, Boswell became convinced he was rooming with the same Riley Simmons who tried to cut his throat at Leavenworth. He arrived at this conclusion not only from what the man said about going to Birger's place and working for Helen Holbrook but also by his actions, which including getting out of bed every few minutes and going to the bathroom—where he put on two shirts and three pairs of pants. And he was always looking for his knife.

Boswell said that as a young man Simmons was about half there, and along with Steve George, he was one of the more dangerous members of the gang. For that reason, Boswell, who was in the hospital to have his eyes operated on, got no sleep that night.

On the surface, Boswell and Simmons had little in common—one personable, philosophical, a fountain of hard-won wisdom and the other a recluse, unkempt and unloved—and yet the orbits of their sometimes violent lives were oddly in conjunction. At the beginning of our telephone conversation, Boswell asked if I believed in coincidence, and when I said I did, he said he did, too. Both men died within a month of each other, in Marion, Illinois, the county seat of "Bloody Williamson." And both men were helpful to me in writing the book.

Years earlier, both Dan Malkovich and Arlie O. Boswell warned me about visiting Simmons at his isolated home. (He was the overseer of a coon dog club located near Colp—which explains why so many hounds were running about and yapping.) Their words came vividly to mind when, during an interview with the man, I noticed that Riley was trying to repair a pair of big wire pliers. At one point when he was standing directly behind me, it was all I could do not to turn around to better watch him, but doing so would have made my fears too obvious. As it turned out, he was friendly enough, though certainly not effusive. He even gave short answers to a few of my many questions. Only once did he show irritation, and that was when I asked if his career in crime had left emotional scars on his parents.

"You know it did," he said.

He told about seeing Lory Price at "one hundred nightclubs"; he mentioned Mother Lee's, a famous sporting house located on the south side of Benton. There were a lot of sporting houses in those days, he said.

I would see him once more. Dying of cancer in the same hospital room where Boswell had been his roommate a few days earlier,

Riley said he was present during the fight at the Masonic Temple in Herrin in 1926. Yes, he was there when "Highpockets" McQuay was shot, but he did not know who killed him, nor did he know who killed Ethel Price. He did mumble something about a Shawneetown incident, which led me to believe he may have killed the man found north of that town and whose body was never identified.

Riley and I had a mutual friend, a much-tattooed ex-moonshiner, ex–train robber who was nicknamed "Terrible" while in the slammer at Menard. Once while "Alabama" and "Terrible" were standing at a urinal, Simmons asked if he had ever killed a man. Stunned by the question, "Terrible" said no.

One ex-gangster thought Simmons had it easy when in the pen, because while the rest of them did hard labor, Riley posed as a psychotic and thus got to sit around staring at the wall alongside the true psychotics. But "Terrible" recalled that "'Bama had trouble at Menard." The following account is based on my July 23, 1983, journal entry:

There was the time Riley sat down in the middle of the long table they called the cutting table. They had been eating watermelon and, as usual, a truck was parked nearby. The rinds were to be thrown into the truck bed, but Riley who was fed up with the arrangement threw the rind and his cap in the box where the silverware went and threw his silverware in the truck. Then he started running. They caught him of course and added some extra time to his sentence.

"'Bama was very uneducated," his friend said.

Simmons had been dead for nearly a month. "Terrible" did not get to the cemetery for the burial because of car transmission trouble in Zeigler, but he did go to the funeral home where he met Simmons's younger sister. He felt she was the one who saw that the final rites were kept low key. She was nice, though, and asked how long he had known her brother.

He replied, "Since the early 1920s."

She also talked with two other men as they stood before her brother's casket. One was a coon hunter.

Riley's white shirt was open at the collar, and he wore checkered pants. He looked "real good" in the casket, his friend recalled.

"We weren't put here to stay," he added. Sure enough, within a year and a half "Terrible" was also gone.

Some months later a relative of another friend of Riley Simmons delivered a chilling account of Ethel Price's death that allegedly came from Simmons himself. The plan had been to frighten Lory's wife, not murder her. However, as soon as they arrived at the site of the abandoned mine, Connie Ritter insisted Ethel walk with him a certain distance. After she refused to have sex with him and began crying and screaming, he either killed her or had someone do it.

"Cold, cold, double cold," said a St. Louis policeman in reference to the dark deeds attributed to Charles "Blackie" Harris. He could just have easily have been talking about the relatively young man in the 1920s, who, as a very old man in Harrisburg in the 1970s, proved to be one of my best sources.

He told a chilling tale of how he had gotten his friend drunk, lured him into a cornfield, and shot him in the back of the head. The killer was tried and acquitted.

"Why did you do it?" I asked, thinking he would use self-defense as justification for such a terrible crime.

"Because he snitched," was his casual reply. In my naive way, I then asked if this killing troubled his conscience these many years since.

"No," he said. "I never think about it unless somebody brings it up."

He is dead now, as are almost all of the gang members who contributed to the book, but I still wonder if his conscience ever caught up with him before he died. I do know he was an avowedly religious man, often testifying at length during revivals.

One of Birger's bartenders told of having his own roadhouse bombed by a rival gangster—he blamed the explosion on Pat Pulliam—and how, following the excitement, he walked down the highway as "naked as a jaybird." After all, he was in the building when it was blown up. He still remembered the name of the woman who saw him on the road.

A longtime buddy of this man remembered seeing Lyle "Shag" Worsham sitting in a car parked outside the barbecue stand at Shady Rest while Birger's men were inside the building deciding Worsham's fate.

"He just sat there," said the old man, shaking his head at the absurdity of it all. "In his place, I would have run."

A friend of Birger from Saline County recalled how he was offered several thousand dollars to kill a man during the coal mine wars of the early 1930s, but declined, saying if he did the killing, his life would not be worth a nickel. At long last, here was a man who stood for reason and common decency. Yet hardly had those words left his lips, when he broke the spell by voicing his one regret regarding the Herrin Massacre in 1922.

"I arrived too late to get in on the fun," said the old gentleman, who, even as we talked, knew he was dying of lung cancer.

An elderly Marion man barely suppressed a chuckle as he recalled the night some of the Birger Gang drove a corpse around town to show off their workmanship. Seeing the cigar clenched between the victim's teeth as he sat propped up in the back seat of the automobile was an extra touch that rendered the scene unforgettable.

One day I went to see Beatrice to deliver an important message that was long overdue. For more than a half century, the old lady had yearned to known what had happened to her daughter Charline but feared she would die before learning the answer. A day or so before my visit with the ailing Beatrice, my wife, Judy, and I found Charline's tombstone near that of her father in the Chesed Shel Emeth Cemetery in University City, Missouri. A newspaper article revealed she had died in childbirth in 1949. After I told Beatrice of our discovery, she said that shortly before my visit, her long lost daughter had appeared to her in a dream. That my news followed her dream so closely, she felt, was more than mere coincidence.

Perhaps she was right. I don't know. I do know Arlie O. Boswell thought it no accident that he and Riley Simmons shared the same hospital room. Odd, odd, double odd.

Over the years, I heard from two daughters of "Hoghead" Davis, Birger's bodyguard. "Hoghead" had disappeared after killing a man named Montgomery. The daughters wondered what happened to their father. It was rumored he had fled to Europe, and there were other tales, equally improbable. But the daughters were right in their belief that they would probably never know the truth. I was sorry not to be able to help them in their quest.

As an old woman, the former "Blonde Bombshell" was more attuned to ailments and prayers to the Lord than to spicy details of her misspent youth. At my prompting, she did recall riding the interurban at Muddy and being too intoxicated to stand up. She also had keen recollection of that night in Harrisburg when somebody followed her home in an automobile. She was terrified.

On another occasion, she, Birger, and two women from St. Louis were riding in Birger's armored car when gunmen opened fire. Naturally, the two from St. Louis were scared, and so was the "Bombshell." She tried to get under the cushions, realizing even while doing so that such action would be futile if the bullets broke through the armor. Thanks to Charlie, who was always thinking ahead, the gas tank was fixed so it would not ignite.

She feared the Sheltons were after her. And she had reason to be afraid. She had stumbled over the body of Ward "Casey" Jones as it lay near the power plant at Shady Rest. The body was wrapped in a gunnysack. Her version of the gangster's killing differed sharply from the one carried in the newspapers. Yes, Rado Millich shot him and was hanged for the deed, but the reason he shot him was a secret the "Bombshell" kept for many years.

United States Marshal Zachary Taylor Sweeney Leitch was a known womanizer and a frequent visitor at Shady Rest. He loved to drink almost as much as he loved to watch the "Blonde Bombshell" perform her unique rendition of the hoochy koochy. He also had a yen for a big blonde out of St. Louis, who happened to be romantically involved with Ward "Casey" Jones. (The "Bombshell" said they were married.) After Jones discovered his loved one was seeing Leitch on the side, he proceeded to beat up the lawman to such an extent that the marshal's clothes were in shreds.

Ever one to help out a friend who represented law and order, Birger drove the dancer back to Zack's house in Harrisburg to get his shirt, pants, and underwear. Because the "Bombshell" lived near Zack's estranged wife and often looked after her, the United States marshal figured she was the one to rummage through his house. He had official documents scattered about, and it would not do for a known gangster to be nosing through them.

Later, at the cabin, she overheard Zack tell gun-happy Art Newman that he would be pleased to see Jones out of the picture. A short time after that conversation Millich killed Jones.

Is the story true? I only know she believed it.

In defense of Zachary Taylor Sweeney Leitch, it should be mentioned that he persuaded his nephew Wilbur Leitch not to get involved in Birger's liquor selling operation. Earlier, thinking he and the young man might go into business together, Birger had given Wilbur a .32 pistol. There were two notches on one side of the handle and a missing part on the other side. Concerning the missing part, Charlie said that came about when he ran out of bullets and had to use the pistol as a billy club. When Wilbur said he wanted to get rid of the notches, Birger said, "Leave them to remember me by."

Although Wilbur kept the pistol for the rest of his life, he never developed a close friendship with Birger and chose to lay the blame for this on his Uncle Zack. Charlie told him twice not to come into Shady Rest, saying, much to Wilbur's chagrin at the time, "You don't belong here."

One day the former hoochy koochy star and I were discussing black-eyed peas and the luck these oddities are supposed to bring if cooked on New Year's Day.

"Well," said I, "you kept Birger's dice all these years, and they didn't bring you good luck." She paused. Good Lord, I had hurt the old woman's feelings.

"I'm going to give you those dice," she said at last. "After I'm gone they will probably be thrown away anyway." And, so, she give me the "lucky dice" Charlie had given her down at the cabin and at a time his own luck had just about run out.

Many people believed Birger never hanged, the "Blonde Bombshell" among them. She based her conclusion solely on the word of Jess Jones (the same Jess Jones who got lost in Centralia that time he was trying to drive Beatrice and the children to visit Charlie in Danville). I believe it made her feel more secure to think

Charlie was still among the living. In her world, Birger was one of the good guys, and for all I know, she went to her grave still convinced he was out there somewhere watching over her.

She had no such illusions about Art Newman. When asked about one of the least publicized of the murders occurring at Shady Rest, that of a young man named Richey who apparently "knew too much," she responded by indicating Art Newman took credit for the deed.

"He had nose trouble," she heard Newman say.

To use one of Arlie O. Boswell's favorite phrases, when Art Newman was "salted away," his wife Bessie turned her affections to a young man in Harrisburg who happened to be the latest boyfriend of the "Bombshell." So it was that Harrisburg, county seat of Saline County and home of Dairy Brand, saw a free-for-all between two angry women, complete with hair pulling and no shortage of scratching. My, how the old woman enjoyed telling that particular story.

After *A Knight of Another Sort* was published in 1981, we heard from a woman who, as a girl in 1928, had played on Birger's scaffold with some of her friends. Charlie stepped to the window of his cell and shooed them away.

"Get off there! That's mine," he shouted from his jail cell.

In another time and place, he might have tossed shiny nickels and dimes to the children just to hear the squeals and to watch the kids scramble for their paltry treasure. Now all he had left in the world was a shred of dignity—which he was not about to squander on a bunch of bratty kids—that, and a scaffold, his scaffold, the one he had watched the carpenters hammer into useful, and dreadful, form.

Elsewhere in Egypt, private grief greeted the dawn of April 19, 1928, a day some would remember for its circuslike atmosphere, marking as it did the last public hanging in Illinois. It is known that a mother and daughter wept that day—and for good reason. The mother was a former sweetheart of Birger, and the daughter was their illegitimate child. Beatrice had little use for the mother but felt sorry for the girl, remembering how people in Harrisburg with prying minds were always bothering her. Their story was not told in the first edition of this book, and their names are not being printed here. Both are deceased.

Arlie O. Boswell told me a lot but, purposely, not everything. Of course, he had forgotten quite a bit, thanks to his prodigious intake of alcohol over the years. In the relaxed atmosphere of a barbershop in Harrisburg, he was overheard bragging he that "had spilled more booze than most people drank." In a more private setting, he freely lamented that alcoholism was the curse of his life, but he had quit drinking many years before we met.

A prime example of a certain "holding back" on the part of Boswell was his version of the shoot-out in Herrin in 1925 between S. Glenn Young and Ora Thomas. Boswell would drop hints or become strangely vague when discussing details of this infamous event in Williamson County history. Why all the secrecy about something that had happened more than a half century earlier? I could only conclude that he believed the "mystery man" who allegedly killed Thomas might still be alive. He had no doubt that Ora Thomas had, indeed, shot and killed S. Glenn Young only a moment or so before his own death.

After I told Boswell that I was going to Kinmundy to visit Maude Nall, the former Mrs. S. Glenn Young, he observed with something of a smile that her husband Taylor Nall might be able to answer some of my questions. He seemed a little surprised when I told him that fellow alcoholic Taylor Nall was already dead.

Certainly, Mrs. Nall did not indicate that her second husband had any connection with the shooting that claimed the life of her first husband, but she did make an observation of her own. Were S. Glenn Young to return from the grave and knock on the door, she would not let him in. She had failed to heed her parents' warning about him, and it was only after their marriage that she discovered the arrogant, publicity-hungry nature of the man she called husband.

It was what she said next that I found most shocking of all. This woman, who had long ago been blinded by shotgun blasts while riding with Young on the highway near Okawville and who still carried some of the shot in her face even as we spoke, believed the ambush might have been planned by Young. (My notes show she also thought noted Klansman and bank robber Harry Steyer might have been involved.) Why her husband drove so slowly just before the shooting occurred had always remained a mystery to her. I believe she was mistaken as to Young's involvement in the matter, but I also believe her dark suspicion about the character of the man tells us more than the laudatory book or the favorable articles written about him.

Meanwhile, for the ever-controversial Arlie O. Boswell, she had nothing but praise. She recalled how kind he was to her in those chaotic days following her husband's death.

Mrs. Ora Thomas suffered a hard time as well, following the celebrated shoot-out that took her husband's life. The Ku Klux Klan was now in control, and bitter men in grimy sheets patrolled the streets of Herrin. They determined who could and could not visit the grieving widow. A friend of Mrs. Thomas, who had earlier seen Ora's corpse on the sidewalk near the European Hotel, solved the problem of getting $500 to the widow by hiding the money in her hair, then bluffing her way past the Klansmen who were guarding the house.

Again, my interest in the life of Charlie Birger began as a very young boy, listening to my grandfather, Guy A. DeNeal, and his sister, Mary Parks, talk about the bitterly cold night late in 1925 when Grandpa and Hosea Parks captured Steve George. George's fate was a cruel one and is so described in the text. Hosea Parks died in a boating accident in Arkansas in 1955. My grandfather lived another twenty-eight years, dying in 1984 at the age of eighty-seven.

Listening to the minister preach at his funeral in the Rudement Social Brethren Church, I realized I was hearing a bit of necessary fiction. Oh, that fiction was not the preacher's fault, because any man of the cloth bold enough and foolish enough to tell half the truth or even a tenth of the truth about any deceased individual would probably be chased from the church—and probably the county as well.

My father's father told wild stories, some of them off color, and on at least three occasions found himself in a situation where he could easily have killed a man. On one occasion, his weapon was a stone. Naturally, none of these juicy tidbits were mentioned during the funeral oration. Instead, family and friends heard about a pillar of the community—which Grandpa was, no doubt about it. We were painted a proper and sanitized portrait of a highly intelligent individual who had made an indelible impression on so many people, especially me. The oldest grandchild, I sat there and obeyed the family rule I had spent a lifetime learning: Do not contradict, with distinguished others present, the "official" version of things. As much as it is possible, I have tried to break that rule and to tell the truth as I have perceived it.

"IT"—Clara Bow had that quality, and so did Charlie Birger. Never fair, this indefinable distinction follows no edict of logic or morality in making a few individuals unforgettable while ten thousand others, perhaps brighter and better than the chosen ones, are forgotten even before their obituaries yellow on the back pages of yesterday's discarded newspapers. Teachers search in vain to find a moral in these rare, meteoric lives, while priests and preachers wring limp sermons from contemplating the convoluted patterns these lives display. Such lives just HAPPEN, and happening, leave the rest of us shaking our heads.

# Chronology

THE KILLING OF CECIL KNIGHTON MARKED THE REAL BEGINning of Birger's notoriety in southern Illinois. The growing impression that a dangerous man held forth beneath a winning smile was reinforced a week later when Birger was credited with killing a second man, the St. Louis gangster William F. "Whitey" Doering. Beginning with Knighton's killing, this chronology extends to and beyond Birger's own death on the gallows.

## 1923

Nov. 15    Cecil Knighton is killed at Halfway. Birger is acquitted of the killing by a coroner's jury on grounds of self-defense.

Nov. 18    "Whitey" Doering is killed and Birger is wounded in a shoot-out at Halfway. Because there is some question as to who actually shot Doering, Birger is once again acquitted by a coroner's jury.

Dec. 22    The first big Ku Klux Klan raid takes place. Two others follow on Jan. 5 and Jan. 7, 1925.

## 1924

Mar. 26    Birger's trial for bootlegging begins at Danville. The defendant is sentenced to a year in jail and fined a total of $2,500.

Apr. 22     Once again in Federal Court at Danville, Birger pleads guilty to charges of possessing liquor and counterfeit revenue stamps and is fined $300 plus court costs and sentenced to ten months in jail. Both sentences are to run concurrently.

August     In the latter part of the month, Beatrice departs for Pennsylvania, leaving Minnie and Charline at her parents' home.

Sept. 24     On Judge Lindley's order, Birger is allowed to return to Harrisburg for a week in order to untangle some property matters.

Oct. 2     Birger returns to Danville.

Oct. 6     Released from jail, Birger returns to Harrisburg.

Nov. 13     In Harrisburg, Birger is sentenced to six months in the county jail and fined $1,000 but remains free on bail.

## 1925

Jan. 24     S. Glenn Young, Ora Thomas, and two other men are killed in Herrin.

Feb. 6     Birger enters the jail at Harrisburg.

Mar. 9     Birger's petition of *habeas corpus* succeeds in gaining his release from jail. In the summer and autumn of 1925, Shady Rest becomes a reality.

December     Birger and the Sheltons form a partnership in slot machine operations.

## 1926

Apr. 13     The battle on the Masonic Temple lawn in Herrin takes six lives and destroys the Ku Klux Klan in Williamson County.

Summer     Several killings in and around Herrin indicate a gang war is brewing. Those "in the know" credit the trouble to friction between the Shelton and Birger elements, but the reading public is not made aware of this development until later in the year.

Aug. 16     John Howard, one of Birger's men, is killed in a fight at Harco. There is no evidence that Howard's death is gang war related.

| | |
|---|---|
| Aug. 22 | In a roadhouse fight north of Marion, former Klansman Harry Walker and one Everett Smith are killed. |
| Sept. 6 | Williamson County State's Attorney Arlie O. Boswell receives a bullet wound in the leg. |
| Sept. 12 | Leaving Grover's Place, a roadhouse between Johnston City and Herrin, Pat Pulliam, his wife, and their friend "Wild Bill" Holland are machine-gunned. Holland is killed; the Pulliams survive. |
| Sept. 14 | On his way to Benton in an ambulance, Pulliam is again "set upon" by gangsters. Miraculously he survives, suffering only bruises. |
| Sept. 17 | Lyle "Shag" Worsham is murdered. |
| Sept. 18 | A body is found in the woods north of Shawneetown. Although the death is thought to be gang war related, the man is not identified. |
| Oct. 4 | On Route 13 west of Harrisburg, Art Newman's car is fired upon from the Sheltons' armored truck. Mrs. Newman is wounded. |
| Oct. 14 | The former Shelton roadhouse is fired upon. |
| Oct. 16 | Machine guns are stolen from a spar mine at Rosiclare. The Birger gang is believed to be responsible. |
| Oct. 25 | Birger demands that Adams surrender the Sheltons' armored truck. |
| Oct. 26 | "High Pockets" McQuay is found shot to death in an automobile on a roadside near Herrin. The body of Ward "Casey" Jones is discovered in the middle fork of the Saline River, near Equality. |
| Oct. 28 | The County Line roadhouse between Johnston City and West Frankfort is fired into and burned to the ground. At the time, it is believed that Shelton gangsters are responsible. |
| Nov. 6 | Colp Mayor Jeff Stone and John "Apie" Milroy are killed in Colp. |
| Nov. 10 | A homemade bomb is tossed from a passing automobile toward the barbecue stand at Shady Rest but misses its mark. |
| Nov. 12 | Joe Adams' home is fired upon. Bombs are dropped from an airplane upon Shady Rest, but little damage results. |

Nov. 25    Bootlegger Virgil Hunsaker's home is bombed in Harrisburg. Later that day, Hunsaker and two companions are machine-gunned on a road west of Harrisburg. All survive.
Nov. 30    A bank robbery takes place at Pocahontas, Illinois.
Dec. 12    Joe Adams is murdered.
Dec. 28    Birger is charged with the Adams killing.

## 1927

Jan. 8     Shady Rest is destroyed around midnight.
Jan. 17    Lory and Ethel Price are abducted from their home.
Jan. 31    The Sheltons' mail robbery trial begins at Quincy.
Feb. 5     The body of Lory Price is discovered in some weeds in Washington County, Illinois. Each of the Shelton brothers receives a twenty-five-year sentence to Leavenworth.
Feb. 8     Birger is arrested by Saline County Sheriff Lige Turner.
Feb. 10    Birger is turned over to Franklin County Sheriff Jim Pritchard.
Mar. 10    Birger is free on bond from Benton jail pending trial.
Mar. 16    Arlie O. Boswell is shot in his garage. He survives.
Apr. 28    In an affidavit, Marion bootlegger Harvey Dungey confesses that he lied on the witness stand during the Sheltons' trial at Quincy.
Apr. 29    Birger is arrested again for the Adams killing.
Apr. 30    Harry Thomasson confesses in Benton courtroom that he and his brother Elmo murdered Joe Adams on Birger's orders.
May 22     Art Newman is arrested in Long Beach, California.
May 26     Due largely to the confession of Harvey Dungey, the Shelton brothers are granted a new trial.
June 13    Following a detailed confession by Art Newman on June 11 at Nashville, Illinois, the body of Ethel Price is found in an abandoned mine near Johnston City.
June 18    Boswell is again fired upon, this time near his home in Marion.

| | |
|---|---|
| June 24 | The trial of Rado Millich and Eural Gowan begins in Marion. They are charged with the murder of Ward "Casey" Jones. |
| July 6 | The trial of Birger, Newman, and Ray Hyland begins at Benton. They are charged with the murder of Joe Adams. |
| July 7 | Millich and Gowan are found guilty of the Jones murder, but only Millich receives the death penalty. |
| July 24 | Birger, Newman, and Ray Hyland are found guilty of the Adams murder, but only Birger is given the death penalty. |
| July 26 | Birger's hanging is set for Oct. 15, 1927. |
| Aug. 7 | There is another attempt on Boswell's life, this one at Crab Orchard. |
| Aug. 12 | Fred Thomasson and Joe Booher are captured near Metropolis. |
| Aug. 13 | Harvey Dungey, Fred Thomasson, and Joe Booher are charged with killing "Shag" Worsham. |
| Oct. 7 | Birger gets a stay of execution. |
| Oct. 21 | Rado Millich is hanged at Marion. |
| Nov. 9 | Harvey Dungey escapes from the Marion jail. |
| Nov. 12 | Harvey Dungey is captured at Ray Thomasson's home in West Frankfort. |
| Dec. 12 | Dungey, Booher, and Thomasson are acquitted in the Worsham trial. |

## 1928

| | |
|---|---|
| Feb. 24 | The Illinois supreme court sets April 13 as the new date for Birger's hanging. |
| Apr. 12 | After a heated session during which Arlie O. Boswell pleads for Birger's life, the Illinois Board of Pardons and Paroles refuses to delay Birger's hanging. Birger's attorney, R. E. Smith, files for a sanity hearing in Benton. The date of the hearing is April 16. |
| Apr. 16 | Out only twelve minutes, the jury at the sanity hearing finds Birger sane. |
| Apr. 19 | At 9:48 A.M., Birger is hanged. |

Aug. 22     Clarence Rone dies at age twenty of natural causes.

Nov. 16     Boswell and other officials are indicted in U.S. District Court at East St. Louis.

## 1929

Jan. 7     Charged with the murder of Ethel Price, Birger gangsters go on trial at Marion. All plead guilty.

Jan. 9     Each defendant in the Price trial is sentenced to a total of 157 years.

Jan. 21     Boswell's trial begins.

Feb. 2     After being found guilty on Jan. 25, Boswell is sentenced to two years at Leavenworth Penitentiary and fined $5,000.

Oct. 18     Following a long search, Connie Ritter is finally arrested in Gulfport, Mississippi.

*1929*     Saline County Sheriff Lige Turner dies of a blood infection.

*1930*     After pleading guilty to the Joe Adams murder, Connie Ritter is sentenced to life imprisonment on May 25.

*1933*     Judge D. T. Hartwell dies following a lingering illness.

*1937*     Following financial reverses, fifty-two-year-old Charles Miller, a former circuit court judge of the second judicial district, leaps to his death from the twenty-second story of the hotel in Chicago where he and his family are living.

*1939*     Former Williamson County Sheriff Oren Coleman dies of a heart attack in Carterville, where he is a bank president.

*1944*     In the White Castle Tavern, just south of Herrin, Monroe "Blackie" Armes, thirty-eight, is mortally wounded by the tavern's owner, Thomas Propes. Thinking his victim dead or at least beyond retaliation, Propes turns his back only to be shot through the head by the dying Armes. Propes is dead by the time police officers arrive.

*1948*     Connie Ritter dies at Menard.

1949  The former Charline Birger dies in childbirth in St. Louis. She is buried near her father.

1954  Rachel Shamsky dies in St. Louis and is buried near her brother, Charlie Birger.

1955  A semi-invalid due to arthritis, J. Milo Pruett dies in Harrisburg at the age of seventy-three.

1957  Former Franklin County State's Attorney Roy Martin dies in Benton. He is seventy-four.

1958  While trying to rob the Midway Tavern near DeSoto, Harvey Dungey is shot and killed by the night watchman. Prior to his death, Dungey was promoting his slide show presentation, which purported to tell the true story of the Birger gang.

1976  Retired attorney Alpheus Gustin, ninety-two, and members of his family are killed in a car-train wreck in Tennessee.

1976  Former Franklin County Sheriff Jim Pritchard dies in Danville at the age of seventy-seven.

1992  The former Minnie Birger dies in Wyoming.

# A KNIGHT OF ANOTHER SORT

# 1
# Birger's Early Years

SON OF LOUIS AND MARY (WIELANSKY) BIRGER AND GRANDSON of Charles and Anna Birger, Shachna Itzik Birger, later to be known as Charles, by his own account was born in Guanbainy, Russia, on January 1, 1880. Sister Rachel, who was older, gave his birth date as October, 1882, and his birth place as Kovno, Russia (now Kaunas, Lithuania). Relying, no doubt, on information supplied by Birger himself, military records indicate the subject was born on January 11, 1880, in Gambany, Russia. Birger's tombstone has 1883 as the year of his birth.

Birger family tradition indicates that the first to arrive in America was Charlie's older brother Samuel. Fleeing Russia in 1887 to avoid serving in the Russian army, the seventeen-year-old wasted no time once in this country; he peddled supplies from a pack on his back. From such a humble beginning, the young man prospered enough to send first for brother Oscar and later for other family members, including his parents and younger brother Charlie. It is believed that Samuel also had twin brothers who may have died in Russia. In the Madison County, Illinois Census for 1900, he is described as a salesman and druggist but is best remembered in Glen Carbon as the proprietor of a general store. Unlike his infamous younger brother, Sam Birger lived to see his American dream come true, and it is only fitting that Glen Carbon named a street in his honor.

1

Charlie's own account of his early years as gleaned from the interviews he gave reporters, fails to give credit to his enterprising older sibling or, indeed, to provide much information at all. He did mention living in New York City and moving from there to St. Louis, where he spent part of his youth. Although his family lived in various places, Charlie remembered in particular a house on the 2200 block of Biddle Street and the nearby school that he attended. Equally vivid were memories of working as a newsboy in St. Louis. It is interesting, in light of his later career, that he spoke of fights with other news carriers in the *Post-Dispatch* alley.

Little is known of his family, due largely to Birger's reluctance to reminisce about the less dramatic aspects of his past. He would say in years to follow that his mother died when he was young, but he failed to mention that he was in his twenties and had already served a stint in the cavalry when she passed away, November 16, 1905. His father, he said, found work as a drayman. Louis Birger is still remembered as being an observant Jew who never really learned to speak English. People close to Charlie got the impression that his family life was marked by a measure of hardship, thus his unwillingness to share the details with the public.

The latter part of Birger's youth was spent in Glen Carbon, a hamlet in Madison County, Illinois, named for, built around, and nourished by the mining of coal. This was home until he joined the 13th United States Cavalry on July 5, 1901. (Unless, of course, there is some truth to the story that in 1896 to 1897 he worked on a ranch in Montana where, as luck would have it, he managed to rub shoulders with Harvey Logan, also known as "Kid Curry," and Harry Longabaugh, the legendary "Sundance Kid." Sad to say, this writer has not been able to verify this tale—or quite believe it.) At the time of enlistment, Birger gave his occupation in Glen Carbon as bricklayer.

Years before, upon learning that the family was moving from New York to St. Louis, Charlie had been thrilled, thinking at last he would see Indians and buffalo. But the century was too far along for that, and in any event, St. Louis was too far east. Now, as a private in the 13th Cavalry, Charlie would ride where only a few years earlier the Sioux and the woolly bison had lorded over the plains. Even the names of the posts where he would serve seemed to keep alive the illusion of the frontier: Fort Meade, South Dakota; Fort Assinniboine and Fort Keogh, Montana. A quarter of a century later, the former cavalryman would boast, "Out of 53 guard mounts that I stood, I was orderly 52 times. It took a good soldier to be an orderly."

The muster roll for the 13th United States Cavalry Troop G shows that from June 3 until July 25, 1902, the unit was "engaged in carbine target practice," while the month of August was chiefly devoted to "revolver practice, mounting and dismounting."

Earlier Birger had twice been thrown from the back of an unwilling steed:

December 5 and 6, 1901, a moderate contusion of left ankle, anterior surface, due to being thrown from horse at Fort Assinniboine, Montana. April 24 and 28, 1902, slight contusion of right hip due to fall from horse at Fort Assinniboine, Montana. Both injuries were incurred in line of duty.

Stationed in the high plains and blasting away with an army carbine while suffering still from falls off two renegade mounts, young Charlie Birger was living the hard outdoor life of his dreams. The muster roll reports it well:

The troop, consisting of three officers and 37 enlisted men, three six-mule teams and one escort wagon as transportation, left Fort Keogh, Montana at 2:30 P.M., October 18, 1902, crossed the Yellowstone River at Kelley's Ferry, and bivouacked the night of the 18th at Cedar Creek, Montana.

On the 19th, 20th and 21st and part of the 22nd, the march up the Yellowstone was continued to Gould Brothers Sheep Ranch above Forsythe, Montana, on the north side of the Yellowstone River.

On the remainder of the 22nd, the 23rd and the 24th, the troop returned to Fort Keogh, crossing the Yellowstone River at Germania Fork and Ferry opposite Miles City. Camps were made on the outward march at McAvoy's Ranch and near Rosebud, Montana. On the return march near Rosebud and at Cameron's Ranch. Total distance of march about 105 miles. A patrol consisting of 1 officer and 3 enlisted men, 1 volunteer guide and 1 escort wagon as transportation was detached October 18th from bivouac at Cedar Creek, and set north to examine country in the vicinity of Sheep Mountain. Montana. Detachment not yet rejoined.

After transfer to Troop B, 6th United States Cavalry, in April 1903, Birger, along with the rest of the troop, was transported by rail to San Francisco where from May 1 to May 4, they performed "camp duty at Presidio of San Francisco." On May 5, they returned to Fort Keogh, Montana, "via Portland on S.P.R.R" (the Southern Pacific Railroad).

At the end of his three-year stint in the army, the young ex-soldier, by his own account, returned to Glen Carbon, where he stayed until 1905. But legend, fed by newspaper accounts (many of which originated with Birger himself), has it otherwise. True or not, his yarns of campfires and roundups set many a reporter to scribbling and many a reader to a fuller appreciation of his checkered career. From branding iron to machine gun, the eras slid past like painted backdrops at a play. Perhaps he did return to the West for a time.

Despite its proximity to East St. Louis and St. Louis, so the story goes, Glen Carbon was far too dull for this young man who had lately arrived from the far reaches of Montana and the Dakotas. So, once again Charlie headed west, this time to become one of an itinerant roundup crew operating out of Deadwood, South Dakota. They rode the cattle country "rounding up cattle and marking them for hire."

Some of the fellows were heard to say one day that they had been told all cavalry horses were "run-down." Cut to the bone by this insensitive remark, Birger quickly let it be known that his company had considered him its best horseman. When word of his brag reached the boss, he was invited to prove his ability by riding "Maneater." "Maneater" was considered by many to be one of the meanest horses east of the Continental Divide, a regular fire-snorting dragon with hooves, this "Maneater," only worse. Boasting to the eager reporters years later, Birger said, "I rode him until my nose bled."

That he could ride him "proved" young Charlie to the others, and from then on, one of his jobs was to break outlaw horses at $1.50 a head. The worst of the lot, he said, were the "somersaulters." About the only way to cure one of those devils was to smash a bottle of salt water across his brow and then let nature do the rest. Thinking the stuff in his eyes was blood, the "somersaulter" became instantly and miraculously cured. The horses did not carry all the scars however, for Birger had a lump on his breast, from being thrown once, and a flattened thumb, from hitting an outlaw horse on the head with his fist.

No less hectic was the time he spent in the boxing ring at Billings, Montana. True, he won $12.50 in the bout, but nearly half of that went for beefsteak for his puffed and blackened eyes.

To go from the storied plains to the plain unstoried prose of a pension questionnaire requires the dousing of the campfires and an end to tales tall or otherwise. In his usual poor penmanship, Charlie, in 1916, wrote this reply to the question, Where have you lived since discharge?

> Glen Carbon, Illinois, from 1904 to 1905. [Note that he couldn't very well say he had been out west breaking horses following service in the army and request a pension for back injuries incurred in the service.] St. Louis, Missouri, from 1905 to 1906. Edgemont, Illinois, from 1906 to 1908. Staunton, Illinois, from 1908 to 1913.

For some reason, he failed to mention living in Virden, Illinois, as revealed in the 1910 census. One Sunday morning, so the story goes, he dressed in colorful attire and rode a bucking bronco down Main Street. That wild ride may have gone unheralded except by wide-eyed boys eager to latch on to heroes, but when Nettie Sheerin and he won a dance contest, the local newspaper considered the event newsworthy enough for publication. The census also lists a wife, Edna.

Another story credits him with mercilessly beating a man in a pool hall. This may have been the reason Charlie and Edna left town.

That Birger did live near Edgemont during the years cited is verified by the Belleville City Directory for the years 1906 to 1907; it lists a Charles Birger and wife Sarah. Actually, they were just within the Belleville city limits but were still considered as being in Edgemont (a small point, but not without importance). The same can be said for "wife Sarah." If she was his wife, Charlie chose not to mention their marriage in future questionnaires. Marriage records from the most likely courthouses are equally reticent. What matters, perhaps, is that the couple lived in a building in French Village, where Birger claimed to have run a lunchroom. It may have been only a candy store.

Ralph Thomas remembered Birger as a "rough, tough character who bummed in Traband's saloon in Edgemont." At the time, Edgemont was the switching point for streetcars traveling to and from Belleville, East St. Louis, O'Fallon, Collinsville, Glen Carbon, and Edwardsville. Located near the switch, Traband's was ideal for accommodating the passengers, many of them miners.

There, on winter days, gamblers like Birger found likely prospects and a warm stove. Fresh from selling sandwiches and/or candy bars at his place across the street, Birger would retire to Traband's. He threw the dice, watched the money change hands, and dreamed with the best of them.

Before moving to Edgemont, he had been a coal miner at the Nigger Hollow Mine near O'Fallon. He had lived in Belleville then, "in a rooming house at the corner of West Main and First Streets," according to the redoubtable Fred J. Kern, editor of the *Belleville News Democrat*. Right on most things, Kern may have been mistaken when he wrote that while in Edgemont, Birger killed a man named Mannie, "son of Supervisor Mannie." My search of the death records in the county clerk's office at Belleville for the years 1905 through 1910 turned up no record of this killing. Kern, who goes on to say, "He too pled self-defense and alibied himself out of the scrape," may have been referring to the killing of William Oughten, and somehow the names were confused.

Charged with several killings during his nearly fifty years, Birger would say near the end of his life, "Yes, I've killed men, but never a good one." Another of his victims, recently deceased, was being discussed at the time, but Birger could just as easily have been talking about William "Chubby" Oughten, his first recorded victim. The year was 1908, the same year that saw William Jennings Bryan's third and last try for the presidency, but probably neither Oughten nor Birger paid much attention to that.

A troublesome individual, all of twenty-six years of age, Oughten had already received a "stay away order" from Belleville, after he was caught stealing some whiskey. Late in August or early in September, he had tangled with a candy store owner named Charlie "Berger," said to be about the same age. The trouble had allegedly begun over some cigars. The stage was set and the curtain drawn. On Sunday night, September 6, Birger and Oughten again began to quarrel, this time in Rollie Rhody's lunch wagon, which was located across the street from Traband's saloon. But for the intervention of a Mr. Keeton, the Edgemont village marshal, and Rhody himself, Oughten and his butcher knife might have finished Charlie early in his career, thus saving southern Illinois much legal expense and many lives. Birger later claimed his enemy had also carried a razor, but a search by the good marshal did not reveal it.

Just after midnight, Phil Traband closed his saloon and was talking with Oughten on the porch, when the latter declared, "I'm going over there and kill that fellow." That fellow, of course, was Birger, and over there was his candy stand in the "old dancing hall," just inside the Belleville city limits. Traband tried to talk Oughten into staying but was unsuccessful.

Before the saloon closed for the night, Birger and Rhody bought two bottles of beer, and Birger carried them across the street, going to the back of the candy store where both men roomed. (Apparently Sarah was out of the picture.) Rhody, who arrived a short time later, was followed by Oughten.

When "Chubby" demanded one of the bottles, Birger said it wasn't his to give, an answer that did not in the least placate Oughten. Following a second demand, Birger handed the bottle over, but this time Oughten said he also wanted an opener. Just as Birger reached for it, Oughten came at him with a knife. Expecting such a play, the candy store owner raised a conveniently placed revolver and fired a warning shot before sending the next three bullets into Oughten's breast. Mortally wounded, the man stumbled across the street, only to fall dead on the porch of Traband's saloon. Following him by moments, his assailant ran over, viewed the body, and then gave himself up to Marshal Keeton. The next morning, the marshal took him into custody. Finding no evidence to the contrary, one assumes that he was acquitted there by a coroner's jury on grounds of self-defense.

It may be that Oughten's death influenced Birger's move to Staunton. Whatever the reason for his going, there is reason to believe that he did not remain in that coal mining town from 1908 until 1913, as stated on his pension questionnaire.

In the autumn of 1927, Birger was visited in jail by the famed evangelist Billy Sunday, who at that time was conducting revival services in West Frankfort, Illinois. During the conversation that took place, the gangster said he had met Sunday twenty years before, when the evangelist was conducting a revival at Danville, Illinois. Despite the interval of two decades, neither man had forgotten the preacher's advice to Charlie: "Hit the sawdust trail." But both men sadly concluded that this advice had completely slipped past young Charlie.

An equally significant account concerning those years of obscurity is found in the *Illinois State Journal* (Springfield, Illinois) of April 19, 1928. There it is stated that several months earlier, Birger had mentioned to one of its reporters that he had first arrived in Springfield "from nowhere" nearly twenty years before and had begun working at a "resort" on Seventh and Madison streets.

"I worked down the street several years ago as a bartender," he said. "I did not stay long. It was a little too tough for me. In those days, they said I was 'yellow,' but now they say I am a gunman with several notches on my gun."

Not without cause those notches.

After spending some time in Christopher in 1912, he moved to Saline County, either in the latter part of that year or in 1913. With its coal mines and sizable payrolls, Saline County would be Charlie Birger's home for the rest of his life.

# 2
# Bootlegging Days

I F BIRGER LIVED IN HARRISBURG FOR SOME TIME BEFORE MOV-
ing to Ledford, as some assert, the records fail to show it. The
matter of chronology aside, it was at Ledford, "patches" of coal
miners' houses southwest of Harrisburg, where he first came to
prominence in southern Illinois. With him came wife Edna, a
statuesque blonde from East St. Louis, whom he had married in
Clayton, Missouri, on March 22, 1913.

In the summer of 1913, Charlie Birger bought a lot in Ledford
near the spur of the streetcar line, and soon thereafter, he was in
the business he knew best—that of selling whiskey and beer to
miners. His methods of obtaining the merchandise varied. For
those who patronized his combination saloon-restaurant, he had
the beer barrels shipped to Eldorado via the Chicago, Cleveland,
Cincinnati, and St. Louis Railroad, better known as the Big Four.
At Eldorado, the barrels were "switched off" on the car line and
sent on their way to the Ledford spur. (The conductor at the time
was John Small, a hefty fellow from Harrisburg who would one
day be sheriff of Saline County.) Birger would often hire a team
and wagon from Billy Morris to haul the beer to his saloon. Always packed in sawdust, most of the barrels would end up in his
barn, where there was a cooling device (it was possibly nothing
more than ice packed within the sawdust). Leo Morris recalled

that when his dad's wagon was returned, there would always be one barrel remaining.

Much of the beer he sold to this community of many "patches" was also shipped directly to the Ledford train depot. Only a boy at the time, George Cummins helped Jim Mofield deliver some of the barrels in a horse-drawn hack to the hamlet of Five Patch—some, but not all. According to Cummins:

> It would come up from Mounds, down by Cairo on the passenger train that came through there, and they'd set it off there at the depot, and the miners would come out on paydays or on Saturdays, and they'd get the beer, and they all got across the railroad there along the bank. They had places cleaned off where they'd drink their beer, shoot craps or play poker. They had a little old stand of a thing and laid the barrel down on its side. They drove a spigot in. When they'd drawn so much, it would quit running. They'd take a hammer and knock that side bottom down so it would get air and it would run until the keg went dry.

From the beginning, Charlie's easy manner won him friends. To the children of the village who gathered at the cinder walks to play or to loaf or to lunch on ice cream, soda pop, or candy bars that could be purchased inside his restaurant, Birger was something of an overseer, since most of their fathers worked in the mines. A boy at that time, Leo Morris well remembers how Birger would come out on the porch wearing his usual summer attire of blue serge pants, sheep-lined house shoes, and a BVD undershirt. Usually he was hatless. When enough youngsters were about, he would very often brighten their day by bringing out a cigar box full of change. One of his men—most often John Bard, who actually ran the place—would hold the box while Charlie threw the contents into the air. Cinders would fly as the eager youngsters scrambled for the coins. Above the melee could be heard the guttural laughter of the one whose coins had started it all. It was a great show and, according to Morris, one that occurred almost daily when the weather permitted.

Most of the time, Birger seemed glad to have the children around, but once when he wanted to get them out of his hair, he persuaded them and John Bard to peddle some watermelons. Leo Morris recalled it well:

He used to have a Model "T" roadster made like a pick-up. Charlie always had a few things to sell—just as a blind. He always had watermelons and different things. I can remember one time in particular—I don't know why he wanted us out of the place of business—but he said to John Bard, "You go out there and get those watermelons and put them in that truck and take those boys with you and go peddle them." So we did. We never put in over ten, I guess. We had about that many boys in there. We come down through the Patch and down by the railroad . . . and up to Dorrisville and back down Goat Row and down Liberty Road and back to the railroad station. Well, the railroad station was high off the ground, and there was a ditch in it, and a lot of guys used to slip in there and have their drinks, you know. Now John stopped there. We never stopped nor asked a soul to buy a watermelon, so we had all that he'd had when we left. He said since we couldn't sell the watermelons, we'd just eat them. You know what that meant. We got out of the truck, got the melons, got under there, sat down and ate the whole bunch. When we got back, Charlie asked John how many we had sold. When John told him we hadn't sold any, but ate them all, Charlie said, "That's good."

Birger was no less accommodating with the adults of the community. Few in Ledford had cars, even fewer had telephones, but Birger had both. In the event of an emergency, those cars were available, but one of his men had to do the driving—the cars were never loaned out. If someone needed a doctor and didn't have the money to pay the bill, Birger was the man to see. He would call the doctor and tell him to come down to Ledford and to add the fee to his own bill. When the family got on its feet again—that is, when the man got back to work in the mines—Birger expected to be paid back in full. "I don't guess he got beat out of a dime," said Morris.

On at least one occasion, his generosity was extended to the community, Morris related:

One time they had an ice cream social down here in 14 Patch. Charlie sent a couple of boys down there, and they built a little stand. They got the ice cream from the Busy Bee up on Harrisburg Square. Charlie had them send the ice cream down in five-gallon freezers, and he furnished all the soda pop and everything. When it was going that night, I happened to be there, and Charlie came up and laid down a twenty dollar bill and said to treat the kids until it was all gone. When it was over, he went back down there and picked up all the stuff, took it all back to his place. Damn if he didn't pay for what was left, and he gave it to them in the first place.

Despite his well-advertised generosity, not everyone liked him. In particular, there was a family by the name of Pulley who also had a phone. Mrs. Pulley was especially antagonistic toward Ledford's prime "booze" vendor. Any time she suspected that he was breaking the law, she would ring up the Saline county sheriff.

And even Billy Morris, who considered Birger his friend, had reason not to trust him completely. On one occasion, while sitting in the rocking chair in front of the grate in Morris's home, Birger observed that Billy had not worked much in the mines that summer. To that his host could only nod in agreement. Then came the proposition. With Billy's approval, Birger would build a garage on the corner of Morris's land, drive one of his cars inside, get the car insured, let it set for a time, and then quietly burn the building down. Half the insurance money would come in handy for an out-of-work miner's family, he said. No doubt it would have, but the cool reception from his would-be partner effectively killed the scheme.

Early in 1914, Birger was charged with rape, but on December 21, the charge was stricken from the court docket. Harrisburg businessman and gambler Dan Lockwood provided his bond.

On June 11, 1915, eight witnesses heard Birger threaten to kill Oscar Ridley. After Ridley signed a complaint, a peace warrant was issued, and Perry Cain, a constable from Harrisburg, arrested Birger on June 14. On June 25, Justice of the Peace Edward Stricklin ruled that Birger was to keep the peace toward Oscar Ridley for one month from that day, and if he failed to do so, he would forfeit his bond. The remainder of the bond would be paid by J. Milo Pruett as previously agreed upon. There is no evidence that Charlie "broke" the peace during the ensuing month or that he or his friend Pruett, who was considered one of the wealthiest men in Harrisburg, had to pay the money. Birger did have to pay the court costs.

In addition to his difficulties with the law, problems of a personal nature were now at hand. On November 29, 1915, he and Edna were separated, although their divorce was not official until 1917. Never one to lack for female companionship, Birger would in later years lament the fact that their marriage had not been a success. He would recall the good times, such as the night they were walking home from a christening, and Edna slipped and fell into a pond, all but ruining her gorgeous blue dress. When Charlie tried to pull her to bankside, the pond claimed yet another victim, but they had great fun laughing about their soaking. Of course, Edna was furious the time he brought several chorus girls home. Such stunts as that might have prompted the breakup of the marriage, but never far in the background was Birger's increasing notoriety, which also may have been a factor.

Like many coal-mining communities, Ledford had a reputation for toughness—not totally deserved, according to some local residents. Of course, there were fights, and not "anemic tousles," either. They were real fist-to-nose encounters where the cinder grit got mixed up with bits of tooth and a fair amount of blood and wherein the coal-dust-laden air was ripe with curses that, if edited, could have passed for poetry. Birger's place was the scene of many such bouts, but there were other bootleggers in and around Ledford who could be counted on for the stuff to fuel those free-for-alls. The locals blamed most of the trouble on outsiders who flocked to Birger's and the other less well-known joints for a rollicking good time. Sometimes the rollicking simply got out of hand.

Even without the outsiders, there was sufficient friction to spark an occasional brawl. Unhappily, two elements contributed most to the discord. One element was the people of Eastern Europe—the Lithuanians, the Hungarians, and the Polish. Clannish, they congregated mostly in town. Their ways were strange, but their homes were neat. Some of them never quite learned the language. They were called "hunkies."

The people who called them hunkies, the "Kentucky crackers," were the other element. They lived, for the most part, outside the town. Like the foreigners, they had been drawn to Saline County by the promise of work in the mines. Unlike the Lithuanians and Hungarians and other East Europeans, their homes were often less than presentable. That gibberish-spouting "hunkies," just off the boat, could come to the Midwest and show them up for the slovenly hillbillies they were was a galling fact of life. What the "crackers" usually failed to take into account was that while they had important activities with which to fill their free time, such as hunting and drinking, the foreigners, with their language problem, could best spend their free time fixing up their modest homes—and drinking.

With undercurrents of hostility combined with the ever-present liquor, Ledford was a typical southern Illinois coal-mining community. No less typical was Charlie Birger, who provided the extra touches to what was, after all, the miner's hard and rather drab existence.

For the lonely, he had women. For the thirsty, he had almost every drink imaginable, including champagne. Best of all, he even had a couple of black entertainers who played guitar and banjo. One of them had worked in a carnival, and his specialty was making up songs about real people. All this clever soul needed to set him off on a spasm of creation was a name and the promise of a drink at song's end. He rarely failed to please the customer. Popular with the crowd, many of whom had been "immortalized" on the spot, this black lyricist would invariably end the offerings with the theme song containing the line "Come after breakfast, bring your dinner, and go home before suppertime."

Another notable personage was D. P. (Pat) Bybee, an officious little gentleman who claimed to be an attorney. Usually drunk, Bybee bore an uncanny resemblance to W. C. Fields, with manners to match. Once, a young girl whose mother worked for Birger found a man lying in the window box at Charlie's place and cried out, "Oh, Mama, here's another dead man." It was, however, only the town's "attorney," out from a bout with the bottle. The lass who found him would blossom into quite a drinker herself and would be known as the "Blonde Bombshell." Needless to say, she reappears in this narrative. Little is known of the bartender, one

"Henry Seven Shoe," except that he lent his presence and remarkable nickname to the establishment.

For many people, 1916 meant trenches in France. But for Charlie, it was the year he arrested a man and had five ducks and seven geese stolen. The poultry was taken in the early part of December, on three different occasions. Not content with their meager haul, the thieves then raided the coops of one of Birger's neighbors.

The other incident occurred at Havana, Illinois. It illustrates very clearly what was to be a curious trait of this very genuine gangster, namely his willingness, even eagerness, to cooperate with the local authorities.

In the latter part of 1915, three fellows robbed a store in Carrier Mills, only to be captured a short time later. Two of the men were convicted and jailed. But the third, John Weger, was lucky enough to get "Lige" Gaskins to pay his bond. Weger then disappeared. Later, in a letter sent to some friends or relatives in Saline County, the fugitive wrote that Canada was his new home, but that soon he was planning to enlist in the army. He said he wanted to go overseas. These stirring words were probably penned in Havana, Illinois, where Weger was subsequently "captured" by Charlie Birger. According to the telegram received by Deputy Sheriff Tom Russell, Birger and his "prisoner" were returning to Harrisburg the evening of April 25, 1916.

This curious account has yet another twist. Birger and Weger apparently were close friends or at least enough so for Weger to serve as the witness on two of Birger's pension questionnaires, dated December 15, 1915, and February 22, 1916. The Harrisburg *Daily Register* article of April 25 states that Weger left Saline County "some time ago." This "capture" of his former pal shows Birger at his ambitious best: "booze" vendor, gambler, operator of a "house," but through it all, always a pal of the Saline County law enforcement personnel.

On the night of December 3, 1917, there occurred a more dramatic example of the bond existing between Birger and the lawmen. At about 6:00 P.M., the telephone jingled at the Saline County jail, and Sheriff George Russell answered. He was told that a man and a woman, both drunk, were causing trouble at the Big Four

15

depot in Carrier Mills. Deputies Harve Rann and Tom Russell went to the scene of the disturbance. Meanwhile, another call came. This time the voice on the other end said the couple had boarded the "seven o'clock car" and were heading north. When the sheriff finally got word to his deputies of this change in plans, they managed to get aboard the company streetcar No. 4. The sheriff instructed them to meet car No. 7 at a designated crossing, arrest the pair, and then transfer them to the freight car.

When No. 7 pulled in, however, the deputies were told that the elusive two had disembarked at Ledford. When Rann and Russell arrived at the coal-mining village, they were met by Charlie Birger, who was only too happy to be of service. After he told them the inebriated pair had walked north from the depot, the two officers resumed the chase, this time on foot. By the time they reached the Pauper Crossing southwest of Harrisburg, it became quite clear to the officers that they would have better luck back at Ledford. They managed to "hitch a ride" back there, only to discover that the subjects of all this fuss were, at that moment, celebrating in a saloon operated by Tom "Crip" Yates, a young roughneck of local repute against whom charges of burglary and larceny had been lodged. The two deputies slipped up to either a side or the back door.

"You come in that door and we'll burn you up," someone said when they demanded admittance to Yates's establishment.

The threat apparently carried the ring of truth, for Rann went to place a call to Sheriff Russell in Harrisburg while Tom Russell waited. Rann, upon his return, saw that some of the patrons were running out the front door. There was no time to relay the sheriff's order, which was to wait until he arrived. Reaching the door just as the couple was coming out, Rann took charge of the man while Russell took charge of the woman. Off they went to the depot, Rann and his man taking the lead while Russell and the woman followed closely behind.

As they neared the depot, the woman began to struggle. "I'm not going another step farther with you!" she screamed.

Just then "Crip" Yates stepped up. "See here, Russell," he said. "Let's try to smooth this thing over. Let her go. You know me."

"Yes, I know you too well," Russell snapped. "You get back,

and don't interfere here." To emphasize that remark, he gave the saloon keeper a shove.

Just then, Charlie Birger was approaching the crowd. When he got close enough to see the pistol in Yates's hand, pointed under the deputy's arm, Birger leaped for the man with the gun. Turning, Yates fired one shot that tore through Birger's coat. That shot was followed by three others, but now Birger was doing the shooting. Aware that his bullets had taken effect (all three shots were in the chest), Birger tossed his pistol aside, grabbed Yates around the waist, and held on until the mortally wounded man fell to the ground.

On their way back to the Harrisburg jail with the drunken pair, the officers took the wounded man to the operating table of Dr. C. W. Turner. About half an hour following the shooting, Yates died. There are, of course, other accounts of Yates's death. Birger's family doctor, Joe Lightner, said, "Charlie made arrangements with some of the officers to go down and arrest 'Crip'" (his competitor in the liquor business). "When they went down there, Charlie joined them on some pretext," according to Dr. Lightner. Birger sent the officers away. The rest of the story goes something like this: "While the officers were gone, Charlie shot 'Crip.' They brought 'Crip' into Dr. Turner's, and he was still alive. Charlie came up then. 'Crip' told him what a yellow streak he had up his back. 'Crip' died."

One of those who helped carry Yates into Dr. Turner's office disagrees. According to Ralph Pallister, the dying man never said a word.

Willard St. John, who also knew Birger quite well, was convinced that at least two of the three shots were fired after Yates fell. He recalled a conversation with Birger about the shooting.

"Why did you do it?" St. John asked.

"I wanted to show it was in self-defense, that I was afraid of him," Birger replied. In an undertone he added, "I was afraid of him."

If any fear remained as to his fate, a glance at Harrisburg's *Daily Register* of Tuesday, December 4, surely eased his mind: "Although they regretted very much to do so, Birger was also locked up and is now in the local jail."

He was not there long, however, thanks to the decision of the coroner's jury. Moments after the evidence was presented in the crowded courtroom, the jury gave its verdict as follows: "We, the jury, find that George Thomas Yates came to his death by a gunshot wound at the hands of Charles Birger, and we further find that the said Charles Birger was justified in the shooting."

To the prisoner, these were sweet words; and the fact that at least two of the six who found him guiltless were his close friends, J. Milo Pruett and Med Ledford, made them sweeter still. (Deputy Sheriff John D. Cummins, who would be elected sheriff of Saline County in 1918, was another juror, and still another was H. E. Wills, the next county clerk.) Three bullets had eliminated Birger's competitor and had won him kind words from a local newspaper. Soon, however, his "good guy/bad guy image" would be tarnished by an incident in Massac County.

On the night of March 29, 1918, a Ford and a Buick were stolen in Metropolis. The Ford was found the following morning at a Baptist church near town, where it had apparently "run out of juice." On April 19, Metropolis Chief of Police Isaac Brannon arrested Charles Birger. Accompanying the two back to Massac County were Birger's attorney, Acquilla Lewis, and D. P. Bybee, who paid his $1,000 bond.

On April 22, the Buick along with two other automobiles was finally located in Birger's barn at Ledford. This new evidence seemed sufficient for Metropolis authorities to issue another warrant. This time the Saline County officers said Birger could not be located. On April 28, the day before his preliminary hearing on the first charge, Birger was finally "nailed" by Harve Rann at the Big Four depot in Carrier Mills. Just as the southbound passenger train pulled in, Rann, Tom Russell, and Will Wriston hopped aboard—each man was to search a designated area. Looking through the smoker, Rann found his man, along with Bybee and Attorney Lewis. The fiery-tempered Lewis was so uncooperative that he was later arrested for remarks he made that day on the train. Arriving in Harrisburg on the evening train, Massac County Sheriff Orso Shirk and Metropolis Chief of Police Ike Brannon took charge of Birger, who at that time was in the Saline County jail.

Not satisfied with this one arrest, the Saline County officers proceeded to raid Birger's restaurant at Ledford. There, according to Harve Rann, the bar "was supplied with everything necessary to serve most any kind of a drink a man might call for." Bottles and kegs were emptied outside, leaving a whiskey odor to the village and, according to some witnesses, a "head" on some of the nearby streams.

Next, they raided the Big Four depot at Ledford. The men found four whiskey barrels, sixteen cases of whiskey in half pint bottles, twenty-five kegs of beer, and what was once a case of champagne. The agent said that Birger had receipted all the "wet goods" and that all the shipping charges had been paid. The "haul" was brought to Harrisburg and poured into the gutters.

On all fronts, it seemed that Charlie's problems were mounting. The chief of police of St. Louis wrote Ike Brannon that the suspect had purchased name tags and license plates from a St. Louis firm. Indications were that with Charlie Birger's almost certain conviction following his upcoming trial, an important car theft ring was about to be broken.

Held on the second warrant, Birger now saw his bond raised to $5,000. This time, though, Sheriff Russell believed it was in the prisoner's best interests that the bond not be filled since he was wanted by authorities in Williamson, Franklin, Washington, and Johnson counties in Illinois and also by authorities in Knox County, Indiana. He had been busy.

There are no records to show the length of Birger's stay in the Massac County jail, but he was certainly there long enough to make donations to some of the local charities and to conduct himself as "a model prisoner." What bearing his philanthropy may have had on the trial is not clear, but certainly it did him no harm in the eyes of local citizens. Chief of Police Ike Brannon, for instance, thought him a prince among prisoners and was to say so in later years when Birger's reputation as a gunman was greatly enhanced. Brannon failed to mention that the prisoner had managed to buy two "jackasses from a Metropolis man" and that he promptly gave them to the police chief's young sons. Naturally, the boys were sad when their dad made them give the animals back.

A few Saline countians thought they caught a familiar refrain when they heard of Charlie's doings in that old river town. Yes, he was up to his old tricks again, winning over with charm and "greenbacks" those who should have been clear-eyed enough to see through his strategy.

Similarly, there was a familiar refrain regarding some of the witnesses slated to testify. H. E. Wills, who had recently served on the coroner's jury following the Yates killing, was to have been summoned to testify for the defendant, but there is nothing to indicate he did so. Another member of that jury, J. Milo Pruett, was subpoenaed to testify both for the defendant and for the State, but his travel voucher is given only for the latter. The man who may have owed his life to Birger's quick trigger, Tom Russell, was summoned forth by the State. Oddly enough, Sheriff George Russell's wife was subpoenaed by Birger's attorneys. If the list of witnesses seems confusing, the *Metropolis Herald*'s account of the trial's outcome added its own touch of uncertainty by referring to the defendant as James Birger: "It was found that an agreement could not be reached as to the innocence or guilt of Birger. He was immediately taken in charge by the sheriff of Saline County and taken back to Harrisburg, where it is said there are several charges against him for selling liquor."

Thus concluded the car-stealing case that attracted more than usual notice.

# 3
# Charlie and Beatrice

ARLY JULY 1919 FOUND BARBER SHOPS AND STREET CORNERS
everywhere buzzing with predictions and wagers about the
forthcoming battle between heavyweight boxing champion
Jess Willard and an up and coming slugger named Jack Dempsey.
The fight for the championship was to be fought the Fourth of
July in Toledo, Ohio. Along with other gamblers from Harrisburg, Birger would be in attendance.

In the first round alone, Willard was knocked down seven times,
which was not all that surprising considering that the tall, thirty-
seven-year-old boxer had failed to train for the much younger
Dempsey. The inevitable knockout punch came in round three,
and chances are Birger and buddies saw it all, if not exactly at
ringside, at least as part of the roaring crowd.

However, the real excitement came when he and the others returned to Saline County. No sooner had Charlie arrived back at
Ledford Saturday night, July 5, than he was arrested by Saline
County Sheriff John D. Cummins and his deputy W. O. Warren.
The two had been tipped off about some whiskey that had been
stored in a building belonging to Birger. Their search revealed
nearly six hundred half-pint bottles, not to mention many quart
bottles. Bud Tavender was instructed to stand guard over the booze
until Sunday morning. In the meantime, Birger and his faithful
bartender John Bard were taken to the Saline County jail in Har-

risburg. Upon the filing of the necessary bond, Birger was released, while Bard remained behind bars awhile longer.

The case dragged on until November when Birger was find $100 on each of the three counts and sentenced to thirty days in jail. It appears that the jail sentence was suspended.

That raid was only the beginning of Birger's woes. On July 7, 1919, a trunk marked "Glassware" arrived at the express office in Eldorado. That the trunk was addressed to Charles Birger was of little concern but that it had also been sent from East St. Louis by Charles Birger did seem a little odd to the express agent. Odder still were the flies buzzing about the container, as well as a certain aroma emanating from it. Clearly this was a matter for the law officers. An unnamed reporter for the *Daily Register* left us this thoughtful account:

> When Birger called at the office yesterday and asked about the trunk the express agent had already suspicioned what it contained and had notified the police. Policeman Lamb was in the office when Birger called and when he saw the police he remarked that he would get a dray and call for it and he did not return. They did not count it or disturb it but are of the opinion that it contains about seventy-two quarts. The sheriff was notified, but owing to the newness and unfamiliarity of the new search and seizure laws and the fact that the booze was not yet in Birger's possession they did not seize it, but are guarding it until the attorney general advises them what to do.

As it turned out, the true count was seventy-eight quarts, each of which the court ordered Sheriff Cummins to pour into the water sewer located on the southeast corner of Harrisburg Square on the last day of July. Many years later, old timers would wistfully recall how the whiskey aroma hung around for days.

On Thursday, July 24, the fairground at Shawneetown was the site of "one of the best ever (horse races) witnessed in southern Illinois. Van Dillon succeeded in giving the dust to the field, beating the favorite, H.M. . . . Considerable money changed hands." Some of that money, no doubt, found or fled Birger's pockets.

But that day provided Birger more drama than any celebrated horse race, in that he was charged with contributing to the delinquency to two sisters from Carrier Mills. One was sixteen, the other was fourteen. The two girls had been missing since Wednesday night, prompting their mother to contact Mrs. McCreery, the juvenile officer. Somehow a car was located, and together the two woman journeyed to the Shawneetown fairground, where rumor had it that Birger and the girls might be found.

All missing parties were located, along with at least two others who seemed to be along for the ride. What had at first appeared to be a criminal act of the worst sort now began to look more like a foolish jaunt, but the sisters were handed over to the custody of their mother and a warrant was served. The next day Sheriff Cummins arrested Birger and placed him under a $1,000 bond, which he promptly paid.

Later that year, all charges would be dropped at the request of the girls' mother, leaving the entire matter to be quickly overshadowed by other, more dramatic, episodes in Birger's criminal career. But a certain detail is worth noting. One of Charlie's more mature companions that Thursday at the Shawneetown fairground was eighteen-year-old Beatrice Bainbridge, the woman he would later marry.

Nearly sixty years later I would meet Beatrice and find her to be a grandmotherly, down-to-earth old lady. For my sake, she tried to recall a past she had spent decades trying to suppress, and for that I am grateful. She was quick to admit that her years with Birger had a dreamlike quality about them. Much of what she was able to remember was painful.

"He would tell me anything," she said. And no doubt he did.

So, this is her story. Not every detail adheres to the facts as we know them. For instance, she recalled being married in Clayton, Missouri, shortly after the incident in Shawneetown. The actual marriage certificate is dated March 1921. Perhaps her memory played a trick here; yet from other anecdotes she shared, it is evident she and Birger were together long before the official marriage date. Is it possible Charlie arranged a sham wedding that was convincing enough to fool even the "bride"? Only he could have gotten away with the deception. It is a matter of record that Edna is listed as his wife in the 1910 census, which was compiled three years before they were officially wed. Illusion for illusion's sake was an ideal in the pursuit of which Birger took considerable pride.

In Harrisburg, Illinois, that summer of 1919, few business establishments were more popular than the Busy Bee Candy Kitchen, located near the southwest corner of the Square. That day two girls sat at one of the tables in the confectionery. One wore a homemade hat, "a most gorgeous thing," adorned with a streamer of blue and pink ribbon that hung down her back. Beatrice Bainbridge was proud of that hat.

Bessie, her more fashionably dressed friend, had an admirer who, at that moment, was standing behind the two girls talking to a darkly handsome man of less than average height. During a pause in their conversation, the stranger reached over and cut the ribbon streamer from Beatrice's hat.

It was on November 9, 1976, nearly sixty years after the ribbon cutting event, that I interviewed Beatrice Bainbridge, whom I will hereafter refer to as Beatrice. For purposes of privacy, even after sixty years had passed, I agreed to use only her maiden name.

"It insulted me [when he cut the streamer]," she said, "and he laughed a happy, guttural laugh."

As though his audacity had entitled him to a proper introduction, the man sat down, apologized, and told her that his name was Jack Diamond and that he was a jewelry salesman from Chicago. As for the ribbon cutting, he offered an apology but undercut it by insisting that her beauty had so befogged his senses that he had had no other choice. Because she did not know him "from a sack of rabbits," the recipient of this adulation had no reason to doubt the stranger's word.

The next Sunday afternoon (Beatrice was allowed uptown only on Sunday afternoons), the two couples went for a drive in the country. At Ingram Hill Cemetery, southeast of town, the car came to a stop, and the other couple quickly got out of the car and disappeared among the tombstones, leaving Beatrice alone with her admirer, who seemed once again to be laughing at her. "That was the first time I ever was in the car with him," she recalled, "because a car ride to me then was like somebody giving me a Lincoln Continental now."

Since she had to be home by five o'clock, the other couple was soon summoned for the short drive back to Harrisburg. Even though they were running late, the girls asked to be dropped off uptown, blocks beyond the prying eyes of Beatrice's parents, Bob and Mary Bainbridge. However, it happened that Beatrice's brother, Earl, saw them get out of the car, and he lost no time in conveying this information to their father and mother.

As Beatrice walked home, she met her mother where McKinley and Poplar streets intersect on McKinley Hill. Mary Bainbridge, her German blood raised to a boiling point, whipped her errant daughter all the way to their home in west Harrisburg, and she didn't quit there.

"She whipped me from one end of the house to the other," Beatrice recalled with a laugh (although at the time it was anything but funny). It was not until she was confronted by her family that the young girl learned the reason for the stripes on her back.

When Earl accused her of being in the company of Charlie Birger, "a bad character man" from Ledford, she vigorously denied it, saying her date—if he could be called that—was Jack Diamond, a jewelry salesman from Chicago, and a gentleman. For a moment, poor Earl could only shake his head. Her "gentleman," he said, was a gambler and a bootlegger, a womanizer of no small reputation, and finally, a killer. Convinced by his argument, the parents forbade their daughter to ever see Birger again.

When Bessie brought Charlie word of the whipping, he seemed dismayed and gave her a message in return. "She came up the alley," remembered Beatrice, "through the backyard and got ahold of me." And the message? If she refused to see him elsewhere, Birger would come to her home. She agreed to a meeting just this once, although she was aware that if her parents found out, another—possibly more severe—whipping could be the result.

"Mom and Dad were gone someplace. . . . and I sneaked down through the back alley to see what he wanted," she said.

He suggested that they take a ride, but she refused. When he mentioned the whipping, she downplayed the details, fearing what might happen to her brother Earl if his tattling became known to Birger.

"Don't send any notes," she insisted, "and don't bother me no more, because I'm already in too much trouble. They won't even let me leave the house."

Thinking the matter over for a moment, Birger replied, "Well, you won't have to take another whipping."

Memory of that whipping had not faded when, sometime later,

25

Bessie asked Beatrice if she would accompany her and her beau and some other young people to the Shawneetown Fair to see some of the horse races and, in general, to partake of such festivities as were there. "No," came the reply, "I'll get killed if they find out I'm gone." Not only would they be back by five o'clock, Bessie argued, but their very absence would go unnoticed; besides, the excitement would do her good. Expecting nothing more than an afternoon's diversion, Beatrice Pearl Bainbridge agreed to go along.

Waiting for them at the fairground was the handsome fellow who had caused all the trouble. "He appeared and walked around the fairground there," she recalled. "How fresh," she thought him at one point for brushing the dust from her white, homemade dress. "But that was all—he never even put his arm around me."

That afternoon was still in its prime when juvenile officer Mrs. McCreery arrived with the disheartening news that the woman accompanying her was charging Birger with contributing to the delinquency of her two young daughters. (That story has been told.) For her part, Beatrice forgot pertinent details of the incident but did recall how the subsequent discord and confusion prompted Charlie to drive to Missouri and to take her along. Her life would be changed forever.

"He took me on to Clayton, Missouri. I was too dumb to ask him why he was going in there," she said (referring to the office of the justice of the peace in the St. Louis county courthouse). "He told me to sign my name, and I asked him what for. He said we were getting married. I started to cry. I wanted to go home."

Instead of taking Beatrice back to Harrisburg, Birger took her to the home of his sister, Rachel Shamsky, in St. Louis. Beatrice quickly realized that Ray (as Rachel was called) was not pleased with her brother's choice in a wife. "She raised Cain with him for marrying me." Ray had in mind a Jewish girl from the city, certainly not an underage Gentile who spoke with a strong southern Illinois accent. When Beatrice offered to help with the dishes after supper, she was coldly told that would not be necessary. Much of the conversation that night went past the new bride, as it was in Yiddish. What happened next she remembered clearly:

We went to the American Annex Hotel, and I wouldn't undress to go to bed. Charlie threatened to throw me in the bathtub of water if I didn't get undressed, and when I said, "You wouldn't dare!" he did. He threw me in, clothes, hat, shoes, and all. I was wearing a homemade dress, homemade underwear—you can imagine! The Grapes of Wrath I was!

The bridegroom spent the night at his sister's home, leaving Beatrice back at the hotel to ponder the turn her life had taken in the past few hours: "I just sat there in the room, looking out the window, with my clothes on. I was afraid to go to bed or anything. He had said when he left, 'Now, I'm going over to Ray's. Don't you open this door for nobody. I'll call you.'"

With such an inauspicious beginning, the honeymoon improved very little during their several days' stay in St. Louis. He did buy her some clothes, and every night he would stop by to take her to a restaurant and a movie. Once they even attended a burlesque show. "We walked into this place there, and I didn't want to sit down because they were exposing themselves, and I thought it was terrible," Beatrice remembered. "And Charlie said he shouldn't have brought me there, that he thought it was a movie house—but he could have told me anything." Her husband was also thoughtful enough to stop by a couple of times a day. One day, to relieve the boredom, he suggested that she might like to ride the streetcar, boarding it there at the hotel. After some protest on her part and his scoffing at her fears, Beatrice finally stepped aboard.

"If you get lost," he said, "look up and see Buster Brown. Then you'll know you're at the American Annex Hotel." Most of the day she rode that streetcar, but instead of enjoying the sights, she was constantly on the watch for a sign of Buster and his faithful dog, Tige. "Finally I asked the streetcar conductor, and I guess he wondered what I was doing on that streetcar all that time. I was sick to my stomach."

Amid this series of uncomfortable surprises, the young bride soon realized that she was now the stepmother of Birger's young daughter, Minnie. Fond though he was of the child, Birger could no longer abide the mother, his former sweetheart, Winnie Mofield. Listening to him rant about Winnie's failures as a mother, Beatrice began to realize that Charlie had married her primarily because he wanted someone to help raise his daughter. This, in time, she would do.

Back in Saline County, at last, the newlyweds stopped at Charlie's place in Ledford. Taking Minnie from the housekeeper who had cared for the little girl while Charlie was away in St. Louis getting married again, they drove to a hotel in Eldorado. They lived there only a short time before moving to a small apartment above the Busy Bee Candy Kitchen in Harrisburg.

Charlie Birger

The Big Four Depot at Carrier Mills

Beatrice Birger with stepdaughter Minnie, *left*, and daughter Charline, *right*

Charline Birger as a toddler, behind the Birger home

Wilbur Leitch at his soda fountain in the old streetcar depot in Muddy, 1915

Ora Thomas

S. Glenn Young

*Left to right*: Carl, Earl, and Bernie Shelton

*Left to right*: Minnie, Bernice, and Charline Birger

Joe Chesnas

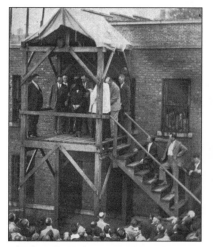

The hanging of Joe Chesnas

Heads bowed prior to Chesnas's hanging

Southern Illinois moonshiners but not members of the Birger gang, 1927

Southern Illinois moonshiners, 1927

The barbecue stand at Shady Rest

The Birger gang at Shady Rest

Birger and his gang at Shady Rest. Standing, *left to right*: Riley "Alabama" Simmons, Rado Millich, "Honest John" Renfro, Eural Gowan, unidentified man, Clarence Rone, unidentified man, and Oral Gowan. Kneeling, *left to right*: Steve George, Art Newman, Connie Ritter, Ernest Blue, Ward "Casey" Jones, Leon Stover, Bert Owens, and Birger.

The Birger gang. Standing, *left to right*: Clarence Rone, Art Newman, Ward "Casey" Jones, and Riley "Alabama" Simmons. Seated on car, *left to right*: "Honest John" Renfro, Steve George, Birger, Connie Ritter, Eural Gowan, unidentified man, and Leon Stover. Foreground, *left to right*: Bert Owens, Rado Millich, Ernest Blue, and Oral Gowan. The man standing below Ritter and Simmons has not been positively identified.

The ruins of the cabin at Shady Rest

PRIMARY, TUESDAY, APRIL 13, 1926

## OREN COLEMAN

CANDIDATE FOR REPUBLICAN NOMINATION FOR

### SHERIFF

OF WILLIAMSON COUNTY

YOUR VOTE AND INFLUENCE SOLICITED
(OVER)

Oren Coleman's political card

Jim Pritchard's political poster

Lory and Ethel Price

Lory Price, an Illinois state
highway patrolman

The home of Lory and Ethel Price

The note that Joe Adams was holding when he was shot

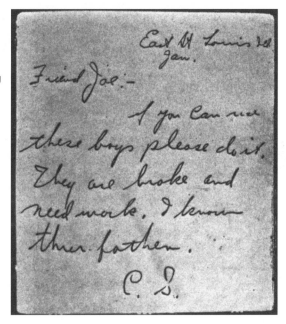

Helen Holbrook

Searching for the body of Ethel Price

Equipment used in the search for Ethel Price's body

*Left to right*: Arlie Sinks, deputy sheriff of Williamson County, unidentified man, and Arlie O. Boswell, state's attorney of Williamson County. The photograph was taken near the mine shaft where Ethel Price's body was finally found.

Digging for the body of Ethel Price

The Franklin County Jail in Benton, Illinois

The Franklin County Courthouse in Benton, Illinois

The crowd outside the courthouse during Birger's trial

# 4
# Booze and Harrisburg

WITH THE NIGHTMARE OF ST. LOUIS BEHIND HER, BEATRICE was faced with a day-by-day existence that was in some ways even worse. She was shunned by most of the members of her family and made to feel that she had disgraced the Bainbridge name beyond redemption. Only her father, Bob Bainbridge, kept in touch.

A mine examiner at Saline 3 Mine, west of Harrisburg, he stopped by almost every day for a short visit, after the Birgers moved to 609 West Poplar. (After leaving their apartment uptown, the three lived in the back rooms of what would be called the "Near Bar." The house the family would call home had its origins in a two-room shack that Charlie had moved to the lot next to the "Near Bar." Once the "building on" was complete, the Birgers had a presentable and livable home.) When Mary Bainbridge finally learned of these visits, Beatrice said she was furious. "I knew he caught heck when he got home," she added.

On the one hand was her family's hostility, and on the other was the attitude of the townspeople. They also shunned her because of Birger's reputation. That left her with Charlie—or more often without him, because he was away from home most of the time. On those rare nights when he was there, he seemed less an open and loving husband than a pleasant stranger. Certainly, he never confided in her, either about his past or his current activities. The extent of his various, usually illegal, enterprises came to the young bride as a series of shocks. Equally shocking—it quickly became clear—was her role in his life. Love had nothing to do with it. He simply wanted a wife to rear Minnie and to provide him with a gloss of respectability. That he would find lovers elsewhere became another of the shocks that awaited her. The nights he did spend at home she best remembered because of his easy laughter, one of the man's outstanding characteristics. More than once he mentioned "The Monkey Cage," presumably a gambling establishment in East St. Louis or St. Louis. But to Beatrice, a monkey cage was where monkeys swung chattering from bar to bar, a misrepresentation that invariably brought forth that laugh of his. Sometimes he called her a hillbilly, and that hurt.

When he became serious, the talk usually centered around money. With Charlie it was always, "Some day—some day I'm going to be somebody." At the time, she thought his chances of ever being anything other than a small-time gambler and bootlegger were minimal, because "he had to be pushed." The words were there and he dressed the part, but the drive was missing or so she thought. Still, there were schemes that grew like weeds in a trash-strewn alley. Once he decided to import a Chinese cook in order to treat Harrisburg to some real Oriental cooking. However, because Harrisburg was strictly a meat and potatoes town—as anyone could have told him had he bothered to ask—the "Hong Kong" soon folded, and the cook returned to St. Louis, where his talents were appreciated.

Birger's presence in west Harrisburg livened up the area in many ways. His neighbors got accustomed to the little Jersey cow he kept for the fresh milk and to the tame duck that followed him around. They were intrigued by the statue of the angel—water spurted from the mouth—in the fish pond west of the house and to the goldfish swimming below. (Later these goldfish would be moved to a larger pond behind the house, where they grew to reveal their true carp-selves.) Needless to say, the kids in the neighborhood were delighted by the pony and wagon Charlie kept, especially when he gave them a ride.

Sad to say, the statue—that symbol of serenity—was years later moved to the yard, there to be used for target practice. When the stray bullets struck his garage, Delbert Balabas was thankful the walls were of concrete and thirteen inches thick at that.

Ever the showman, nothing pleased Charlie more than dressing up in his military garb and participating in yet another of Harrisburg's parades. On at least one occasion he is said to have led a parade while sitting atop a white horse. Before he was a notorious gangster known throughout the Midwest, Birger was a noted character, at least in Harrisburg.

And always there was the question of money. The army pension he had been trying to get since 1915 or earlier finally came through in 1922 or 1923, thanks largely to the efforts of his "true and lawful attorney," Dr. Louis N. Parish of Harrisburg. For the remaining years of his life, Birger would receive the munificent sum of $25 a month for injuries incurred while trying to tame Uncle Sam's bucking broncos, back when he and the century were young. The $25 helped, but only a little.

A glimpse of the furniture in their home seemed to confirm the futility of Birger's lust for wealth. "We burned wood in a cook stove," said his former wife. Still, he had enough to hire someone to do the housework, leaving Beatrice more time to spend with Minnie. Beatrice remembered:

> I always had a housekeeper . . . I didn't have to do anything. They were Hungarians, but I can't remember for the life of me who they were. I also had a colored girl from Carrier Mills. I remember she was almost white, and her sister was black. They did the laundry. One time she dressed up in my clothes and went up in Harrisburg and Charlie saw her. He ripped them off of her, you know, and said if he ever caught her down there again what he'd do to her.

When angry, Charlie was another man. While Beatrice had rarely been the target of his anger, she had seen others who were. One such was Minnie's mother, Winnie Mofield.

Minnie, who was born in 1917, was "taken" at an early age by her father, a man considered by many to be a law violator of the worst sort. Their opinion notwithstanding, he meant to provide his child with a proper upbringing, and for her part, Winnie was to keep her distance. She certainly was not welcome in his home, as ex-wife Edna continued to be long after their separation. Not quite as cold-blooded about such matters as her husband, Beatrice sometimes managed to slip Winnie in for visits with her child. Charlie arrived unexpectedly one day to find his former sweetheart sitting with his wife and child at a table at the back of the Near Bar's restaurant. He was livid. Amid curses, he hit Winnie so hard the poor woman was lifted from her chair and sent sprawling on the dirt outside the open door. When Beatrice moved to help her, Charlie told her to stay put. Winnie, at last regaining her feet, did the most sensible thing possible—she ran. Turning to his wife, who had unlocked the gate of the high board fence in back to let Winnie in, Birger said only, "Don't you ever let her come here again!"

The scene was not lost on the one who watched, too stunned to speak. "I didn't like it when he hit Winnie that time," she said more than half a century later. "I wondered if he would ever do that to me, but he never did."

Even after that, Winnie managed to "drop by," especially when Charlie was away in St. Louis. Not content merely to hold her child, she would complain about her former lover. "When he wanted anything, he took it," she said bitterly. She even tried to tell Beatrice what she should and shouldn't do. Her unsolicited advice was not heeded, according to the one to whom it was aimed: "Charlie did his business at the City National Bank, and I used to take all the money to the bank. Winnie would tell me I was crazy for not taking my share. I told her I'd never taken a thing in my life, and I wasn't about to."

That was good thinking on her part. For one thing, Charlie wouldn't have liked it. For another, neither would bank president T. Y. Gregg, who was usually only too happy to help her carry in the heavy bags.

Those heavy bags meant Charlie was "getting up" in the world. A symbol of his rise was the "Near Bar," with its brick bar in front, where bootleg whiskey and home brew were sold. Topped with green felt, the gambling tables in some of the six back rooms were equally impressive, equally attractive. Beatrice remembered them well:

I'd see people you'd be surprised to see in Harrisburg. If they didn't have any money to gamble, or when they went broke, they'd bring their wives' wedding rings, wristwatches, or necklaces, and he'd put them in a box. He'd say, "Now when the guy gets on his right leg, I'll give them back."

According to numerous stories, Birger did just that. And according to one fellow who occasionally rolled dice with him, the ironclad rule of the house was that any man who was wiped out in the action always left with a dollar bill in his pocket, compliments of the proprietor.

Gambling was not the only game running at the place. While being propositioned by a good-looking young lady who was quick to quote a price, one wit replied, "I just wanted to borrow it, not buy it."

The "Near Bar," as it was sometimes called, was the best-known joint in Harrisburg (remember that the "Hong Kong" failed there in 1920). However, it was not Birger's only place in town. According to his former wife and others, more than one of his "houses ran in the east part of town." Gambling certainly existed in these places, but prostitution was the main attraction. In the extreme west part of town stood yet another "house," one that Beatrice remembered well from her one visit:

> One time, I guess I told you, he had a little Jersey cow he raised and he had a lamb and we run out of feed and I couldn't find John Bard, who was supposed to look after us, him and Jim Kelley. I went out there. It was an old store building down from the Grazulis place on the left side there, and he met me at the door and he ate me alive. And he made me come home, saying, "Don't you ever come out here again. This is no place . . . "

Because he had friends in high places, Beatrice felt Charlie was free to operate with a minimum of interference. She remembered two law officers who came for their weekly payoffs:

> They would come down there in the afternoon when nobody'd be around. Charlie handed each man the box and said, "Help yourself." They never seemed to take too much. I never knew how much

was in the box, a cigar box, but it was full of bills. Each would take so much, and then—Charlie had such a guttural laugh—he would laugh and close it up. They'd take off. They always came in the side door; they never came in the front.

That money crossed the alleged chasm that yawned between those who broke the law and those who were being paid to uphold it was nothing new. Rudy Walker, who also operated outside the law in nearby Eldorado, related his own method of buying protection from Sheriff Lige Turner during 1926 to 1929. "I ran a crap game here on the west end, and I had to pay $100 every Monday to the sheriff," he said.

When asked if that amount seemed excessive, the old man shook his head and said, "My crap game was running me from $5,000 to $15,000 a week profit." The protection extended only to the crap game, however. His moonshining operations out in the country—also a very profitable venture—were fair game. One trip to St. Louis netted Walker from $17,000 to $18,000. Among his many local customers was his old friend, Charlie Birger. Walker remembered:

> When I first sold Birger whiskey, it was at his place over in west Harrisburg. He'd take ten to twenty barrels or kegs at a time off of me. Sometimes he would come to my house and get it or send a truck or car, or lots of times I'd meet him somewhere and transfer it on the road. At one time, on Election Day, I took it over in broad daylight, took it in the back door of his house. Nobody would be thinking anything about it, you know.

Much of the liquor sold in Harrisburg came from the hills to the south and southeast. One ancient fellow fondly recalled the days he helped "run White Mule" for Birger in one of the streams near Williams Hill, just over the line in Pope County.

In full or in partnership, Birger himself once owned a still; it was located about a quarter of a mile west of the Estes Bridge, north of Rudement in Saline County. At one time, my informant and another fellow "packed" two five-gallon bottles of whiskey to the roadside near the bridge for Birger to pick up and take back into Harrisburg, as he did every other night. If the boys needed five hundred pounds of sugar or a ton of "shorts," Birger would drive out from town, pick up the "booze," and be gone. Rarely did he actually visit the still site.

One night, no pickup was made, because by the time he arrived, the bottles were gone. Furious, Birger stormed up the creek to find out why the whiskey wasn't there. Each of the still hands so convincingly swore he had helped the other "pack" it down to the designated spot that Birger finally had no choice but to believe them.

"Come with me," he said to one. Afraid to go, but more afraid not to, the lad dutifully followed, and when they reached the spot where the bottles had been left, Birger knelt and found a set of tracks. They followed those for fifty yards or so into some brush, and in a ditch they found the five-gallon bottles.

"That guy won't come back tonight," Birger said.

As they waited at the same spot the next night, the two heard a buggy arrive. The guilty party was loading the containers when Birger stood up, pistol in hand and said, "Don't run." Quickly setting the bottles down, the thief owned up to the stealing and waited to hear the consequences. This time he would "get off light."

"I want you to take it right back to where you got it," said Birger. In an undertone, he added, "Don't ever let me catch you down here again."

The young man who watched the drama from the underbrush later "teamed" in town, often hauling whiskey from the Big Four depot to Birger's home. He reported that never in all their dealings was Charlie anything less than a gentleman.

The gentleman beneath the swagger was also apparent to Wilbur Leitch:

I started a little place in Muddy, in the old streetcar depot. It was built in with a seven or eight-foot board fence around it, and there used to be a show there, a movie. I ran that that winter [1915]. Birger came up—I had known him before—and wanted me to take orders for whiskey and drinks. Give the customers what they ordered there then, and the order that they would give me would be sent to Cairo, and it would come up the next morning by rail, and he would bring it over from Harrisburg to replace it. That was evading the law. I came awful near doing that, and if it hadn't been for my uncle, Zack Leitch, who was deputy United States marshal at that time, I would have.

While the deal was still a possibility, Birger gave the young man his own .32 Smith and Wesson for, Wilbur felt, his own protection. Two neat notches marked the back of the little gun's handle, and a hefty sliver was missing from the bottom of the handle. Birger did not discuss the notches, but he said that the missing fragment came one night when he ran out of bullets and had to convert the weapon into a billy club. Too smart to inquire further, Wilbur felt that if he had accepted the job, he too would have put that pistol to use.

The two remained friends, but at a distance. After he was married, Wilbur bought a farm south of Raleigh. The premises were soon visited by chicken thieves, one of whom caught a load of Wilbur's buckshot in the backside. The evidence that turned up after the occurrence indicated that Birger had at least condoned the thievery. Birger himself made his appearance on the place after that, accompanied by some of his men. They had been blasting doves out of a nearby tree that happened to stand in the middle of the dirt road. Perched prominently on the front of his Buick coupe, Birger ordered the driver to pull over so he could chat for a moment with an old pal. The chicken snatching episode was fresh on his mind, but Wilbur was the soul of courtesy. "To tell the truth, though, I kept my eye on him all the time," he said.

An enterprising moonshiner from Eagle Creek once tried to sell Birger some of his produce at the place at the west end. "He talked nice and even tried to sell me a distill," the old man recalled. But that deal, too, fell through. Before leaving, the man from the hills noticed two things about the joint: The bottles on the shelves bore recognizable labels, and the women seemed more than merely friendly.

# 5
# A Bad Man, Yet...

DESPITE HIS OPEN DISREGARD FOR THE LAW, BIRGER WAS CALLED friend by some of Harrisburg's leading citizens. Among those who lent him their prestige was J. Milo Pruett, owner of Pruett's Garage and reputed to be one of the wealthiest men in town. Attorney Alpheus Gustin, according to Gustin's diary, often represented the gangster in court. So did Henry Reese Lightfoot. Dr. Joe Lightner, prominent physician and founder of Lightner Hospital, was—according to Beatrice—one of Charlie's closest friends.

Before crossing the street at a restaurant, Birger and his men were in the habit of leaving their guns in the office of another of his friends, Dr. Nicholas A. Hermann. Although Mrs. Hermann finally persuaded her husband to discourage this practice, which was turning the office into a temporary arsenal, she was not quite able to get Birger out of her husband's life. More than once, she returned from a bridge party only to find her husband and his gangster friend chatting before the open fire.

George T. "Talt" Gaskins, businessman and gambler, was a man with whom Birger had real estate dealings over a number of years. Gaskins was a partner with his brother, John Thad, in the Gaskins and Company Clothing Store at 27 East Poplar Street. "Talt," as indicated, was a gambler, and once he lost a diamond ring in one of Birger's games. His wife, Fannie, went to Charlie and got it back, according to John Utter, who said the story was still somewhat of a family tradition.

"Talt" and Charlie had another common interest: Birger's ex-wife, Edna, who for a time—before marrying a carnival man named Jimmy Aarons—ran the Princess Beauty Parlor on West Poplar Street. Separated though they were, Charlie and Edna remained close over the years—so close, in fact, that when it wasn't convenient to meet Gaskins in her beauty parlor, Edna used Charlie's home for the rendezvous.

But "Talt's" gambling and autumnal love affair are of less interest than his land dealings with Birger. To this writer, at least, these dealings are confusing. Land records in the county clerk's office at Harrisburg, Illinois, show that on June 16, 1919, Birger's older sister, Rachel Shamsky, paid $6,000 for "the west half of the N.E.—of Section 28 and the N.E.—of Section 29, all in Township 7 South, Range 6." This is in Long Branch Township, in the north-central part of Saline County. The purchase amounted to approximately 240 acres. On October 20, 1920—the same day that Birger sold Gaskins's Lots 2, 3, and 4 of his land holdings in west Harrisburg for $500—Rachel and her husband, Jacob, sold Gaskins the aforementioned acreage plus thirty acres in Section 32 of the same township for $8,000. On April 12, 1922, these farms were then sold to Birger for $1,000. Beatrice said that Charlie had planned to have a moonshining operation on his farm north of Harrisburg but that nothing came of it. George "Talt" Gaskins died on March 21, 1924.

That community leaders had ties of friendship with this particular gangster might have raised eyebrows at the time, but these ties are not necessarily damning in retrospect. After all, the fellow had class—that indefinable something most gunmen never acquire. His lack of education was smoothly covered by a genial manner. A ready talker, he was also a good listener. And when the "big shots" talked, he listened. Beatrice recalled that he would talk by the hour with this or that businessman, or so it seemed to her as she stood there bored beyond words.

Others in the town found him anything but boring, especially those he helped in various ways. For instance his neighbor Mrs. J. A. (Cynthia) Boatright was happy to see Charlie, especially when he brought a case of ginger ale; he did this about once a month. No doubt he thought highly of her, for he let her pluck his geese for the feathers. Late one night, Mrs. Boatright's lights were on—she had suffered a stroke. Ever the thoughtful one, Charlie took the old lady a bottle of rubbing alcohol for her legs.

Mary Lois Bynum remembered how Charlie used to come to the home of her parents, Mr. and Mrs. James Sullivan, to buy eggs and milk. The father was afraid of Birger; not so the mother. She and Charlie had long talks, where he mused aloud what his life might have been if, as a youngster, he hadn't loitered around the banks of East St. Louis, where he deposited the loot of local gangsters for a fee.

After being warned that her son spent too much time at one of Charlie's joints, Mrs. Sullivan paid her gangster friend a visit and told him never to let her darling boy enter the place again. He gave his word the lad would be banned.

His relations with the very poor were even more congenial. They were much more publicized as well. When a state's attorney of a county in southeastern Missouri who was formerly from Harrisburg invited Birger to move his operations across the Mississippi River, there to run wide open with no fear of interference from the law, Birger respectfully declined the offer, generous though it was. Harrisburg had been too good to him.

On May 7, 1923, Harrisburg's *Daily Register* nixed the rumor that Birger had died of blood poisoning in a St. Louis hospital. Six days later the newspaper printed an update on his condition:

> Charlie Birger now improving. Friends here of Charlie Birger will be pleased to learn that he is now on the road to improvement. As told to our paper several days ago, he is in a hospital in St. Louis suffering with blood poisoning. He underwent an operation which proved successful and he is growing better.

The problem started at Hart's Cafe. A local Harrisburg man named Earl Estes made a remark that hit Birger the wrong way. Wheeling, Charlie swung his fist squarely into the teeth of the "wise-cracker," who—needless to say—was out the door and gone before Charlie realized that he had suffered more damage than had the fleet-footed Estes. As a result of the blow, infection set in; for a time, it was feared that Birger might lose his hand.

One finger was finally amputated. The finger was later preserved in a jar of alcohol, and it sat in a place of prominence in the Birger living room. Thereafter, he wore gray suede gloves.

One compensation resulting from the injury was that the missing finger was mentioned in Birger's pension application, no doubt in the hopes that some trusting soul in Washington would believe it to be the result of a toss from a crazy army stallion on the plains of Montana rather than the result of a petty brawl in a Harrisburg cafe. It also prevented the sufferer from testifying at a trial wherein he was accused of selling a car that he didn't own to Joe Kaytor. Affidavits from Dr. C. W. Turner and Dr. Andrew J. Butner attested that Birger was in great pain and in no position to take the stand. Without that testimony, so his attorneys Alpheus Gustin and H. R. Lightfoot argued, the trial itself would be an exercise in futility. The jury apparently thought otherwise, for in the end, Birger was fined $505, along with court costs.

True, the jury found him guilty, but the sentence seems light and suggests that the patient may have dwarfed the "con man" in the minds of the jurors. If so, the illusion seems fitting, for Birger had long been a charmer, winning friends with his easy smile and his list of good deeds.

One good deed that got little publicity occurred late in 1919— or early in 1920—when he began keeping his aged father, Louis Birger. Shortly after arriving in Harrisburg, the old fellow repaid his son by running away. The elder Birger "escaped" many times while in Harrisburg, but he was always "captured" by Charlie or one of his employees. Although Beatrice found her father-in-law difficult, she liked him and even thought he looked like Santa Claus, if only for his short stature and white beard.

On December 10, 1921, Louis Birger died; "senility" is recorded by Dr. Lightner in the death record. A great believer in show, Charlie favored a casket with all the trimmings. But Rachel and Sam, who had arrived in Harrisburg shortly before their father's death, demanded that the casket be stripped of ostentation. A plain oak box would serve well, they said. And instead of a pillow, they placed a sandstone covered with white satin under the dead man's head. As a Gentile, Beatrice was required to sit in the back during funeral services in Gaskins's Funeral Home. So, too, was Bert Gaskins, who owned the establishment. At one point during the ceremony, the undertaker whispered to her, "Well, this is my first." The body of the deceased was buried in Chesed Shel Emeth Cemetery in University City, Missouri.

Tradition has it that Charlie often placed groceries at the doors of the needy and that he provided coal for families that could not afford it. Willard St. John remembered that a man wanted to attend his mother's funeral in Kentucky but had no car. Hearing of the man's plight, Birger offered him the use of his own Buick. The man was touched, but declined the offer, saying that the roads were too badly rutted for such a fine automobile. "Think nothing of it," Charlie said, pointing out that he had insurance. As a final gesture, he even gave the mourner money to buy gasoline.

Wilbur Leitch was in Charlie Gaskins's poolroom on the south side of Harrisburg Square when a beggar came to the door. Said Leitch:

> Charlie Birger hollered at him, said "Come on in." Charlie picked up a derby hat, which was very common in those days, and he passed it around and took up a collection. He immediately came back and dumped it on the glass showcase, counted it out, and gave it to the man. In the meantime, he called Mr. Horning of the Horning Hotel and told him he was sending a man down there and that he wanted him to give him a bath, a haircut, and a shave, and the man was to report back up there the next morning, at which time he would take up another collection and buy him a suit of clothes.

Beatrice, who was in a position to know him far better than most, remembered those acts of charity:

> When he found out there was a family in need, he didn't make it known. He went and bought this stuff and set it on the porch. He would leave money in envelopes under their doors, and one would tell the other where it came from, of course, and that is where he got the reputation of helping people.

A man who a few years later was to know Birger well painted a more rounded portrait, summing him up with the word "Enigmatic." He added, "He had a wonderful quality, a heart of gold.

There in Harrisburg sometimes he'd support twelve or fifteen families, buy coal, groceries." Pausing a moment, he continued, "He had cold eyes, a killer's eyes. He would kill you for something somebody else would punch you in the nose for. He was usually on dope." Having once been a member of Birger's gang, my informant was in a position to know the truth.

Never a gang member, the paperboy, Bill Yarbrough, had a shoe-shine stall in a poolroom owned by a semipro baseball player named Johnny Dowell. Often, he said, Birger would get his shoes and leather puttees shined. He always paid the lad a dollar. "I can see him now," continued Yarbrough, "marching down the streets of Harrisburg, slapping his leather puttees with a swagger stick. He envisioned himself a Prussian general. One Christmas, he gave Yarbrough a "ten-dollar gold piece" for delivering the paper.

Before the astonished eyes of Kuma McNabb, a young woman who lived in the west part of Harrisburg, the darker side became apparent:

> One night all of our neighborhood was in bed and it was after one o'clock when we heard a terrible crash, and of course, Mother and Dad and my husband, Jim, and myself all ran outside. It was Charlie Birger. He had his lady friend in the car with him. They were going from West Poplar Street to his home, and Jimmy McIntosh and his brother were coming east on Poplar Street and Charlie was going west. They were going up the hill, and the boys were drunk, and they had forced Charlie to run his car off of Poplar Street into the house "kitty-cornered" across from us, and that's what caused us all to jump out of bed and run outside in our nightgowns and pj's.
>
> Charlie jumped out of his car and was going after these boys, but the brother was sober enough that he jumped back in the car and he got away. But Charlie got hold of this boy [Jimmy] just half-way between our house and the house east of us, out on the sidewalk, and he had his pistol and was just beating the boy nearly to death. And all that poor little old Jimmy could say was, "Don't hit me any more, Charlie, please. Please don't hit me any more! I'm sick, don't hit me any more." But he just kept on hitting him, pounding him with his pistol, and I couldn't stand it any longer, and I broke from our group, and I ran over to where Charlie was beating on this boy, and I said, "Don't hit him any more. That's a

sick boy. You're killing him. You stop right now!" And, of course, Charlie immediately turned on me and he said, "Well, goddamn you, you get back in the house or I'll kill you!"

That dispersed all of us, but he did leave the boy alone and got back in his car and left.

The garage just back of Birger's house attracted the attention of Al Rogers, a lad living in west Harrisburg at the time. As he walked past on his way to school, or to a movie, he saw within a large fireplace and an oversized safe and thought them somehow out of place. He was right. A kettle of brown sugar was secured over the flames of the fireplace. When properly "burned," the sugar became the coloring agent for the alcohol brought in by the Shelton brothers, Carl, Earl, and Bernie. When the final product was bottled and labeled, some of it went into the safe. However, what young Al didn't know couldn't hurt him.

Clever fellows, those Sheltons. They even showed Charlie how to convert Beatrice's new washing machine—one of the first in town—into a device for mixing distilled water and 190 proof alcohol. The proper ratio of water and alcohol along with a certain amount of burned brown sugar was poured into a small wooden barrel. This barrel was then placed into the oblong tub with corrugated sides, there to shake for a day and a night. During the interval, Birger and his new friends could be found playing cards in the garage.

Needless to say, the woman for whom the washing machine was originally intended was more than a little "put out." But she knew better than to complain. Instead, she paid attention to what was going on.

There was that time that the Sheltons stole some whiskey labels from a warehouse in St. Louis and delivered them to Charlie. Charlie made a mistake when he put them in the safe. A central attraction in a noted raid, this safe proved to be Birger's undoing, at least in Saline County.

In *Mean Old Jail*, Curtis Small recalls how his father—then sheriff of Saline County—and his deputies instituted a county-wide cleanup of stills and bootlegging joints. In the course of John Small's crusade, a young gambler from Alabama named Cecil Knighton was arrested in May of 1923. Knighton operated one of

Birger's places in the west part of Harrisburg. After pleading guilty
to liquor violations and then posting his bond, Knighton was
fined $500 by Judge A. G. Abbey and was issued a "stay away"
order from Saline County. Bowing to the edict of the law, the gambler moved to Williamson County.

In June, a raid was made on Birger's place. Finding no liquor in
the house, the sheriff and his deputies searched the garage. There
they discovered the safe. When Charlie refused to open it, the unwieldy object was seized and taken away. According to Small, the
contents were finally revealed at George Mitchell's machine shop
on North Jackson. Bottled whiskey was found along with some
uncut liquor. Even more damning were the counterfeit federal liquor stamps. When Birger saw that he was beaten, he promised
John Small to move his operations to Williamson County. He continued to live in Saline County.

However, according to Beatrice, the safe was blown there on
the premises by order of a federal marshal from Danville. She remembered it well, she said, being pregnant at the time, and watching it all from the porch. Frightened by the blast, she fell and later
suffered a miscarriage. The stillborn baby boy caused the would-
be father to plunge into one of his rare drunks, downing bottle
after bottle of Virginia Dare wine and sobbing that he had always
wanted a son. (In fact, before their daughter Edna Charline was
born in 1921, Birger engaged a rabbi from St. Louis for the cir-
cumcision rites, according to Beatrice. A large party was planned,
but when it became clear that the baby was a girl, the ceremony
was canceled.)

Personal tragedy and legal entanglements aside, the "character"
Harrisburg had come to appreciate placed an announcement in
the *Daily Register* on May 18, 1923. He had advertised in the
newspaper before, once to sell Christmas trees. But this time he
had a grievance and was as angry as any law abiding citizen would
be who had been robbed:

A few nights ago a thief stole from under two of my turkey hens on
my farm near Saline #4 mine 29 turkey eggs. One of the hens was
also stolen. I have been given information as to who the guilty
party is. I will not prosecute if eggs and turkey hen is returned. But

if they are not, I am going to make it hot for the thief and I know who he is.

Within six months Birger would be charged with two killings in Williamson County. He would be "written up" at length in newspapers throughout southern Illinois. Even the *Daily Register*, a newspaper noted for exhibiting a certain appreciation of its local celebrity, splashed the bloody details of these killings on page one. Ironically, less than four years earlier, a reporter for the *Daily Register* quoted Charlie as saying he had "cut out his wild ways, and there was no chance of anyone being killed by him."

# 6
# Egan Rats and Hogan's Jellyrolls

T HAT RAID IN JUNE OF 1923 MAY WELL HAVE CLOSED BIRGER'S main establishment in the west end, but it is unlikely that his business interests in Harrisburg and Saline County were terminated quite so neatly. Human nature being the same in Harrisburg as in Singapore, no doubt the houses continued to accommodate the unloved and the gaming tables continued to draw at least a devoted clientele.

It should also be remembered that Birger's financial interests extended beyond those joints associated with him personally. The kingpin of the Saline County underworld, he received weekly payoffs from gamblers such as Harrisburg's Charlie Gaskins and "Hickory" Boatright. Together they paid $100 a week for the privilege of running their crap games. Another man paid $200. The town's "sporting houses," such as the Blue Moon on the east end, paid an average of from $15 to $25 weekly; and one house in the southeast part of the county shelled out $300.

The man who did the collecting—my informant—says he usually kept about a third of the take—but adds that since no books were kept, he never tried to be exact. In fact, sometimes he kept it all. Concerned that his free and easy way with the profits might get him killed, he would occasionally ask around to see if Birger was checking on him, and he was much gratified to learn that he was not.

Whatever his standing in Harrisburg, it is true that in the latter part of 1923, Birger was more and more visible at a resort between Marion and Johnston City, appropriately known as Halfway. His partners in that operation were Ralph Hill, Charles "Chink" Shaffer, and Nathan Riddle. Of the three, Shaffer received the most attention, being a well-known gambler and a snappy dresser. A close friend of Judge D. T. Hartwell, Shaffer was thought to be the supplier of Hartwell's "dope"—probably morphine.

Beatrice remembered Halfway as "a big house with a rounded porch—that was Charlie's bootlegging joint." This house was on the west side of the road; on the east side of the road was the establishment he ran with his partners. One of the bartenders was Cecil Knighton. With his Near Bar in Harrisburg officially closed, thanks to an injunction from the office of State's Attorney Charles Thompson, Birger became a familiar figure at the roadhouse and was often seen in the company of Knighton. Business continued as usual.

The two men were close. One of the few outsiders made welcome in Birger's home, the slender Knighton was more than once heard to remark that he did not want his mother to learn of his activities in Illinois. A neat dresser, thanks mainly to Harrisburg's leading haberdashers, Rathbone and Brown, Knighton was especially proud of his light-colored clothes and was rarely seen in anything else.

Beatrice saw him as "just a young fellow up from Alabama who wanted to be a gambler, and that's what he was. He was the only one allowed around the place because, I guess, he [Birger] figured he was good enough to associate in his home." On the other hand, the young man had a quick temper and was almost never without a pistol.

As depicted in various newspapers, his killing bore an uncanny resemblance to that of William Oughten in Edgemont fifteen years earlier. After an argument between Birger and Knighton at the roadhouse—over a woman, according to tradition—Birger went to his place across the road. Knighton followed, vowing he was going "to get that Jew son of a bitch and run him out of Illinois." After Knighton took a shot at him, Birger grabbed a shotgun and blasted his assailant twice, killing him. After someone summoned

Marion policeman Tom Boyd, Birger stood over the body of his one-time friend. When Boyd arrived, he surrendered. The date was November 15, 1923.

Beatrice remembered that story differently. She and Charlie had just returned from St. Louis; he had bought her a couple of dresses. He had also purchased a large number of boxes from a wholesale house. She didn't know what was in those boxes, but she suspected they contained whiskey bottles.

Upon arriving at Halfway, Birger began counting the proceeds of his business. "Big Jim" Kelly (perhaps the same Jim Kelly with whom he had served time, years earlier in the Metropolis jail) whispered something in his ear. At that point, Birger "packed me up and we came home." When they arrived in Harrisburg, he told her, "Somebody killed Cecil Knighton." Soon afterward he drove back alone to Halfway. "And I thought he [Knighton] was an awful nice fellow," she said.

The coroner's jury, meeting in Marion the afternoon of November 16, exonerated Birger on grounds of self-defense. Officially blameless, yet apparently distraught—according to Harrisburg's *Daily Register*—he met with friends back in Harrisburg and freely discussed the matter. On a bright note, he spoke of the dance hall and park he planned to build on the west side of the road at Halfway and even talked of building a lake between Harrisburg and Marion. He probably had in mind the land he owned five miles west of Harrisburg.

There is a macabre footnote to the Knighton killing. Rathbone and Brown had ordered some silk shirts for the natty Alabama man, but before he could pick them up, fate had intervened. While in the store to order some shirts of his own one day, Birger was shown the silk shirts with the letter "C" monogrammed on the pockets. Delighted, he bought the lot.

Knighton was well known in Harrisburg, and his killing caused no little excitement there. Before the talk could fade away, however, another man, himself no stranger to the town, was killed at Halfway, and again Birger was blamed.

It was Sunday night, November 18. Five men had left Mrs. Effie Ashby's roadhouse, which was located north of Johnston City, and had driven south to Halfway. Meanwhile, in Marion, Charlie

Birger was dining at the home of his friend and business partner Charles "Chink" Shaffer. After supper, they drove to the roadhouse. No sooner had they arrived than the five men appeared. Birger knew four of them: Bailey Martin, Roy Shaw, Ora Thomas, and William F. "Whitey" Doering.

"How's it going?" Doering asked, as he proceeded to shake hands with Birger, whom he had known for years.

Despite his show of affability, the St. Louisan had little to be cheerful about. He had recently been sentenced to thirty years in the federal penitentiary at Atlanta, Georgia, for his involvement in a St. Louis mail robbery that had occurred on April 2, 1923, in which more than $2,400,000 in bonds and securities had been stolen. Acting on a tip, federal officers had raided Doering's fine home in the exclusive Richmond Heights section of St. Louis and had found most of the haul—$2,139,000 of Federal Land Bank bonds. He claimed that he knew nothing about the bonds, but he was arrested along with one Dan Weisman, formerly of Johnston City.

Being much less affluent than his partner, Weisman could not pay the appeal bond of $75,000 and began serving his term soon after the two men were found guilty on October 20 in federal court. On the other hand, Doering promptly filled his bond, set at $90,000, and he then moved to the vicinity of Marion, where his personable and liberal ways made him many friends.

That night, according to Birger, Shaffer began to rib Doering. "Gee, you're looking bad. I bet you've lost thirty pounds since you've been in court." "Whitey" only grinned.

Birger finally told the fellows to let up on him. About fifteen minutes later, "Whitey" called Birger outside. At this point, versions of what followed vary, but this much can be determined: In an exchange of shots, Doering and Birger were wounded. Doering died in the Herrin Hospital.

Birger's deposition was taken at the same hospital. He stated that "Whitey" had asked him a question that he had refused to answer. In the deposition, Birger stated, "When I said I didn't know the answer, he cursed and whipped out his automatic. Before I could run, he had shot me and I fell forward, grabbing him." (Birger would not say at the time just what the question was, but it was assumed that Doering wanted to know the time of the payroll distribution at the Harco mine near Harrisburg. Later, Birger denied Doering had asked any question at all.)

During the ensuing struggle, three of the men who had accompanied Doering ran outside. Birger said he knew Shaw and Martin, but the third man remained a mystery. Meanwhile, the shooting became general. But through it all, Birger claimed to hear someone say, "Kill Birger. Make a good job of it."

The bullet that was sent to do just that had struck Doering instead, Birger said, sending both wounded men to the porch. Unconscious, Birger at this point could relate only what he heard later: that the three lifted Doering into his car and drove him to Herrin, leaving the other two men to fend for themselves—in other words, to exit by the back door and flee across the fields. Finally, only Birger was left lying on the porch, with a bullet lodged just below his heart. As he told a reporter:

> After I had laid there for awhile, my strength came back, and I got to my feet. Everything was quiet, and there was not a soul in sight. So I started out to Marion, crossing the fields on the way. I got there about half an hour later and went to the sheriff's house. After I woke him up, he called the ambulance, and they took me to Herrin.

At two o'clock Monday morning, November 19, word of the shooting reached Harrisburg, according to the *Daily Register*. A call was placed to the Canary Taxi Company requesting that someone there notify Beatrice and drive her to the Herrin Hospital, where her husband lay gravely, possibly mortally, wounded. A short time later, Beatrice and Minnie got into the taxi and started out.

The driver of the car, Glen McCoy, reported later to the paper that Birger was sitting up in bed talking to his wife and anyone else who would listen. He told how the men, supposedly his friends, had come to the roadhouse and how that visit had resulted in a quarrel and the fatal shooting of Doering. McCoy said the wounded man insisted he would have gladly loaned them any amount of money had they only asked.

The incoming calls from all over the county requesting more

information about the shooting prompted the *Daily Register* to run a long article taken from the *St. Louis Post-Dispatch*, detailing Doering's spectacular criminal career. On November 21, the newspaper reported receiving information that carloads of Egan Rats and Hogan's Jellyrolls—"two of the most dangerous gunmen gangs in the country" (and deadly enemies)—were converging on Herrin, presumably drawn by the presence there of the "dangerously wounded" Charlie Birger. Perhaps one faction came to praise and the other to bury. If the St. Louis gunmen did really arrive in Herrin, they blended so well with the local citizenry that their presence was hardly noticed.

Sometime after the death of Doering, Birger came to the office of Marion attorney Arlie O. Boswell to ask a favor of the young man. He said that he had received an invitation over the telephone from one of the Egan Rats requesting that he come to St. Louis for a showdown. Bound by his own peculiar code of honor, the gangster felt compelled to go, but he wondered if, in the meantime, Boswell would keep his diamond ring in the office safe. In the event of death as a result of the shootout, the ring was to be turned over to Mrs. Birger; otherwise, he would pick it up upon his return.

Boswell thanked his visitor for placing so much confidence in him, and then the young attorney declined the offer. He believed that once the ring was in his possession, there it would stay, thus obligating him to Birger. As for the fight, he doubted that it ever took place.

Let's backtrack for a moment to the Herrin Hospital, when Birger was still a patient there. When Beatrice came in the door, she saw a young woman leave the room. She was curious. "When I went in to see Charlie, I said, 'Did you have any visitors?'" The man in bandages said no at first, but upon further questioning, snapped back, "Don't worry about that. You're my wife. You're the only woman I want!"

Beatrice later learned that the woman at the hospital was the one he had been seeing for some time. All along, of course, she had suspected that there were others to account for the nights Charlie spent away from home, but until that moment, she had considered herself the "kingpin." Now, bitterly, she knew she was only the wife, the figurehead, the woman he needed as a mother for Minnie and Charline. "He always had those other women," she said.

As for poor "Whitey"—whom she had all but forgotten in the wake of this emotional crisis—Beatrice might have shed some light upon his relationship with her husband, had anyone bothered to ask. Certainly, Doering was no stranger to the establishment on West Poplar or to the nearby garage, which in a sense was Birger's headquarters. Once, she recalled, he even brought stolen furs and diamonds there to be sold in Harrisburg.

But she did not testify. Others who did, including some of the men who accompanied Doering to the Halfway that night, convinced the coroner's jury that the victim had died at the hands of parties unknown.

Slow to recover from his wound (one which he was said to suffer from for the rest of his life), Birger was, as ever, busy with projects. And, as always, trouble was near at hand.

On June 28, 1923, he bought from McKinley Graves forty acres of land east of Crab Orchard in Williamson County, paying $1,650 for it. Sometime later, he and his wife inspected the place. She recalled that they talked about it when they got home:

> He was planning what he called the barbecue stand, and we were sitting in the front room. He said, "Let's think of some names." I said, "Well, let's call it, being there's so many trees, Shady Rest." He said, "Well, I'll think about it." Just like that. It never did mature while I was with him.

What she did remember, however, was "an old, tumbledown shanty across the highway where he had women. It was more of a cow shed, because there was no floor. He had rugs instead." The one time she was there is memorable, thanks to the woman she had glimpsed leaving Charlie's hospital room at Herrin. One day that thoughtful soul told her that Birger wanted to see her out at the shack. Beatrice thought the request was odd, especially since Charlie tried so hard to keep his family and his business life in separate compartments. But she finally decided that something was wrong and headed to the shack in the taxicab her rival had hired.

"When I got there," she said with the slightest bit of a smile, "I saw these women and men drinking and what have you, and I remembered from the time before and thought to myself, 'You'd better not go near there.'" She told the cab driver to take her back to Harrisburg. The only part Birger played in the affair was to "beat the daylights" out of the woman who set Beatrice up.

# 7
# The Arrival of S. Glenn Young

**M**ENTIONED EARLIER FOR HIS REFUSAL TO KEEP BIRGER'S RING in his office, Marion attorney Arlie O. Boswell would in later years regret that he had ever known Birger at all. They were first introduced by Sheriff George Galligan of Williamson County, back in the days before Boswell and Galligan found themselves on opposite ends of the political spectrum and before otherwise decent citizens were taking potshots at each other in the name of the Klan and the anti-Klan forces. Still in bandages from the Doering affair, Birger seemed a nice fellow, despite his swagger. His thick, black hair, dark skin, and high cheekbones suggested to the lawyer more an American Indian than a middle-aged Jew.

There was a certain irony in that meeting in front of the old Cline–Vick Pharmacy in Marion. With the blessing of Sam Stearns, chairman of the Williamson County Board, and John Whitesides, a member of that Board, Boswell was even then running for the office of Williamson County state's attorney. Stearns and White-sides were leaders of an organization known as the Marion Law Enforcement League, considered by many to be synonymous with the Ku Klux Klan. Because the avowed purpose of the Law Enforcement League was to destroy the criminal element in the county, especially the bootleggers, it is not too surprising that several of the local ministers were members. Rightly or wrongly, it was felt at the time that the county's failure to prosecute the alleged perpetrators of the Herrin Massacre had given the green light to criminals of every sort who had flocked to Williamson County in order to pursue their various callings. Boswell recalled:

Sam Stearns and John Whitesides came to my office with a gentleman whom they introduced to me as Glenn Young, and they told me at one time he had been a United States deputy marshal, and most of his work was with the federal government, and that he wanted me to advise him how to get warrants and how they could be served by the State.

They went out and followed my instructions, making "buys" with the purpose of predicating a search warrant. One day those three men again came to my office and said they wanted to go to Washington to talk to the federal people. They advised me they had over a hundred "buys."

I went with them, and they paid my expenses—$100 a day, and, boy, that was the most money I had ever seen in my life.

Praising their candidate, the two board members probably gave an overblown account of Young's accomplishments. As verified by a letter from J. Edgar Hoover to Paul M. Angle, dated December 31, 1947, and made available to this writer by the Chicago Historical Society, Young worked for the Bureau of Investigation for the Justice Department only from the autumn of 1918 until early March 1919. His job was to track down draft dodgers, mostly in the Appalachians. Resigning from the Bureau—a few years later under the leadership of J. Edgar Hoover, it would receive wide publicity as the FBI—Young joined (on June 25, 1920) the fledgling Prohibition Unit, a creation of the Treasury Department designed to battle those who chose to ignore the Volstead Act. This time his territory was southern Illinois, a region rife with moonshiners and bootleggers. On November 7, 1920, during a raid in Madison, Illinois, he killed one Luke Vukovic.

Tried in Springfield, Young was found innocent on July 10, 1921. Whatever joy the decision may have given Young was overshadowed by the fact that two weeks later he was dismissed by the Prohibition Unit. For a time, he worked as an agent for the Illinois Central Railroad in New Orleans.

Early in October 1923, word came from Rev. A. M. Stickney

that Williamson County needed Young. A Methodist minister in Marion, Stickney was a prime mover in the Marion Law Enforcement League.

To establish his credibility with the group, S. Glenn Young introduced them to Congressman W. S. Hammer of Asheville, North Carolina. Hammer's more than ample girth impressed Boswell almost as much as his praise of an old friend.

Early in the night of December 22, 1923, the Oddfellows Hall in Carbondale was the scene of an unusual gathering. Hundreds of men, recruited earlier by Young and others, began filing in. Young was waiting for them, as was the division chief of prohibition enforcement, Gus J. Simons, and two men from the Chicago branch, Joseph L. Loeffler and Victor Armitage.

Calling for silence and getting it, Simons finally began to give the men their instructions. They were to leave the hall in small groups, heading for their various destinations. A federal search warrant signed by United States Commissioner William Hart was to be carried by each group. They were given a communal oath, and at 7:00 A.M. they departed in automobiles, each man with his gun and tin star.

In Monday's newspaper print, the results seemed encouraging. Nearly a hundred bootlegging establishments had been raided. Much liquor had been confiscated. Many law violators had been arrested and transported to Benton to be arraigned before Commissioner Hart. S. Glenn Young, who had flushed the moonshiners from the mountains of Georgia and North Carolina with marked success, was now the man of the hour in southern Illinois.

One who saw it differently was Leonard Stearns, son of the Klan's grand cyclops Sam Stearns. Leonard had been among the party that raided the mining community of Colp: "They broke into those people's homes, and regardless of where the wine was, if they found any, they knocked the heads of the barrels in and let the wine run all over everything."

Later he heard that personal property was stolen, and while he saw no stealing himself, Stearns did not doubt that it had occurred. His father had helped plan that first raid, and Leonard himself had been a willing participant, but in the midst of the mostly pointless wreckage, he was thoroughly disillusioned and disgusted. Most of the raiders followed up their "success" by escorting their prisoners at gunpoint to the commissioner's office in Benton for arraignment, but Leonard returned home.

He did not participate in the four additional raids of January 5, 7, and 20 and February 1, 1924, where even the semblance of legality was missing, the "warrants" being issued by local constables and justices of the peace. Rumors of robberies and brutality associated with these raids were numerous.

# 8
# The Klan

On February 8, anti-Klansmen who gathered at Herrin's Rome Club were startled to learn that the Klan was on its way, ostensibly for a confrontation. Actually only two men, Police Chief John Ford and the young policeman Harold Crain, were approaching. Both men were taken into custody and might have come to harm if Sheriff Galligan and his deputy John Layman had not intervened. Tensions being high and guns plentiful, a scuffle ensued that resulted in the wounding of Layman. As the violence spilled into the streets and gunmen searched the alleys and back ways for their enemies, the so-called Rome Club Riot darkened another page of Herrin's unenviable history.

Remarkably enough, the only recorded casualty that night was Caesar Cagle, a prominent Klansman who was shot to death near the Jefferson Hotel. As word of Cagle's death spread quickly among his former associates, so did the news that one of Layman's visitors in the Herrin Hospital was his fellow deputy Ora Thomas. Gambler and bootlegger though he was, Thomas had the pluck of a storybook hero and a delicacy of manner and appearance that is usually found in better men. His strange combination of misdeeds and assets had won him the enmity of S. Glenn Young and his zealots. That he was one of those they accused of killing Cagle seems only fitting.

Art Newman—remember that name—stated that Earl Shelton shot Cagle in the ear after ordering him to raise his hands. The incident was in retaliation for the Klansman's treatment of Shelton during a raid by Young and his followers on a roadhouse—located at the Carterville crossroads west of Herrin—operated by Shelton and one Jack Skelcher. Young had demanded to know whom they were paying for the privilege of operating and had threatened to "put out their lights" if that information was not forthcoming. (Newman claimed that Shelton told him Young had specifically asked if Sheriff Galligan and State's Attorney Delos Duty were the recipients of the payoffs.) When no answer came, Cagle began to count to three. At "two," he slugged Earl with his pistol and continued to strike him. As a final insult, the raiders chased the two from their business place, wrecked the premises, and then set it afire.

True to his word that night, when Earl Shelton next met Cagle, the Klan constable paid in full for his actions of a few months earlier—or so reads the gospel according to Newman, which appeared in the *St. Louis Post-Dispatch* early in 1927. He fails to mention, however, that Cagle died from wounds in the chest, not in the head. It should be remembered that Newman was never one to let the truth interfere with a story that would damage his enemies.

Whatever the truth of the matter, it was the prospect of killing Thomas and Herrin Mayor C. E. "Mage" Anderson, another of those accused in the Cagle killing, that drew Young and several hundred of his gunmen to the hospital. There, for most of the night, they blasted away at those within, often trading bullets with Thomas and the others. By some miracle, no one on either side was killed. (In a footnote in his *Bloody Williamson*, Paul M. Angle mentions that a lad who underwent an operation for appendicitis during the affray died the next morning, presumably from shock.) With the arrival of the militia from Carbondale, the shooting ceased.

The guardsmen and their bayonets notwithstanding, S. Glenn Young now controlled Herrin. On the morning of February 9, after proclaiming himself "acting police chief" of that city, he ordered the arrest and jailing of Mayor Anderson, charging him with being a participant in Cagle's murder. He also ordered the arrest of Sheriff Galligan on the same charge. For a time, it appeared that Galligan might be killed.

In spite of Young's grip on Herrin and Williamson County, discordant voices were heard, none more clearly than Delos Duty's. The state's attorney poured out his vitriol against the interloper with the pearl-handled automatics, albeit anonymously, in Fred J. Kern's *Belleville News-Democrat*, and wisely packed an automatic of his own. Busy plotting Young's demise were the bootlegging Sheltons, whose base of operation was in East St. Louis but who were becoming more and more visible in Williamson County, where they had formerly lived. Despite his title of Grand Cyclops, Sam Stearns had friends in the Italian communities; they confirmed the episodes he had first learned of from his son Leonard. Still, it was only after he and John Whitesides and others had done some investigation of their own and found to their satisfaction that Leonard's stories were substantially true that they finally cut off Young's salary.

Following the elaborate funeral for Caesar Cagle on February 10, 1924, stability of a sort returned to Herrin. Two days later, Young turned the office of police chief back over to John Ford, who had just been released from the jail at Belleville, as had Harold Crain. Missing for a time and feared dead, Galligan, along with four of his men, stepped from—of all places—the county jail at Urbana. Mayor Anderson was released from the Marion jail.

As a result of the hospital shooting, ninety-nine indictments were returned against the Klansmen by a grand jury in the Herrin City Court on March 14. The charges included conspiracy, kidnapping, and assault with attempt to murder. On the other side, only Carl and Earl Shelton were indicted for the killing of Caesar Cagle.

With the support of the Klan, twenty-seven-year-old Arlie O. Boswell had won the Republican nomination for Williamson County state's attorney. He had also succeeded in getting the cases of some of his clients transferred from the Herrin City Court, where Judge Bowen was definitely hostile to the Klan, to the United States District Court in East St. Louis. "I was up there on a motion to dismiss them," he said, adding with no small amount of pride, "and I got them dismissed." While in that storied river city, he also received a lunch invitation from Earl Lingle, a boyhood chum and classmate.

Something of a celebrity in the red hills around Anna, Illinois, from whence he and Boswell came, Lingle owned a highly successful insurance agency that was located across the street from the East St. Louis police station and below the law offices of the well-known attorney Joe McGlynn. At the last minute, Lingle remembered a noon appointment back at the office—such are the pitfalls of success. So back they went, the insurance man to see his client and the attorney to wait in an outer office.

While cooling his heels, Boswell saw a tall, somewhat handsome man walk past, enter another room, and close the door. After Lingle saw his client off, he also went into the other room, but after a few moments, he came out and motioned to his friend to enter.

"When I went in there," said Boswell, "this gentleman was standing up and Lingle introduced him. 'Arlie, I want you to meet Mr. Shelton.'"

"Shelton! Are you one of the famous Shelton boys?"

The tall man studied the floor for a moment. "I don't know how famous we are," he said at last, "but I'm a Shelton, all right. Carl Shelton."

After the two men shook hands, Boswell said, "I'm damn glad to meet you, Carl, because I understand you were going to kill me when you laid eyes on me."

"Oh, no, you're not on the list," the tall man said with a quiet laugh.

The attorney said he was pleased to hear that; Shelton said they needed to talk. In essence, he had learned through their mutual friend, Earl Lingle, that Boswell, with the Klan's support, would be the next state's attorney of Williamson County. Since the Sheltons planned to be in Williamson County, he thought it wise to get to know the man Lingle had characterized as "a vicious prosecutor who wasn't afraid of the devil and all his imps."

Boswell, flattered by this remark, replied that he didn't see how he could be called vicious since he hadn't prosecuted anybody yet.

Evidently bored by the small talk, Shelton came straight to the point:

We make our living by violating the law, and I want you to know that we expect that if we come down in your county sooner or later, we'll be charged with some crime and you'll prosecute us and we expect that. But I also want you to know that we hire the best attorneys in the country. You know one of them, Joe McGlynn upstairs. I want to say that you'll never have any trouble with us in the prosecution as long as you do it according to law. If you try to frame us, you're going to be in very, very bad shape.

After assuring him that the frame would not be a part of his legal artillery, Boswell said that if Carl or his brothers violated the law and were caught in his county, he and not one of his associates would do the prosecuting. Shelton said he appreciated that. Throughout their brief encounter, Boswell found him to be friendly, courteous, and with more of the manner of a banker than of a bootlegger. Certainly, he possessed none of the swagger that marked Charlie Birger. Boswell, however, was not deceived into believing that Carl Shelton was some "teddy bear" of a fellow with an overblown reputation.

When we sat down and were doing this talking, he got up and pulled out this German Luger and laid it on the table. Well, I got up and pulled out my little old .38 automatic pistol and I said, "Mr. Shelton, your pistol is a little bit bigger than mine," and he said, "Yours will shoot as many times and probably just as hard." And we laughed about it.

Do you know, when I left, I left my pistol on the table and Earl Lingle had to ship it to me by express. In those days, you couldn't ship it by mail. Don't think I wasn't just a little bit "shook up" by all this conversation.

No doubt a residue of that fear remained when he and Lingle were having lunch later in the White Way Restaurant, nor was he undisturbed when he saw two men of less than average height standing near the cash register at the front of the restaurant and staring at him. Busy with his lunch, Lingle noticed them only after Boswell nudged him, requesting that he identify the pair who had, it seemed, been eyeing him for at least five minutes. Without drawing attention to himself, the insurance man glanced up before going back to his sandwich and soup.

"That's Art Newman and Freddie Wooten," came his whispered reply. Boswell swallowed a quick breath. Like Carl Shelton, both men were known to him by reputation. As owner-proprietor of the notorious Arlington Hotel in East St. Louis, as bootlegger, gambler, avowed enemy of the Klan, and bosom friend and patron of the Shelton Boys, Newman had made his mark in the local underworld. Likewise, Wooten, his fellow gambler and frequent companion, had not gone unnoticed.

Not only had Boswell heard of them, he had also heard they were planning to kill him at the first opportunity. Over the protests of his luncheon companion, he got up and walked to where they were.

"I'm Arlie Boswell," he said. "I'm from Marion, Illinois, and I'm sure you guys know who I am and where I'm from because you have been watching me like a hawk for five minutes." As casually as possible, he mentioned the rumor of their plans to kill him, adding, "I just want to look into the eyes of any son of a bitch that has got that idea, to see what they look like."

Both men insisted that they were bothering no one. As for doing him harm, that was the farthest thing from their minds—they were just looking, that's all. In that case, said their accuser, using as much sarcasm as he dared, he would gladly forward them his photograph upon his return to Marion. They did not smile.

"It's a wonder they didn't slap me down," he observed in retrospect.

"You know," said Lingle after Boswell had returned to their table, "you're the craziest son-of-a-bitch I ever heard of." He shook his head in disbelief, looking down at his food, which had suddenly lost its savor. "Why, they could have shot you in the back, Arlie."

The attorney shook his head. No, he said, people of that stripe did their killing from behind doorways, from back alleys, and from all the shadows and oblique corners that abundantly darken and complicate their landscape. True, he had put on a show for a friend from home, but more than that, he had tricked Newman and Wooten into feeling that they could not frighten him.

As luck would have it, Art Newman has left his own account of the meeting with Boswell in the White Way Restaurant. According to him, Carl Shelton had suggested that he meet the man who was almost certain to be the next Williamson County state's attorney.

Shelton, according to Newman, had more up his sleeve than idle conversation. That night, as Boswell prepared to board the train at the railway station, who should be crouching behind a nearby boxcar but the Sheltons and their henchman, Charlie Briggs. It was only at Newman's urging that they called off their plans to "bump off" the reputed Klansman. Why this sudden concern on the part of a man who had devoted his best years to thwarting the law? It was the little gambler's studied belief that Boswell's sudden demise would cause him and his friends more trouble than it was worth. No doubt he was thinking about the Klan's reaction in the wake of such a killing.

When informed of the gangster's version of their encounter more than fifty years later, Boswell smiled broadly and labeled it just another of Newman's lies—but a good story, nevertheless.

# 9
# Bloody Williamson

THIS SCENE SHIFTS TO A SLIGHTLY EARLIER TIME AND ANOTHER
locale; however, the characters remain the same. On March 3,
1924, in the federal courtroom of Judge Walter C. Lindley at
Danville, the trials began of more than two hundred liquor violators. Conspicuous among them were Ora Thomas and Charlie
Birger. Also present in the courtroom were some spectators who
should have remained in Herrin, notably S. Glenn Young and a
few of his men. Young even wore his famous pearl-handled automatics.

In the hallway before the trial convened, Young called Birger an
unprintable name and, by so doing, nearly caused a riot. Birger
asked United States Marshal James J. White for protection, adding that he had left his .38 in his hotel room. As it turned out,
though, he had little to worry about, because Young was not permitted to carry his guns into the courtroom. Danville, as the
Klansman learned to his dismay, was a long way from Marion and
Herrin.

Another who found that so as the trials progressed was Ora
Thomas. After being sentenced to one of the longer jail terms, the
errant deputy was forced to listen as Judge Lindley denounced
him at length.

Birger, who was supposed to appear in court the afternoon of
Wednesday, March 25, did not do so until the next day, at which

time he was asked by the judge why the forfeiture of his bond should not be revoked. There had been a misunderstanding at the time, Birger said. He further requested that the trial be postponed until Thursday, since his witnesses could not arrive before that time. Both requests were agreed to by Special Prosecutor Lawrence T. Allen, and Judge Lindley concurred. Birger's attorneys were S. Murray Clark of Danville and his long-time friend from Harrisburg, Alpheus Gustin.

To the witness stand at last came George B. Simcox, father-in-law of S. Glenn Young and a former deputy United States marshal at Danville—but presently a federal court bailiff in East St. Louis. Simcox testified that on the morning of November 7 and on the nights of November 8 and 14, he had bought liquor at Halfway. Birger, he testified, was behind the bar pouring drinks on all three occasions.

Convincing as his testimony was, there was a problem. Why had Birger not recognized Simcox, a man he had known by sight for years?

*Simcox:* I was considerably lighter in weight and did not have my teeth.
*Allen:* Would you object to taking your teeth out, Mr. Simcox, so the jury may see how you look without them?
*Simcox:* It's rather embarrassing, but I'll do it.

At this point, Birger's attorney, S. Murray Clark of Danville, raised an objection.

*Simcox:* I sincerely hope your objection may be sustained.
*Judge Lindley:* Objection sustained. I see no good in Mr. Simcox taking his teeth out.
*Simcox:* Thank you, Judge.

As the laughter subsided, Simcox stepped down from the witness stand.

His son-in-law, S. Glenn Young, stated that on November 16, he and two deputies, John Frothingham and J. W. Munday, both of Pope County, had purchased liquor at Halfway. Birger, he said, was not there at the time. (Note: Frothingham along with two other Klansmen robbed the bank at Brownfield, in Pope county, later in 1924. Captured, they were sent to the Southern Illinois Penitentiary at Menard.)

Conspicuous among Birger's witnesses was Charles Cisney of Marion, an employee in the restaurant area; Cisney testified that he had never seen Birger behind the bar. As far as he knew, the owners were "Mitch" Wood, Charles Irving, and the late Cecil Knighton.

Birger himself stated that the three were running Halfway and that he had no interest in the place, although he had bought twenty acres across the road in July of 1923. He claimed he was not even on the premises at those times Simcox asserted he made the "buys."

Judge Lindley was not only convinced, he was furious. After the jury returned a verdict of guilty, he exercised his right to make a speech, as he had done earlier in the case of Ora Thomas.

"I am determined to stop this lying on the part of defense witnesses who seek to discredit government witnesses," he said. "Somebody will go to the penitentiary if that practice continues."

Then he zeroed in on the man standing before him, saying:

> I don't know what to do with so-called citizens like you. You have money to hire lawyers. You have been defended as ably as any man could be. You've taken the witness stand and perjured yourself. Maybe I can stop you people from doing these things. I don't know. I am going to give you the limit. I will fine you $500 on the possession count, $1,000 on the sale count, and send you to jail for one year on the nuisance count. You are going to jail now. I will give your attorney 60 days to file a bill of exceptions in, but you cannot have one minute of delay in starting your sentence.

Birger's was the heaviest sentence meted out to any of the 178 defendants.

On April 22, he was in federal court again. In September of the previous year, he had been indicted on two counts—possession of liquor and possession of counterfeit revenue strip stamps. Both indictments had resulted from the raid at his premises on June 26, 1923.

The defendant took this occasion to appeal his first conviction of March 27, claiming that on the morning of November 7, the time George Simcox testified that he made the first buy, he (Birger) was in the office of Saline County State's Attorney Charles Thompson. He further stated that on the night of November 8, he was aboard a train. The judge just shook his head. "The jury passed on the evidence in your case," he said. "I can do nothing for you."

To the current charges, he pleaded guilty and was sentenced to ten months in jail and a fine of $300, plus the court costs. He took what consolation he could from the fact that the two jail sentences were to run concurrently.

Some days earlier, Beatrice and the two girls had gone to Danville in an attempt to persuade the judge to reduce the one-year sentence. Judge Lindley refused to reduce the sentence, but he did make reference to the visit in his parting remarks to the defendant: "If anything on earth should wake a man up," he said, "it should be the possession of the wife and children you have." Judge Lindley added that it was hard for him to deprive wives and children of the support to which they were entitled, but he insisted that the law was supreme in such matters.

Then it was Birger's turn. "Your Honor," he said, "I have learned my lesson, and you will never see me in this court again. But I will claim that I am innocent of the charge the jury convicted me on."

Following the sentencing, Birger was taken to the United States marshal's office where he told a reporter:

> I have been pretty much of a rotter in my life, but I never lied about anybody. I had rather take a man out and shoot him than to lie about him and get him in jail. If they would give me the chance, I could prove that the whole charge against me at Halfway Roadhouse was "framed," and I want George Simcox to think about what he has done all the time I am lying in jail away from my family.

The man who was credited with putting the lights out for Knighton and Doering and who had fleeced the miners at his crap tables was getting as good as he gave, or so it seemed to those who read the newspapers. Actually, he fared quite well—the cold and damp of a jail cell were not for him. According to Beatrice, he

68

made himself quite comfortable in part of the jailer's quarters. Moreover, his stretch at Danville kept him safely out of the gun sights of S. Glenn Young and his henchmen.

Not that Young was doing all that well himself, as evidenced by the incident on May 23 when the Klansman and his pretty wife, Maude, were fired upon from a passing car while driving through the Okawville Bottoms on their way to East St. Louis following a successful Klan rally in Harrisburg. Although Young was hit only in the leg, his wife was blinded for life.

Later, Judge Lindley's ruling that S. Glenn Young would be tried on indictments stemming from his raid tactics surely brought a smile to Birger's face. And just as surely a chuckle of satisfaction came when, in September, he learned of a dismissal he considered long overdue: S. Glenn Young had been officially expelled from the Klan.

Even those bits of good cheer, however, did not so much hold his attention as did the newspaper account of an incident at a Herrin garage owned by John Smith, one of that town's leading Klansmen. It had started with a car, the side-curtained Dodge in which Jack Skelcher was mortally wounded in a roadblock on the Carterville-Herrin road the day following the Young shooting. A few hours earlier, word had reached the Klan that Skelcher, along with Charlie Briggs and the two Sheltons, Carl and Earl, were the ones who had ambushed the Youngs the day before. Somehow they learned that some or all of the men were headed back into the county and set up their roadblocks accordingly. As stated, Skelcher died as a result of the gunfire, but Charlie Briggs, the only other person in the car, would live to fight another day despite his wounds.

Bullet holes and all, the Dodge was taken to John Smith's garage, and there it remained until August 30, the day that Carl and Earl Shelton were to go on trial before Judge E. N. Bowen in the Herrin City Court for the killing of Caesar Cagle. They did not appear in court that day. Their attorney, the much-shot-at Delos Duty, rose to announce that the one witness against the brothers had vanished, and for that reason, the case should be dismissed. That Tim Cagle, the dead man's father, should agree with Duty no doubt influenced Judge Bowen in his decision to dismiss the case.

Being more prudent than courageous, the judge was probably eager to be rid of the case. And, besides that, the Sheltons were fellow anti-Klansmen.

With this victory of sorts behind them, the Sheltons, accompanied by Sheriff Galligan, his special deputies, Ora Thomas, and "Bud" Allison, as well as other ardent anti-Klansmen, went to the Smith garage for the purpose of retrieving the Dodge that had been held until that time as possible evidence to be used in the trial. John Smith was not in the building at the time, and one of the workmen there seemed less than eager to let the car go. Words were exchanged, and then a fistfight broke out.

With uncommon slowness, a car filled with Klansmen drove past. Some of those in the sheriff's party stepped outside to talk with a passerby who recklessly advised them to pocket their pistols. Instead, they forced the passengers out of the car. Then a shot rang out. Whether it came from the garage or from the street, this lone shot sparked a barrage of gunfire that left six men dead.

Among the dead were Chester Reid, the man who had urged restraint only a few moments earlier, and a fellow bystander, Otto Rowland. The three dead or dying Klansmen were Dewey Newbold, Charles Wollard, and Green Dunning. From Sheriff Galligan's entourage, only "Bud" Allison was killed, but another man, Herman Phemister, later died from his wounds. Luckier were Carl Shelton, who had only a bullet hole in his hand, and his brother Earl, who was shot in the right leg, just under the knee.

With Birger at Danville and S. Glenn Young in Atlanta, Georgia, for medical treatment, Williamson County was clearly maintaining its unenviable reputation for sudden violence. But even with the latest incident, there were many in the county who cursed the newspapers for carrying accounts of the shootings. Especially to blame, they felt, were the metropolitan dailies that seemed to revel in the county's misfortunes. Chief among the culprits was the *Chicago Tribune*. Ever since the Herrin Massacre in 1922, it had sent down its most prying reporters to sniff out the latest gun smoke and send back to the Windy City all the details, and then some. Not far behind in their low esteem were the *St. Louis Post-Dispatch* and its rival, the *Globe-Democrat*. Thanks to these and numerous other newspapers, the county was seen across the nation as living up to its description as "Bloody Williamson," a description that had besmirched its name since the murderous days of the "Vendetta" back in the 1870s.

Removed as he was from the battle itself and the smell of a just-fired pistol or the searing flight of the bullet as it slammed into a man's body or a brick wall—and learning of the details primarily through newsprint—Birger was, for the moment, preoccupied with personal matters. First, there was the problem of Beatrice. He felt that she was drawing away from him. From the beginning, of course, he had been jealous. Once when her two male cousins came to visit from Pennsylvania, he became furious, seeing in their easy laughter more than the camaraderie of friendship and kinship. Because she rarely answered his letters now, he believed the worst and insisted on seeing her.

She recalled that first time that she tried to see him in jail. The two girls went along, and so did Beatrice's father. Driving the car was Jess Jones, one of Charlie's hired hands. She said with a smile: "Jess got lost. We got as far as Centralia, and we didn't know which way to go. So we turned around and came back. But I wrote him a letter in a restaurant in Centralia, and told him that was as far as we got."

Far from pleased when he learned of their turning back, Charlie made reference to that and other matters in a letter postmarked May 29, 1924. No changes have been made in either the wording or the spelling of that letter:

Dear Mrs. Birger and babies:

I know you are blowed up. I can't blame you a bit, but listen girley, it's partly your fault; when you was going anyplace you ought to have set down and wrote me a letter and telling me where you were going and who with. I am going to ask you to move up here. You ignored my letter never said you would or wouldn't. You ought have sat down and wrote me a letter and told me you would rather stay with the folks. I would have said alright.

I asked you to send me a telegram and you didn't do it. I have written half a dozen times and ask you to come up to see me and you never said nothing about that. I got a letter from you saying you got $300 for the register and then I got another letter from you postmarked Centralia saying that you was going to ship the dogs and the honey Thursday. The dogs were already here. If you had sat down and wrote me and told me you was taking your father and mother somewhere you know I would have been satisfied as you know I don't care where you go as long as your people go with you.

Instead of that you always write and tell me your looking for a job, either wanting to go to Detroit or St. Louis. You know that your credit is good in Harrisburg and don't have to work.

Instead of writing and saying Dear Hubby or something of that sort you always address your letters Mr. Charles Birger and always in a hurry. Spend about thirty minutes a day and maybe I won't be so suspicious and I wouldn't blow up so much.

The jailer here has tried to call you several times but could never get you. He is my friend and will let me talk to you over long distance anytime. So don't forget me woman, cause you know I'm in love with you or I wouldn't blow up, and don't make me live hard because you know it.

I'll have to admit that jealously is the worst sickeness in the world, and I sure am jealous of you.

So I will try and close. Try and keep my little family together. So when you come up here bring a big club with you and hit me right between the eyes.

> I remain your loving hubby
> Chas.

The dogs Charlie mentioned, she said, were a couple of bird dogs he had given the sheriff.

Another surviving letter is dated August 2, 1924 and addressed to his wife at her parents' home at 302 North Sherman in Harrisburg:

Dear Bea and babies:

I feel a great deal better since I got to talk to you. I am sending this letter special so you will get it tomorrow. I am sending Hart one special delivery to so you can get that money tomorrow night and leave Monday morning. So lets try and forget what we both have done and try and raise our two babies. All these hard times and notoriety should learn us both a good lesson.

Bring enough clothes with you so you can stay three or four days. If babies need anything we can buy it here. Wire me when

you leave so I can arrange a room for you. Hoping this will find
you in good humor and the babies in good health I remain,
                              Your Old Pal
                              Chas.


Monday morning, or soon thereafter, Beatrice and the two girls
were on a train bound for Danville. "At Danville, he had the run
of the place," she said, looking back over the years. "They didn't
lock him up. He had an apartment, because I went up there, me
and the children, and stayed a week with him."

This homelike scene was but an interlude in an increasingly
difficult situation. For some time, Bob Bainbridge had warned his
daughter about Charlie's new-found friends, the Sheltons. They
would get him killed, he said, and her too, if she stayed around
long enough.

Before going to jail, Charlie had heard similar lectures from his
father-in-law about choosing well one's companions, but there is
nothing to indicate that he really listened. How could he? In jail
or out, Birger had grand visions of really being someone important, someone like C. V. Parker, who owned a string of stores in
Harrisburg and Saline County, or his longtime friend J. Milo
Pruett, a Buick dealer and, like Parker, a director of the First Trust
and Savings Bank. When these visions were evoked in his conversation, as they often were, Bob Bainbridge heard him out, adding,
when he got the chance, "Charlie, you're going to die with your
boots on—that's what you're going to do."

Despite their differences, the two men got along, or they could
at least pass the time of day with each other. Not so with Charlie
and his mother-in-law, because—purely and simply—she hated
every fiber in his body. Once, when he was driving one of his
"women" to work at a place in the west end, Mrs. Bainbridge
happened to see them. Furious, she hurled a brick through the
car's windshield. Birger, at whom the missile was aimed, thought
the scene wildly hilarious and even expressed admiration for the
woman's spunk. Once on a street in Harrisburg when he had the
audacity to speak to her in public, she hit him in the face with a
brand new alarm clock. Some woman!

With Beatrice it was different, especially after she delivered that strong-willed woman a granddaughter. Actually, the reconciliation between mother and daughter occurred just before Charline's birth or just after Bob Bainbridge told his wife of the cars he had seen at the Birger's as he was on his way home from work. Sensing that something was wrong, Mary Bainbridge hurried over only to find her daughter having a difficult delivery. After the nearly lifeless baby was finally delivered with forceps, the grandmother immersed the poor child in hot and cold water in the bathtub, thus, according to Beatrice, saving the child's life.

Bob Bainbridge's insistence that Beatrice flee far outweighed the influence of her short visit to Danville. Charming as ever and outwardly kind, Birger still dreamed aloud that "someday, someday I'll be worth my weight in gold." There was about this man—so fascinating to many—something of the grating monotony of a stuck record. Over and over in the early days of their marriage, he had played on the Victrola a record that seemed to mean a great deal to him. Beatrice could recall only the refrain: "I'm in the inside looking out, waiting for the evening mail." While he dreamed in Danville, she was in Harrisburg packing her bags.

Her brother-in-law, Howard Boatright, who worked for the O. L. Baker Furniture Store in Harrisburg, had left a trunk at her parents' home. Little by little, she took her clothes over until one night she and her father and brother-in-law drove to Eldorado in the furniture truck. There, Beatrice boarded the train that would carry her to Shamokin, Pennsylvania, the home of her father's brother. Minnie and Charline were left with the Bainbridges. Too clearly she remembered: "I had a layover there in Pittsburgh, and I was almost sure when I changed from one train to another I saw him [Birger] and this Jess Jones. I was scared to death. Every time a stranger would come along, I thought it was him after me."

In the wake of his wife's disappearance, Birger got permission from Judge Lindley to personally attend to some property entanglements in Harrisburg. True to his word, the prisoner returned to Danville on October 2, after a week's absence. Following an investigation of the charges by Prosecuting Attorney Lawrence T. Allen, Birger was freed on October 6 by order of the United States Court, Judge Lindley presiding.

Three letters from Birger to his friend and attorney Alpheus

Gustin detail his efforts to win that release and also demonstrate his quite genuine concern for his children. They also introduce to us one Jack Davis, better known as "Hoghead" Davis, a little-known but deadly character. As with the other letters, Birger's spelling is unchanged:

Danville, Ill. June 25, 1924

Mr. Alvin Guston
Harrisburg, Ill.
Dear Sir:-
Have you ever done anything with that petition you had for me? There has been one made up against me, but send the other anyway. It may do some good.

The judge has cut fines and sentences down on all but two here, but he seems hard at me. There must have been a great many letters come in against me—

Write all the news and let me know what you can do,
As ever Your Friend<br>Chas. Birger

Danville Aug. 26–24

Dear Friend Gustin
I received a letter from Bea today she said she was going to some other country and left the children with her mother. Well I would like to have the children up hear for about two weeks go and see her father and see if he will get the kids and bring them up here to stay with me for about two weeks. I will pay his fare when I get ready to send them back home. I will wire him to come and get them. If he doesn't want to do that put Minnie on the morning train and wire me and I will meet her. Get my car and put it in Pruett's garage. L. T. Allen Dist. Prosc. Attorney has taken my case up again. He is convinced that I am innocent. I want afidavets covering the eight of November. The night of the eight I met Jack Davis at Parker City. I got off the night train and John M. Boden, and there were several others I just don't remember their names. They were coon hunting with me the night of the eight and I went back to Harrisburg the morning of the ninth we have found out. The date that Simcox testified against me he was at Utopia hunting. L. T. Allen is writting to Lee Barnes and Gaskins to get affivadits that they saw me the

75

night of the eight get off at Parker city for they were on the train. Get that Rokes affivadit that he swore to either Jack or Rumsey [Note: probably Darce F. Rumsey, an attorney in Saline County, later a state's attorney and circuit judge] have it and get the county court records where I paid Cecil fine on the day of the seventh. I want you to take a day off and tend to this as I would like to get this tended to this week. Court starts on the first and I would like to have the affidavits here by that time. I will appreciate this favor very much answer at once

Your friend
Chas. Birger

Sept. 4, 1923

Dear Friend

Recieved your letter. I haven't received Roakes affidavit. I am writing Jack—trying to get an affidavit from him. I want you to go to the Horseman [sic] School and get Minnies grade and transfer card. I started Minnie to school yesterday. If you are coming up here before long I want you to bring the baby up.

Write and tell me all the news.

Your Friend
Chas.

The "Jack" referred to in the letters of August 26 and September 4 is the aforementioned "Hoghead" Davis. In the entry in his diary for April 4, 1924, Gustin writes: "Jack Davis up P.M. with petition for federal judge."

How effective this petition was in persuading Judge Lindley to let the prisoner go is not known, but it does seem clear that Davis helped win Birger's release. The entry in Gustin's diary for September 26 shows that Birger and Davis visited the attorney in his office that afternoon or night.

Not until 1928 was it intimated that Davis was the man credited by the underworld with the killing of "Whitey" Doering. But by this time, "Hoghead" was long gone, having fled after shooting Roy Montgomery in a poolroom in Harrisburg's west end on Christmas Eve, 1924. Montgomery died two days later. (That John Bard was one of the two operators of this poolroom indicates that Charlie Birger may have had an interest in the establishment.) At the time of the Doering killing, Davis was Birger's paid body-guard and was said to be the best shot in Williamson County. Following Davis's disappearance, his two daughters lived at Birger's home for a time before being transferred to an orphanage.

Under the date of January 15, 1925, we find this entry in Alf Gustin's diary: "Jack Davis policies #T20174T20178 and Fire 4388 returned. . . . cancelled—to Earl L. Lingle." As stated earlier, Lingle was a markedly successful insurance man in East St. Louis.

Settled as she was in Pennsylvania (although afraid to leave her uncle's home and living under an assumed name), Beatrice began noticing something very odd about the letters her father sent. She wrote to him about it. Convinced that his letters were being steamed open and read at the post office in Harrisburg at Birger's request, Bob Bainbridge went to the local postmaster and threatened to go straight to the postmaster general if further tampering occurred. From that time on, to assure that his messages would not be inspected by unwanted parties, he walked from his home in west Harrisburg to the Big Four depot on the other side of town and shipped the letters by rail.

For fear that the news might bring his daughter back, Bob Bainbridge failed to mention that upon his return to Harrisburg, Charlie had reclaimed Charline. Prior to the little girl's departure, Birger had frequently stopped by the Bainbridge home on the pretext of seeing Charline but actually, Mr. Bainbridge felt, to learn of Beatrice's whereabouts so that he could kill her or have her killed. Less suspicious of her husband's motives, Beatrice nevertheless was canny enough to heed her father's advice to stay away from Harrisburg.

As for the girls, Minnie lived in Danville for a year, staying at the home of H. M. Culp, who was chief probation officer. Charline, too, lived in the Culp home—but for only three months. After that time, she was brought to Harrisburg to live with her father. Later Minnie joined her.

After the terrible tornado struck Murphysboro and West Frankfort in March of 1925, Birger learned of an unidentified woman who had been killed in West Frankfort and persuaded his father-in-law to check out the story. Although he knew better, of course, but thinking it prudent to appear ignorant about the matter, Bob Bainbridge drove to West Frankfort, viewed the girl's body, and reported to his anxious son-in-law that Beatrice was not among the dead. That piece of information seemed to ease Birger's mind.

A divorce was granted in Harrisburg. It became official on September 19, 1925.

# 10

# "Don't Pull That Gun, Ora"

**B**EATRICE WAS GONE. MINNIE WAS STILL IN DANVILLE. CHARLINE was now in her father's custody, given over to him by Bob Bainbridge, who no longer wanted Birger stopping by the house asking questions about Beatrice. Despite the freedom accorded him, Birger was no better able to manage his affairs than during the months in Danville. As it always had and always would, trouble clung to him like a virus.

Less than a month after his release, he again appeared in a courtroom as a defendant, this time before Saline County Judge A. G. Abney, on a charge of possessing intoxicating liquor. He pled guilty and on November 13 was sentenced to six months in the county jail and fined $1,000. By his own account, he paid that fine on January 28. On February 6, Birger stepped into his cell.

Between the sentencing and the serving of that sentence, Herrin witnessed another shootout, this one involving two of her most noted antagonists. In the background of this murderous throwback to the Old West may well have been Charlie Birger—who had seen the western frontier in its twilight years.

It was no secret in Williamson County that Birger's friend, Ora Thomas, had vowed to kill S. Glenn Young. According to Leonard Stearns, Thomas had even told Sam Stearns—who happened to be a relative by marriage—that the time would come, and soon, when either he or Young would kill the other. On the night of

January 24, one observer watched Thomas as he cleaned his guns in the sheriff's quarters at Marion. Mentioning casually that he might not be returning, Thomas made it very clear that a confrontation was imminent.

That knowledge was possibly shared by others, Charlie Birger among them. A man who once served as Birger's "collector" and bodyguard claims that he, Birger, John Howard, and two other men were in or near the European Hotel in Herrin the night of January 24, 1925.

Days before, so his story goes, Birger heard that a battle was in the offing, that S. Glenn Young, the man who had insulted him at Danville and who had insulted and pistol-whipped his way out of the good graces of Williamson County residents, was to be repaid in full for the wreckage he had caused. A price had been on Young's head even before he came to Williamson County. The attempt on his life in the Okawville Bottoms in 1924—resulting in the blinding of Mrs. Young but only minor wounds to Young himself—was an effort by bootleggers to rid themselves of this dry raider with a craving for publicity.

With Thomas, however, it was a personal matter. More than once, this very proud man had publicly been insulted by Young. "I think when Ora Thomas walked into the Canary Cigar Store, he was crazy with hatred for Glenn Young," said Arlie O. Boswell, who—though on opposite sides of the political fence from Thomas—liked the man and thought him an effective law officer. (In contrast, Boswell, along with many other Klansmen, had grown to appreciate S. Glenn Young "about as much as a rattlesnake.")

The night of January 2 found Herrin policeman Ross Lizenby firing a pistol into one of the columns in front of Gualdoni's Drug Store in Herrin. (For what it's worth, Sam Stearns once told Boswell that Lizenby was a crack shot who could shoot the very sparrows off a telephone wire while leaning out the window of a speeding automobile.) After they heard the shot, Young and some of his subordinates drove over to investigate, but apparently they found nothing, because a few minutes later they drove away.

Later in the evening, while patrolling the streets, Young and friends saw a young man, Elias Green, in the Canary Cigar Store, which was located on the ground floor of the European Hotel.

Convinced that Green had spread tales that he was one of the strikebreakers at the Lester Strip Mine in 1922, Young swaggered in and began to curse the fellow.

Walking down the street following his attendance as bailiff in Judge Bowen's city court, Ora Thomas heard the commotion and went to investigate. When he saw his longtime enemy standing in the doorway, Young warned, "Don't pull that gun, Ora."

Despite the warning, Ora's as well as other guns were pulled, and shots were fired. Then only smoke and silence ensued. When the curious arrived, they found a dying S. Glenn Young with two bullets in his chest and two of his bodyguards, Ed Forbes and Homer Warren, dead or dying. Dying, too, was their enemy, the delicately handsome Ora Thomas, a man whose questionable associations were offset by his defiance of Young even at the cost of his life. Thomas died in the Herrin Hospital, presumably Young's last victim. But was he?

When the firing ceased, someone who had been lying on the settee between the two antagonists, in order to protect himself, raised up, saw the somewhat dazed Ora Thomas—standing, staring, and holding a smoking pistol—and in his panic, shot the anti-Klansman through the head. So said Arlie O. Boswell, who presented the evidence to the coroner's jury, and Leonard Stearns, who was a member of that jury. Later, State's Attorney Boswell, like those on the jury, did nothing to discourage the widespread belief that Young and Thomas had neatly eliminated each other. It was felt through the county that the two deaths might bring an end to the bloodshed that had made Herrin a dirty word throughout the United States. In consequence, Young's much publicized funeral was almost a celebration, according to Stearns, who was S. Glenn Young's last surviving pallbearer.

This, then, is the bare bones account, one that is held to be true and probably is true as far as it goes. But there is more—much more. Arlie O. Boswell said that his one regret from the four years he served as Williamson County's state's attorney was that he did not investigate more fully the Young-Thomas killings. He had his reasons for not doing so, of course. As stated, the citizens were sick of the killings and wanted desperately to return to "normalcy." Mrs. Thomas, in particular, had requested that the inquiry be completed as quickly as possible. "And I believed that poor woman had suffered enough," added Boswell. He placed little credence in the rumor that Young was one of the strikebreakers in the Lester Mine Riot of 1922, but that rumor has survived the years.

Equally intriguing, the account given by Birger's "collector" points to a conspiracy rather than a fatal, chance encounter, as Boswell and numerous others believe. Days before the shootout, he asserted, Birger tried to dissuade Thomas from killing Young but was unsuccessful. Perhaps the gangster thought such an act would only inflame the Klan forces, uniting them once again into a concentrated effort against the bootleggers. At last, however, Birger relented. On the night of the shooting, four of his men were positioned in the lobby of the European Hotel, while he, oddly enough, sat in a car parked nearby. Following the shooting, his men jumped in that car, but rather than depart from the scene, they drove around the streets of Herrin observing developments while reveling in the fact that they had helped make history in typical Williamson County fashion.

Even if at the time Harrisburg was alive with rumors that Birger might be involved in the Young-Thomas killings, with one exception his name escaped mention in the area newspapers in that connection. The Klan newspaper, the *Herrin Herald*, suggested that he might have been the stranger that Herrin policeman Harry Walker had seen in the company of Judge E. N. Bowen just before the shooting. From the issue of January 29, 1925, there is the following:

Buried deep in the flow of words from Harry Walker was a statement that was not followed out, but which indicated the presence in the chambers of City Judge Bowen, in the company of Bowen and Deputy Sheriff Thomas, of a very mysterious stranger who remained until the end of the hearing and then was lost sight of. This mysterious stranger did not leave the city hall with the party, and was not mentioned except by Walker. Judge Bowen, who was questioned only briefly and not at all upon this point, mentioned the presence of a neighbor but was the only witness to name such a man. Walker swore that the man was a stranger to whom he had been introduced by Judge Bowen or Thomas, whose name he had forgotten and whom he thought was from Chicago. Walker testified that himself, Lizenby and Thomas were in the judge's chambers at intervals with the stranger who, of course, might have been the neighbor of Judge Bowen, but did not show himself before the others in the courtroom. That this man may have been Charles Birger, former roadhouse and gambling house owner of the Halfway house last fall, the killer of another man at the same place a few days previously, and credited with having killed a total of six or eight men, there is a suspicion. In addition, Birger is said to have been seen in the proximity of the county jail in Marion an hour or so after the shooting here. Mention was also made of the presence of strangers, well-dressed youths with the unmistakable stamp of gangsters, who arrived in Herrin in pairs on trains from different directions, were seen about the streets Saturday afternoon in a group or in pairs and at different times in the company of Ora Thomas, and then vanished.

Interviewed by many reporters over the years, Birger was rarely if ever questioned about the killing of S. Glenn Young. Later, while maintaining his innocence of committing a certain crime, he did admit that a kind of justice might be at work after all, since he had gone unpunished for similar offenses in the past. At the time he made the statement, the charge was murder.

# 11

# The Start of Shady Rest

ITH THE CLANGING SHUT OF THE CELL DOOR ON FEBRUARY 6, Birger once again found himself in a familiar environment. This time, however, the facilities were far less grand than those that had been provided by his host in Vermilion County. This was the kind of jail that put prisoners in their places—alongside winged roaches and the grime of the ages.

In a *habeas corpus* petition dated March 4, 1925, that he sent to Judge D. T. Hartwell of Marion, one of the circuit judges of the First Judicial District, the prisoner states his case:

> On the 6th day of February, A.D. your petitioner was incarcerated in the county jail of said Saline County by the said sheriff of said county, John Small, and has been detained of his liberties since that time. Your petitioner is now suffering with tuberculosis and has continued to grow worse ever since his said incarceration. [The] said jail of said Saline County is in an unhealthy condition, that about 2 weeks ago a fire occurred in said jail by the burning of old filthy and diseased mattresses whereby your petitioner was overcome by the poisonous gases in consequence of said fire and fell helpless to the floor and has been suffering extreme pain thereafter in consequence of said fire.

In his booklet, *Mean Old Jail*, Curtis Small tells how a disgruntled prisoner had set fire to a mattress that had been liberally soaked with "bug juice." The ensuing smoke billowing forth, filling the narrow quarters, sent Birger and fellow prisoners to the floor. When John Small's wife Cora heard the gasping and crying for help, she ran to see what was the matter. Being there alone—her husband and his deputies were busy "bird-dogging" moonshiners at the time—she was at first reluctant to open the door. But when Charlie gave his word that any escapee would answer to him, she finally turned the key that released the prisoners into the fresh air. No one escaped.

Sheriff Small and his prisoner appeared before Judge Hartwell in the Saline County courthouse on March 7. There the sheriff gave his reason for jailing Birger. On March 9, Judge Hartwell ruled that since the prisoner had already paid the $1,000 fine, "both sentences and judgments of the court could not be legally imposed on the defendant under the information in this case. It is ordered that the defendant Charles Birger be now released and fully discharged from jail." Lifting his spirit like a tonic, freedom allowed the former prisoner to fulfill a dream of long standing—the building of Shady Rest.

North of Route 13, where the oak trees stood, would be the barbecue stand—so Beatrice was told. He did not tell her of the roadhouse. South of the road stood a ramshackle shed, the abode of prostitutes Charlie brought in from St. Louis. From such humble beginnings came what was to be, for its kind and time, an entertainment complex of note throughout southern Illinois.

What did he really have in mind at the time? Like everyone else in the area, Birger knew that a concrete highway would soon connect Harrisburg and Marion. Except for "no man's land," a two-mile stretch of grade on the Williamson-Saline line, and another short stretch just west of Harrisburg, this highway was a fact by the close of 1923. Unfortunately for Birger, the months of lounging in Danville had delayed his building plans.

Sometime in 1925, work began on what later would be called, with justification, "the most notorious resort in the south end of the state." Serving the needs of the casual motorist, the barbecue stand near the highway provided sandwiches, soda pop, and candy bars. The floor was sawdust. Mitchell Oil Station of Marion, where Birger and his men bought their gasoline, had a gas pump set up in front. Outside, picnic tables completed the decor.

If by chance the customer wanted something stronger than soda pop, the man in charge (often "Honest John" Renfro, formerly of Hardin County) would pull up from the cooler a bottle of beer. And, if something even stronger was desired, "Honest John" could be counted on to step out to the back to fetch a jar or jug of moonshine. To passing motorists, the barbecue stand with its sawdust floor came to symbolize Shady Rest, a fact, no doubt, that pleased Birger immensely. Apart from the power plant, the real center, however, was the cabin in the woods.

It was set in a clearing north of the road. Built in the autumn of 1925 at a cost of several thousand dollars, it combined a rustic decor with modern conveniences. Once past the chinked logs and the overalled farm boys clutching their rifles, a visitor realized that it was quite a piece of workmanship.

Gracing the east and west ends of the cabin were deer heads and elk antlers, the former staring glassily above either of the two stone fireplaces. Other antlers could be seen along the log walls, as well as numerous old guns. Offsetting the rustic appearance were such modern conveniences as running water, a bathroom, and electric lights, the latter supplied by the power plant on the premises. Off limits to visitors, the basement was used for the "cutting" and coloring of whiskey. Stolen goods were stored there.

Behind the cabin was a large building made of corrugated metal, where dogfights and cockfights were held. Gamblers from the nearby towns and from as far away as Indiana and Tennessee gathered here in the autumn months to place their bets and to coax on the fighters of their choice.

In addition to keeping the local citizenry entertained, Shady Rest served as one of several layover stations for the booze-running Shelton gang. The route from Daytona Beach, Florida, to East St. Louis was first described by one "Ralph Johnson" in a series that appeared in the *St. Louis Star*. "Johnson," a one-time member of the Shelton Gang, chose a pseudonym for the information he gave.

There was, he said, an inlet approximately ten miles south of Daytona Beach and just north of New Smyrna, Florida, where a boat from West End Island in the Bahamas would deliver the whiskey to various rumrunners, among them the Sheltons. Not until the cargo was unloaded at the dock into the Shelton's specially redesigned coupe did the money actually change hands. To avoid the very real possibility of a robbery en route, Carl Shelton would usually telegraph the amount from East St. Louis to his brother, Earl, in Florida.

Loaded down with as many as four hundred quart bottles each, the cars would head north toward Jacksonville. Avoiding that city, as they did most larger ones, they cut back onto the Dixie Highway north of Jacksonville, following it through Waycross and Ocilla, Georgia, traveling northeast into Alabama. At some point, they caught Highway 31. Through Heflin and Aniston and Gadson they drove, and on through the mountains of northeast Alabama, entering Tennessee at the little town of South Pittsburg. Highway 41 led them to a "little plantation" near Smyrna that was owned by a black man. Here the cars were driven into a garage. In a barn nearby, the weary drivers literally "hit the hay."

Avoiding Nashville the next day, they motored along Highway 41 until they reached another garage approximately twenty miles south of Henderson, Kentucky. Here tires and other accessories were available. Also available were the "tails" or touring cars carrying armed men that followed closely behind as they journeyed over the "hot" state of Indiana. The "tails" were there to guard against the twin dangers of the liquor hauling trade: prohibition agents and hijackers. If either began pursuit, they were to block the road. Because these cars contained no liquor, the occupants had little to fear if arrested.

Into Indiana by ferry at Henderson, the liquor runners traveled on toward Princeton, avoiding Evansville. At Princeton, they drove west toward Mt. Carmel, Illinois, crossing the Wabash on a ferry.

For those who earned their daily bread by transporting booze over the highways and back roads of the Southeast and the Midwest, Mt. Carmel, on the Wabash, signaled a parting of the ways. Those bound for Chicago drove north while the Shelton brothers headed west toward East St. Louis or south into Williamson County. From shortly before Christmas of 1924, when the Sheltons made their survey of the route, until the spring of 1925, when Georgia joined Indiana as being a "hot" state, the Daytona Beach-East St. Louis excursion provided much of southern Illinois's liquor supply.

Tropical breezes and shore-lapping waves were far from the minds of those who downed their drinks and ordered others, but from seashore to roadhouse, it was a neat and profitable operation. A case of Canadian Club or Burke's Irish Moss, which sold for approximately $30 a case on the docks, brought from $75 to $85 in East St. Louis. The journey of four or five days often netted the rumrunners from $1,000 to $1,500.

According to "Johnson," Bernie Shelton and Charlie Briggs did most of the hauling. My own source names—in addition to the two just mentioned and himself—Ray Walker, Freddie Wooten, and Monroe "Blackie" Armes. Like "Johnson," my source insisted on anonymity:

> The liquor was bought from a man known as "Big Bill" at Daytona Beach, who supposedly paid off the Coast Guard to let his boats bring in the stuff from the ships lying outside the three-mile limit. The cars used were big lumbering sedans with the back seats removed. And, since the liquor was in tightly wrapped gunnysacks, one car could easily haul fifty cases. There were two men to a car and they drove straight through. One would drive while the other slept, and they stopped only for gas and food [usually lunch meat bought at a country store]. They kept to the back roads, bypassing the larger towns.

These cars were equipped with smoke dispensers capable of emitting "an impassable fog if they were pursued by the police or hijackers."

Surrounded by henchmen as armed as they were ignorant, mean-tempered bulldogs, eagles, and even a monkey named "Jocko," Birger would always take a part of the delivery that he then sold to his own area, "after cutting the Scotch twenty-five percent, of course." Most of the merchandise went to a garage the Sheltons ran in the East St. Louis suburb of Fairmont. From there, it was distributed to various points throughout southern Illinois.

Meanwhile, the moonshiners and bootleggers of southern Illinois were not idle, and among their many customers was, of course, Charlie Birger. Using a team and wagon, one driver hauled half-gallon fruit jars and crock jugs of whiskey, all packed in straw, from Eagle Creek in Gallatin County to the east door of the cabin at Shady Rest. He would make this trip once a week. Around sundown, he would arrive at a point near the still site, where another fellow would be waiting to take charge of the horses and drive them into the woods. Just where this was, the lad never learned, because he was not invited along. When the loaded wagon rattled back into view, he pocketed the cash, stepped up to the driver's seat, and was gone.

Except for Equality, he skirted the towns. Skirting the towns didn't take much doing, since only Eldorado and Harrisburg stood between the hollows of Eagle Creek and Birger's place, as far as he was concerned. Because the horses knew the way, the driver found time to sleep during the all-night journey. For each load, he received $25, plus the amount to be paid the moonshiners for the next batch the next trip around.

The driver turned to coal mining after Prohibition faded into history and in time became a family man and a Mason. Memory of hauling whiskey to a gangster weighed little on his conscience, yet something from that era did prove troubling down the years. The man who took the whisky at Shady Rest seemed to have no last name—everybody called him "Smoky." One day "Smoky" was not there, and his former cohorts seemed unable to recall him. Like smoke, the man had vanished. Listening to the story, I almost had the impression that the informant half believed he had dealt with a phantom.

Tim Hopson, also from the Eagle Creek area, did not forget his former customer:

Charlie bought his whiskey from St. Louis and from a couple of brothers in New Haven. And I sold him a right smart of whiskey, too, off and on. He bought it here and there. He would come and get it and most of the time, he was by himself. Drove a big Cadillac car. He had two or three cars, Charlie did, had a big Buick touring car, a Hudson, and the Cadillac. He'd buy as high as fifty gallons at a time when he'd come. I sold it for eight dollars a gallon.

Hopson said he made a lot of money in his time, but spent most of it on fines.

# 12
# Bloodshed, Cockfights, and Bulldogs

ROM HARRISBURG AND HERRIN AND MARION CAME THE BORED
businessmen and thirsty attorneys, the women whose easy
laughter complemented the clinking of the glasses, and the
miners who tried but could never quite wipe clean the coal dust
from under their eyes. They came to drink, to laugh, and to seize
the excitement Charlie had taken such pains to provide at Shady
Rest.

To help them along, Birger hired local bands. He was lucky
once when a medicine show came through Harrisburg, boasting
surefire cures for age-old ills and a band composed of silver strings.
The latter he hired to entertain his clientele—he himself provided
the medicine. Usually, however, the talent came from the nearby
towns. One popular black group came from Harrisburg's east end
or "colored section." It included Alvin Woods on saxophone and
Charles Lennox on drums. What finally happened when the music
and laughter became one under a whiskey mist could have been
foretold by any street-corner seer. Fully primed with a portion of
the cargo from Daytona or the equally potent corn squeezings
manufactured in the Illinois hills, some fellow or girl all but broke
Charlie Lennox's heart by stepping through his drum. Hardly
anyone else even noticed.

However, few of the customers failed to notice when the "Blonde
Bombshell" favored the crowd, as she often did, with her strik-

ingly uninhibited version of the "hoochy koochy." (She actually wanted to dance in the nude, but Charlie wouldn't permit that.) Even as a child in the days of World War I, she had entertained, singing for the lads of Harrisburg who were soon to be shipped to the trenches of France. Now, a buxom young lady of less than twenty, she savored the attention that was abundantly hers, thinking, no doubt, that it, like the 1920s, would last forever. Moreover, she was grateful for the friendship of her employer. Charlie was almost like a father to her. And she was no less grateful to Alpheus Gustin and H. R. Lightfoot, who often drove her to work. After the applause faded into the cracks in the logs, she resumed her duties as hostess by greeting the customers at the door.

With its women and booze available for a price and with its pseudo-rustic atmosphere—logs without and mounted deer heads within—the cabin appealed to a certain clientele. Out at the back and down in the woods, the bleachers around the fighting pits drew the gamblers, both professional and amateur. For them, bared fangs and a silver spur promised more thrills than a bought kiss or a turn on the dance floor. Willard St. John had cause to remember one cockfight in particular:

> I never did bet on but one rooster. In fact, he was the gamest-looking rooster I ever saw. Boy, he was a strutter. I told Charlie, I said, "I believe I'll bet on him." Charlie said, "I will, too." Now, a rooster, if you know anything about the history of a rooster fight, they don't gain much reputation because they don't live long enough. They put them buckle spurs on them and they fight to the finish. But that son of a gun, when they put the other rooster in there with him, he wouldn't fight at all. He ran. Lost my bet. Charlie grabbed that durn rooster up and just twisted his head off, and threw it right out as far as he could.

For the amount of blood shed, cockfights could not compare with the bouts between bulldogs, St. John added. Although roosters were noted for their short, frantic lives in the pits and while the losing canines did not always die, the dogfights did seem more brutal. Often the combatants would lock, burying their teeth into each other's necks. They could be separated only by having "the wind choked out of them." Having watched many a cockfight with barely a blink, St. John observed that bulldog fights should never have been allowed.

For sure, there was one that should never have been. Rudy Walker, who was there, thought it might even have been the cause of the trouble with the Sheltons later on. While that seems unlikely, the incident was, at least, an omen of the dark days ahead.

Walker, "Boots" Dillard, and "Pink" Whitehouse, all of whom "fought all the chickens we could get matches for," had taken their victorious fowl back to a cage in the back of "Pink" Whitehouse's pickup truck. They then returned to the arena, where yet another contest was soon to begin—this one between bulldogs belonging to Earl Shelton and Charlie Birger. According to Walker, after Shelton requested the fight, Birger, as a matter of course, asked the dog's weight.

"Sixty-two pounds," came the quick reply. As a courtesy, Birger took Earl's word on the weight. After all, they were old friends and business partners, having spent many an hour at the card table in Birger's garage while Beatrice's washing machine did its work. The fight was on.

In the arena, it was customary for the dogs to battle "until their owners gave them up or they died." After a remarkably short "battle," Birger's dog did the latter, causing Charlie to remark that the assertedly "equal size mutt" had handled his dog like a toy. Much too late, he insisted that the victor be placed on the scales. With obvious reluctance, "Big Earl" obliged. His dog weighed in at a hefty 73 pounds, while what was left of the loser only weighed 62 pounds. Clearly, this was a matter to be resolved on the spot. Walker mused, more than half a century later:

They had a shootout there in the chicken arena. Me and "Boots" stood behind one of those big, old-fashioned pot-bellied stoves and the bullets were going clink-clink as they hit the corrugated metal on the building, you know. "Boots," I said, "can you get out through that hole there?" That was where Birger had cut an oval place for his little puppy to get in for the night. He said, "I don't know." "Well," I said, "I'm going out through there. I can't get out through the door." Just one door to the place. And I got out there, so I pulled "Boots" through. He got hung in it and I pulled him through and took all the skin off his back. Well, "Pink" was still bigger than "Boots," and he crawled on his hands and knees till he got around to the door, and he never got hit. Me and "Boots" beat him out of there. They was still shooting inside. I don't know how many was hit. I got out of there as quick as I could. I never will forget what "Pink" said when he got in his truck. "By golly, that ain't no place for a preacher's son, is it?"

# 13
# Charles "Hardrock" Davis and the Anti-Horse Thief Association

ANY BURGLARIES IN THE AREA SOUTH OF HARRISBURG IN the summer of 1925 led to the establishment of the Anti–Horse Thief Association. Meeting regularly, its members were versed in such useful procedures as how to set up a successful roadblock, when to fire the warning shot, and when to shoot in earnest. The items most commonly stolen were chickens and tires, but cars were also taken; in fact, too many of them. Angry, the farmers and storekeepers were not impressed with Sheriff John Small's protests that he and his few deputies could hardly patrol the county's back roads from dusk until the morning hours and maintain any kind of order in the daytime, too. No, the locals would have to work together, insisted Small. They had a choice, either cooperation or chaos, take it or leave it, goodbye and good day.

The Association's first attempts at policing were as disheartening as the portly sheriff's parting words. So, while their chickens boiled in other men's pots, they fumed at fate, at John Small, and at the rising tide of barbarism. But on the night of December 5, 1925, the Rudement chapter of the Anti–Horse Thief Association captured two robbery suspects and, by so doing, played an unwitting role in the fate of Birger and his gang. Much of this account came from my grandfather, Guy A. DeNeal, who was a member of the Association; he was also a special deputy of John Small.

Three nights earlier, someone had tried to break into Hosea Parks's general store ten miles south of Harrisburg. From his home across the road, the store owner heard the noise, grabbed a gun, and went to investigate. When they heard him coming, the would-be robbers fled, taking nothing—so far as Parks could discern.

The next two nights found Parks and his shotgun in a second-story niche of the store building, waiting. He heard the questioning cry of an owl from across the cold pastures and the scratching of a mouse as it skittered across the hardwood floor, its nose alert for crumbs. But he did not hear the robbers return.

Late Saturday afternoon of December 5, there came a prewinter storm with hard winds and bitter cold. On a night like that, Parks reasoned, even a dedicated thief would not venture out. By staying home that night, he badly misread the criminal mind.

The storm broke around midnight, leaving a frozen world in the glow of a very cold moon. Around 1:30 A.M., Parks's bird dog began to bark. The weary storekeeper pulled on his clothes, grabbed the shotgun and the .32 long-barreled revolver, and slipped out into the yard. Across the road was an automobile with its hood raised. Very clearly in the moonlight, he could see the figure of a man standing on the porch of the store. One of the two pistol shots Parks fired toward that figure seemed to find its mark, but the man shot back before disappearing on foot down Travelstead Lane that led north from Rudement.

With lights off, the car sped west on what was soon to be "hard-road" Route 34. At the time, however, the roadbed had merely been graded as step one in a process that would soon transform this horse-and-buggy route into a splendid thoroughfare for Model T's, if not for today's coal trucks.

Meanwhile, Mrs. Parks rang up Sheriff Small in Harrisburg to tell him that the automobile was headed his way. Assuming that the sheriff would set up the necessary roadblock, she next called her brother, Guy A. DeNeal, a schoolteacher in Saline County.

Following the jangling of the various telephones, several men armed with shotguns arrived at the store, ready for action. Minutes earlier, Parks had poured antifreeze, cranked the car, and then "lit out" in pursuit. Perhaps a quarter of a mile west of Rudement, the car he was pursuing suddenly swerved, flashed its lights, and passed its pursuer, barreling east. Wheeling his own car's headlights in the same direction, Parks resumed the chase and quickly found that the other car was outdistancing him. He pulled in at the store, telephoned the sheriff the disconcerting news that the fellows had switched direction, and then, taking some of the newly arrived Association members with him, once again "lit out" down the road.

Beyond the crest of Lockwood Hill, they found a car, a Ford, parked beside the highway. In the back seat, shivering under a quilt, was a fellow who claimed he had been hunting that bone-cold night, had come upon this parked car, and had just got in. With men from two cars holding shotguns on him, he was unable to explain why the engine was warm or why the license plates were missing. (The next day, overcoats taken in the store robbery were found stuffed in a nearby culvert.) One of the men drove this car to Harrisburg while the "hunter" was taken in the other car to the Saline County jail. Escorting him were Parks, DeNeal, and two other men.

About three miles west of Rudement, on what is known as Blackman Hill, Parks and friends met a car that slowed as if to stop, then sped on. At the time, they gave little thought to the incident, being more concerned with the prisoner in their custody.

When they arrived at the jail, these men were angered to find Sheriff Small still in bed. Apparently he had not taken Parks's call seriously. Still, their night's work culminated in a cell door clanging shut, and the weary fellows headed back toward the heavy quilts of their homes at Rudement. Or so they thought.

About six miles south of town, they noticed a pedestrian walking their way. He wore a sheepskin coat with the collar upturned, a style that was fitting, considering the night. But Parks thought he detected a resemblance between this person and the figure on the porch that he had surely "winged." He slowed the car to find out. One good look was satisfactory. From the driver's side, he and DeNeal slid out of the car, since a luggage carrier made an exit almost impossible from the other side. As the suspect reached for what seemed to be a pistol, the storekeeper shoved the .32 in his face and threatened to use it. As it turned out, the man had been reaching for a syringe filled with morphine. While Hosea Parks's index finger danced dangerously near the trigger of his gun, his brother-in-law retrieved a .45 automatic from the pedestrian's pocket, along with a chisel.

Once again, it was back to town, this time with a prisoner who refused to say more than his name, which he claimed was Steve George. His look of dejection was heightened by the cut on his lip (for which Parks took credit, marking it up to his years of sighting down a rifle in squirrel season) and the burrs that clung to his sheepskin coat. They had no way of knowing it, of course, but these amateur crime fighters from the Rudement hills had just captured the most feared of Charlie Birger's gangsters. What they didn't know made for sweeter dreams.

Considered to be of less than average intelligence, this gold-toothed Bulgarian actually seemed to enjoy killing, according to some who would have known. No Sunday-school superintendent himself, Art Newman was to tell a reporter more than a year later that Steve's reverence for human life was practically nonexistent. Somewhat wary of this particular gangster himself, Birger once told Arlie O. Boswell that while most of his men were "harmless punks," he had one "really bad character" named Steve George, a man he had "to watch like a hawk." Bragged Birger, "I believe I could get him to kill anybody for maybe a cigar or at least a five-dollar bill."

Formerly a miner at Harco, Steve was no stranger to the Harrisburg police. They probably knew of his past, particularly the four years he had served in the Missouri State Penitentiary for the killing of his wife, Rosa, and her lover, Fred Bolittle, at Desloge, Missouri, during a Labor Day picnic in 1915. They were equally well acquainted with John Howard, the man at whose home Steve stayed in Dorrisville. For some time, the police chief, Walter Jackson, had wanted to inspect Howard's home. Now with Steve's arrest, he had the opportunity, and despite the late hour of 3:00 A.M., he intended to use it. With fellow officer Charles "Hardrock" Davis and the Anti–Horse Thief group crowding the shadows, Jackson knocked on Howard's door.

"John Howard had his clothes on," recalled Guy A. DeNeal.

"Just had his shoes off, was in his sock feet, and he was laying on the couch. He'd just got back, he said, from St. Louis, but actually he was the one we met on Blackman Hill." They had recognized his car.

That predawn raid revealed a loaded automatic in a dresser drawer and also some medical paraphernalia that DeNeal believes was used to induce abortions. In one room, they found perhaps a hundred women's coats. Luckily for Howard and pals, the labels had been ripped out, making identification impossible, especially since none of the coats had come from Parks's store. More important to the issue at hand, they found a cushion belonging to a Ford car and fitted it perfectly into the automobile found at the roadside earlier.

In the interval between the raid and the trial of his two cohorts early in January, 1926, John Howard managed to get into a shooting scrape, on Harrisburg Square, with the redoubtable Charles "Hardrock" Davis. Howard had just pulled into a parking place, when Davis, who happened to be standing nearby, noticed a pistol laying in the front seat. Many officers would have chosen to overlook the weapon, considering the owner's reputation, but to "Hardrock," that pistol might as well have been a fuse sizzling down to dynamite or a naked woman, shameless in her glory. It had no business on the Square, his Square. Guy A. DeNeal was not there, but he heard about what happened. "'Hardrock' just reached in, and as he started to get it, John Howard grabbed it. Old 'Hardrock' was quick on the trigger. He had a big .44. He jerked it out and shot John. All that saved Howard's life was a gold watch, but it knocked the wind out of him." The next time bullets flew, John Howard would not be so lucky.

Meanwhile, "Hardrock" had problems of his own. The moonshiners from Eagle Creek—that hilly region where the southeastern part of Saline County joins Gallatin—found that Davis was a man to avoid when delivering their goods in Harrisburg. One notable exception, however, managed to walk past the policeman with the bottles strapped around his waist, hidden under his shirt.

No less accommodating to the Birger gang, Davis once made the mistake of trying to search one of Birger's cars that happened to be parked on the Square. Displaying his usual calm, Birger told one of his bodyguards (my informant) to take care of the matter, which he did. Slipping up behind "Hardrock," he delivered him a blow on the head with the butt of his pistol. About to follow through, he was told by Birger merely to empty the cartridges from the policeman's gun and let him be. To this day, Charles "Hardrock" Davis is remembered as an uncompromising police officer, almost one of a kind.

On January 5, 1926, the trial of Steve George and his accomplice was held in the Saline County Courthouse, with Judge Abney presiding. The prosecutor was State's Attorney Charles T. Flota. George's attorney was former State's Attorney Charles H. Thompson, a man who would later serve as a justice on the Illinois Supreme Court. According to DeNeal, who was present during the trial, Thompson did not appear altogether pleased to have this murderer, drug addict, and petty thief for a client but went through the motions of defending him with as much professional aplomb as he could muster.

That one of his men should be the focus of the Court's attention was disconcerting to Birger, who, in his heavy overcoat, was conspicuous at the trial. From Harrisburg gambler and businessman Dan Lockwood, Parks learned that Birger had threatened to kill him. Having reason to believe that under his overcoat, the gang leader carried a gun, possibly even a machine gun, the storekeeper managed to borrow a pistol from Deputy Sheriff Henry Mitchell.

Nor did DeNeal rest easy after the trial, especially when he noticed that Steve George's brother seemed to be following him wherever he went. The schoolteacher was not too worried, however, thinking probably the fellow only wanted back his brother's pistol, then in DeNeal's possession. He did not get it.

As for Birger, my grandfather found him more a puzzle than a threat. As the proceedings droned on, he thought back a few months to his first sight of the gangster; it occurred just after one of Small's deputies, Royce Cline, had been killed by a black moonshiner near Carrier Mills. While Cline's body lay within the Gaskins's Funeral Parlor, "a little runt of a fellow was 'raising Cain'" on the sidewalk outside the establishment. Indeed, the talk that flew through the town of storming the jail and lynching the prisoner could be traced, in part, to haranguing like that of "Citizen Charlie." Yet here he was in court, as well dressed as any haberdasher and looking about as deadly. This time he was only listening.

A torn lip and a coat full of burrs did not constitute guilt, of course, nor did Parks's testimony that George was the one who had stood on the porch, firing back at him. Circumstantial though it was, the evidence must have been convincing, because the day after the trial began, the jury returned guilty verdicts. Already an accomplished car thief, the younger defendant was sentenced to an indeterminate term at the Illinois State Reformatory at Pontiac, while his more seasoned partner received a life sentence to the Southern Illinois Penitentiary at Menard. Even so, Birger had no intention of letting Steve George spend one day behind bars. Under pressure, the man with the gold teeth could divulge enough of what he had seen and heard to destroy Charlie Birger.

At the moment, however, Birger had more on his mind than keeping the murderous Steve George free of prison bars and prying lawmen. He needed someone to fill the space left by Beatrice's departure—not that the house had been empty of female presence following the night his former wife and her suitcase had journeyed east. Housekeepers had come and gone, but he needed someone to serve as wife and mother, to share his name and his nights at home. Presently employed as housekeeper was Sibyle Dee Davis, widow of Sam Davis. Davis, along with his son and others from the Harrisburg area, had drowned in a boating accident on the Mississippi, near Memphis, in 1919. Following the tragedy, Birger took pity on the Davis family, providing them with coal and groceries. Mrs. Davis's daughter, Bernice, a beauty, as Beatrice had been, meanwhile caught the eye of the family's benefactor and began to share his life. Tradition has it that they were married in February 1926. She would find that Charlie could be the soul of kindness, both to the children and to her.

Even Hosea Parks had occasion to see Birger at his enigmatic best. Early one morning while in Pankey's Bakery in Harrisburg to buy bread for resale at his own store, Parks discovered that his smallest bill was a twenty, an enormous sum at the time and certainly more than the baker could change so early in the day. At that point, Charlie Birger walked in. "What's the problem, Mr. Parks?" he asked. Parks said that making change was the problem; he did not—could not—say that the real problem at hand was having to engage in polite conversation with the man who had threatened to kill him and may be about to do so now. Instead of a gun, Birger pulled out his wallet and extracted from the wad of bills within enough to change the twenty. Their paths never crossed again.

# 14
# Trouble in Herrin

DUE LARGELY TO THE EFFORTS OF HERRIN NEWSPAPERMAN HAL Trovillion, evangelist Howard S. Williams came to Herrin to conduct a series of revivals, the purpose being to heal the wounds caused by the recent Klan and anti-Klan conflict. Judging from those who stepped forth to proclaim their part in the recent hostilities before asking the Lord for forgiveness, the revival was a success. So pleased was Trovillion that he published a booklet, *Persuading God Back to Herrin*. In it, the Bible-bearing Williams was favorably compared with the late, unlamented gunman, S. Glenn Young.

Doing his part to bring about reconciliation, State's Attorney Arlie O. Boswell struck from the court docket 145 cases resulting from the Klan war. In later years, Boswell would cite the landmark Castree and Elias decisions as his reason for dismissing the liquor cases. In its ruling of February 19, 1925, the Illinois Supreme Court sharply defined the limitations of a search warrant.

Three jugs of liquor had been found in the home of Sam Castree of Rockford, but the search warrant legitimizing that raid had been issued only for Castree's store, which adjoined his home. This oversight on the part of the raiders was a boon for the bootleggers of Illinois and Williamson County.

The very legitimacy of the search warrant was at the heart of the Elias decision, filed April 24, 1925, or just a month before the beginning of Herrin's much-heralded revival. Before the Elias decision, "information and belief" were enough to secure a warrant; following it, a search warrant could be issued "only upon affidavit of facts within the knowledge of affiant." Clearly, the methods of S. Glenn Young and his fellow zealots were already archaic, a fact of life that failed to impress the latter or to remove from the books some of the cases resulting from their illegal raids.

For his part, Young's one-time advocate, Boswell, had before him numerous liquor cases, many of them inherited from his predecessor, the anti-Klansman, Delos Duty. "I'd say I had a hundred when I went in. He [Duty] wasn't about to prosecute them," Boswell said. He added:

When the Elias case came in, I had to dismiss those cases. And then, when the law-enforcing agency—I'm not going to say it was the Klan, because I don't believe that—O.K., be that as it may, we'll call it the Klan—the Klan raised hell with me, saying I was in league with the bootleggers. You could tell them all you damn pleased and show them the Elias case and the Castree case all you wanted to. And then the question is with fellows like that goddamned Young, they said it makes no difference, that the end always justifies the means.

(Note: It must be pointed out that Young had been dead for three months when these cases were dismissed.)

Finally, as if once and for all to close that bloody chapter in American history, on July 3, 1925, the Klan's *Herrin Herald* ceased its financially harried existence. A new era?

The signs were right and the future seemed promising, but even Trovillion saw reason to include in his prayerfully optimistic booklet a warning that violence might again beset Herrin and Williamson County:

It may not be over yet—the volcano may not only send up smoke from time to time, but it may again spout destruction and death, but surely not if this wasted and exhausted community heed the last resort to remedy presented by the editor-evangelist, Howard S.

Williams, the little man from Mississippi who came to us a little while ago bearing a gospel of love into this wilderness of hate.

Unfortunately, Trovillion's darkest fears became a reality.

In Herrin, on April 6, 1926, an election for township offices resulted in a decisive victory for the Klan, and the school board election four days later was similarly one sided. The final balloting for nomination of county and state officers to be held on April 13 was dreaded by some because a Klan victory here would leave no doubt that the organization was once again flourishing in Williamson County.

On the morning of April 13, tension was heightened when John Smith, a poll watcher for the Klan, challenged several Catholic voters, among them a nun who had been a resident of Herrin for two decades. This last insult sent clenched fists flying, and Smith, no fool, returned to his bullet-scarred garage.

There he should have stayed, but strolling out that afternoon, Smith became the target of a gunman in a passing car. Only grazed, he darted back into his garage and slammed the door. Other shots rang out from the European Hotel. Closer at hand, still other gunmen in automobiles and on foot thoroughly shot up his place of business, including some of the automobiles inside, but neither Smith nor his armed guards were wounded.

Shortly after the barrage of fifteen minutes or so had died away, the militia, consisting of twenty guardsmen from Carbondale, arrived and quickly took positions in front of the bullet-pocked facade of Smith's garage. Grim faced in their khaki, their bayonets poised, these young men presented an unwelcome sight to the gunmen who even then were returning on foot to continue their assault. Upon seeing the militia, they hastened to their automobiles—which were parked about a block from the garage—and drove away.

They did not drive far. Near the Masonic Temple, one of several polling places in the city, the gunmen emerged from their cars—which were left parked and running in the street—and proceeded to walk toward the building. On the lawn before them stood several men, among them John Ford, a leading Klansman and that day a special constable guarding the polls.

Warned earlier in the day by the "old army doctor," Frank Murrah, that trouble was brewing, Herrin policemen George Wright and John Stamm parked their car at a street corner a short distance east of the polling place. From this vantage point, Wright saw Noble Weaver walk up to Ford, throw a gun on him, then take his pistol. While walking back to one of the gangster's cars parked on the street just east of and adjacent to the Masonic Hall, Weaver was shot in the back by Klansman Mack Sizemore. As Weaver fell to the lawn, a shot rang out, felling Ben Sizemore, Mack's brother. When Bob Greer stuck his head out the door, Weaver "got on his elbow and cut down on Bob" but did not hit him. "Bob dodged back out of the way," Wright added. (The bullet remained in the concrete for years and, despite efforts at patching, was still discernible in 1979.)

Across the street, on a public green east of the Herrin Hospital, lay Harland Ford with his rifle. As a "turtle-back roadster" turned the corner, a shot rang out, presumably from Harland's rifle, causing one of the men in the car to throw up his arms and fall back against the seat.

Meanwhile, Ford himself had been hit. Lying on his back, trying to unjam his rifle, the dying Klansman "finally got that shell ejected and it went off, shot up in the air. He just turned loose and that was the last of him," said Wright.

Harland Ford was dead. Dead or dying on the lawn lay Noble Weaver and the two Sizemores. In a Buick coupe were two other corpses, Aubrey "Orb" Treadway, the man reputed to have loaned Charlie Birger the money with which to build Shady Rest, and Charlie Briggs, considered to be one of the men who had fired on the Youngs in the Okawville Bottoms. The car belonged to Birger. Wright continued in his narrative:

We were under military orders. Whoever the commanding officer was [Major Robert W. Davis of Carbondale], he sent us back out here to the hospital to guard the entrance. We did the best we could. I remember one woman—she was permitted an entrance—who came in with her husband. She said, "If I was a man and had a gun, I'd kill you." I said, "Lady, if you were a man and had a gun, you wouldn't have gotten in." Feelings ran high.

It might be mentioned that the aforesaid woman supported the Klan.

Conspicuously absent from Herrin that day was the state's attorney. The previous night found Boswell in Stonefort, just across the line in Saline County. Years later he would claim that he had hired cars there on behalf of Oren Coleman, the Republican candidate for sheriff of Williamson County.

The next day, Boswell was in Equality with his old friend, Sam Bunker, to electioneer for another old friend, Oscar Carlstrom, attorney general of Illinois. (A newspaper account states that he and Bunker drove to Shawneetown that April 13 to transact some business for the American Legion.)

From either Shawneetown or Equality (depending on the source), Boswell made a telephone call. Recognizing his name, the operator said, "Oh, my God, wasn't it awful how many people were really killed over there?" Boswell claimed ignorance of the affair that already had provided headlines in a number of newspapers and instructed her to connect him with the Herrin city hall. There the woman's account of the tragedy was confirmed with details. Said the former state's attorney:

> I had to make it back over there. I didn't have a gun. Sam wanted to go with me. I said no. He loaned me two guns and ammunition. He talked me into driving his car instead of my car so they wouldn't recognize me. When I got to Herrin, I was the happiest guy in the world that I got there alive.

Alive, yes, but his absence that day not only from Herrin but also from the county itself, when many had predicted violence, would later be noted, and the most dedicated of his enemies would charge him with more than negligence.

For many in the county, the shock of the battle with its half dozen dead was of greatest concern. Some, like John Smith, who sold what remained of his garage and moved to Florida, realized that the Ku Klux Klan could not withstand the machine guns of the gangsters. What had begun as an idealistic crusade by ministers had degenerated into an exercise in destruction and general lawlessness under the leadership of S. Glenn Young. As if to symbolize the defeat of the Klan, Harland Ford's relatively modest tombstone in the Herrin Cemetery was erected in the shadow of Young's bullet-scarred slab of concrete.

Other changes were in order, not the least being the nomination of Oren Coleman as Republican candidate for sheriff. A school-teacher and former principal of the Marion High School, Coleman was a far cry from the gregarious ex-coal miner, George Galligan, whose friends included the Shelton brothers. Coleman, a loner noted for his austere manner, was doubly lucky that bloody Election Day, because just minutes before the shooting began, he had left the Masonic Temple to get a shave at the nearby Jones's Barber Shop. While the bullets flew, the future Williamson County sheriff lay under a warm towel in that shop.

Not so lucky was Charlie Birger, who mourned the loss of one of his closest friends. With Charles "Chink" Shaffer and Alpheus Gustin, he attended the funeral of "Orb" Treadway in Paragould, Arkansas. In his sorrow, however, Birger had reason to be grateful, because he was there when the shooting raged—he and the Sheltons and a host of other bootleggers. It might have been him lying in the coffin, surrounded by flowers and the subject of loving words such as are always bestowed upon the dead no matter what their station in life.

The "calm" following the Klan's demise was tenuous, actually hardly more than an illusion. In July, the body of a man was found lying at a roadside just north of Herrin. In Herrin, a flurry of shootings and beatings prompted Mayor Marshall McCormick to issue an order that all unemployed persons carrying guns within the city limits would be jailed. He particularly had in mind the Shelton brothers who ran a joint "on the north end of North Park Avenue," as well as some of their men. Prominent among these were the two Walkers, Harry and Ray, and the two Armes boys, Floyd and Monroe, better known as "Jardown" and "Blackie." After all, "Blackie" had the distinction of being the only one arrested following the Masonic Temple shooting; but a quick check with George Galligan had shown Armes to be one of his special deputies, and therefore he was released.

In the early hours of July 12, Harry Walker was talking to Ed Rocassi in a bedroom of the latter's "Mildred's Place"—a road-house at the edge of Herrin—just before Boyd Hartin, better known as "Oklahoma Curley," was killed in a gunfight. The following day, Rocassi gave himself up. Not one to discern a message in the shooting death of a drunken troublemaker, Walker continued to frequent roadhouses.

Son of former Herrin Police Chief Matthew Walker and himself a former policeman and Klansman, Harry gained notoriety when Galligan accused him of withholding liquor that had been confiscated in Klan raids. Now it seemed that his name was cropping up in print with unusual frequency, and it was rumored that Harry had a hand in the 1925 killing of Otis Clark, one of the defendants in the Herrin Massacre trial.

Meanwhile, back in Harrisburg, a man with another familiar name (one that was soon to become better known due to the trouble brewing in Williamson County) was helping the local authorities solve a murder. Charlie Birger always liked to be of service to the men who wore badges.

On the night of August 5, 1926, Joe Chesnas and two other young men robbed William Unsell, an elderly rural mail carrier living in Harrisburg. Fearful of identification by the victim, Chesnas shot and killed the old man in Unsell's home three nights after the robbery. The next day, Chesnas was arrested.

Alpheus Gustin, into whose custody Chesnas had been released once before, had told Joe at that time that when he was in trouble to come to him. Now the young man was in real trouble, and as luck would have it, Gustin was one of the three attorneys appointed by the court to represent the impoverished ne'er-do-well.

In jail, Chesnas was comforted by his longtime friend Charlie Birger, who claimed to be, as usual, under arrest himself. Outside, Birger said, was a mob ready to storm the jail for the purpose of dragging Joe off to his own lynching. Confess to him, Birger continued, and he would pull the necessary strings to effect his release, gather his gunmen, and free the young murderer. Fearing that he had little choice in the matter, Chesnas told how he had gone through the window screen—knocking down two chairs in the process—and how in panic he had flashed on the light in his hand and shot Unsell in his bed.

It is doubtful if Birger's efforts in the cell actually decided the young man's fate, although Chesnas did sign a confession following their conversation. But it did prove once again the lengths to which the gangster would go to ingratiate himself with the law. Joe Chesnas was finally hanged in Harrisburg on June 17, 1927.

One who watched from atop a building located near the scaffold was Arlie O. Boswell. Years later, he said that seeing Chesnas drop through the trapdoor was such a shock that he came close to fainting and might have fallen to his own death if his companion hadn't caught him.

# 15
# "Blonde Bombshell"

O N AUGUST 22, 1926, HARRY WALKER AND EVERETT SMITH were killed in a roadhouse north of Marion. Shot through the head, Smith fell near the door, and moments later Walker came running, only to be felled by a bullet in the back that penetrated his heart. He, too, lay near the doorway. When charged with these killings some months later, Art Newman would say only that a "tough gangster" had killed the pair. But with becoming reticence, the little gambler failed to attach a name to his allegation. Nothing came of the charges against Newman.

Of the several witnesses, most contracted temporary amnesia when their time came to testify before the coroner's jury. Some didn't stick around long enough even for that. A woman "entertainer" who had registered earlier at a Marion hotel, arrived at her room following the shootings, packed her bags, and fled, saying over her shoulder as she left that there had been trouble at the roadhouse. Waiting for her in an automobile were two men and another frantic woman.

While little real information came forth concerning the two killings, Arlie O. Boswell remembered well their aftermath:

> After the killing of these two boys at this little hamburger place right north of the cemetery, when we were to have the inquest on the following Monday, I was visited by Ray Walker and Carl

Shelton, who had driven up in front of my house in two cars. Carl Shelton introduced himself to me again and said Mr. Walker wanted to talk to me, and that he came along. I took them up to my office, but at the time, I noticed that four guys got out, two out of each car, with guns. When I later looked out and saw them sitting in the yard, I asked Mr. Shelton to make those guys get back in the car with those guns and not create a scene there in front of my house. In this conversation, Ray Walker came to inform me that I was not to have any inquest in the death of his brother, that he knew who killed him and they would take care of them in the usual fashion. I advised him that we would have an inquest and that I wished he would not attend. He said, "Well, you aren't going to have an inquest, that's what I came here to advise you. When I say that I mean it." And then his hand began to shake and that's when Carl said, "If you move that hand another inch, I'll kill you right here in this man's house." And he apologized to me.

The inquest was graced by the presence of "Blackie" Armes and "one of the Sheltons." Whether their attendance in any way affected the findings of the coroner's jury—that the two men had "met their deaths at the hands of parties unknown"—is not known. Quite aware that the full story was not being told, the state's attorney felt that the killings were committed by members of the Birger gang. And Ray Walker, he is convinced, held the same opinion.

"I'm telling you it was really a very hushed-mouth affair," Boswell said. "But you can't make them testify if they don't want to testify. There was a hell of a lot of heat put on."

That a gang war was brewing became increasingly clear to anyone who opened a newspaper or loitered on a street corner. Some even bothered to ask why.

One popular account credits the Birger-Shelton break to the fickle nature of Helen (Richeson) Holbrook of Shawneetown. While Birger was in Florida buying whiskey, so the story goes, his wealthy sweetheart was having a "whing-ding" with his erstwhile friend, Carl Shelton, in St. Louis. Jealous as usual, Birger learned of their frolic and saw red—Carl's blood, preferably. So neat is the tale and so hauntingly symmetrical, it begs to be authenticated— but cannot be.

Twice married, Helen probably had flings with both men, as

well as with several others. Of the two, the soft-spoken Carl seems to have been her favorite, as indicated by the number of times their names are linked in print. Old timers in Gallatin County's High Knob region talk of their retreat there, now an abandoned farm. Still, the "Blonde Bombshell," no "fizzled dud" herself, remembered the time she found Charlie and Helen together in the latter's Shawneetown mansion. In her inimitable and uninhibited way, she piped, "Helen, what have you done, gone and changed gangsters?" Helen's laughing reply was that the arrangement was only temporary.

No stranger to Shawneetown herself, or to the company of gangsters, the "Blonde Bombshell" once found herself on a houseboat belonging to "Pink" Whitehouse, the cockfighter of renown and brother of "Dock" Whitehouse, another well-known gambler of the area. The boat was docked near town. With her were Attorneys Alpheus Gustin and H. R. Lightfoot, the latter so drunk he could not get out of bed. Somewhat intoxicated herself, the young lady managed to lose her shoes in the water and, as a result, had to dance barefoot on the wood floor of the dance hall uptown that night. When the "Blonde Bombshell" complained about the splinters, Helen, who was having a rather good time herself, shot back with a laugh, "Don't worry, a few more drinks and you won't know the difference."

What blasts the Holbrook legend to the skies is that too many of Helen's "arrangements" were of a temporary nature. For instance, Birger's one-time henchman Riley Simmons claimed he lived with her for two years. Over from West Frankfort for a week's fishing in the lake region north of Shawneetown, Simmons found time between strikes to attend a dance at a nearby dance hall, where, oddly enough, a large tree grew from the center of the dance floor. Amid the whirling skirts, the wearers of which were fueled by the moonshine manufactured in the surrounding hills and hollows, he met Helen, ex-wife of veterinarian J. B. Holbrook and the liveliest and richest dancer of them all. When the music broke, they began to talk, and as it often does, "one thing led to another." Soon this one-time tramp mule driver from Alabama was living in the richly appointed Richeson mansion overlooking the Ohio.

In time, Simmons would stay with her in St. Petersburg, Florida. But two years into blossoming, their idyllic affair fell apart. Helen then "took up" with a baseball player from near Shawnee-town whose goal of breaking into the big leagues would never be realized, some said because of his ties with the Birger gang.

Another veteran of the Birger gang saw Helen more as a misfit than a sex symbol:

> She was an oversexed screwball of a woman who seemed to get turned on by hoodlums. She was nobody's sweetheart in the sense that she could form an attachment to any one person. She was no raving beauty, just a voluptuous woman whose unnatural sex drive guided her to the bed of any hoodlum, be he Birger or Shelton.

If not a woman, then perhaps a diamond?

J. Milo Pruett, director of the First Trust and Savings Bank in Harrisburg and owner of the Pruett Garage, had been a friend of Birger's for many years. A gruff, profane fellow who, according to one who knew him, "spoke to you like he hated you," Pruett was one of moonshiner Tim Hopson's more distinguished customers. Pillars of the community are, after all, only human.

Seeing Milo at her husband's place in Harrisburg's west end, Beatrice Birger naturally assumed he was there to gamble. Perhaps he was, but an elderly ex-gambler who would not even allow this writer to take notes of their conversation maintained that Pruett was too "tight" and too shrewd to risk money on a pair of dice or a deck of cards. No doubt girls hovering about the place learned, much to their chagrin, that their well-advertised favors appealed less to the banker than the crackle of a dollar bill. A man of power, albeit local, he possessed an iron will—bad news for the easy money crowd who, nevertheless, continued to lust after his money. As stained glass appeals to parsons, men of another stripe were much taken with his diamonds. The glitter of the big one he wore on his finger spoke volumes to certain gangsters.

When the banker was robbed at gunpoint of his ring, Pruett rang up Birger, requesting that he bring $1,000 to bolster the $500 in ransom he had already paid to the gunmen glowering in the office of his garage. True to his word as given over the phone, Birger soon arrived, cash in hand. When he slapped the bills down on the table, the ring was returned to its owner. But before the robbers could pocket the loot, Birger grabbed it up, saying, "The hell with you guys. You won't get a dime."

Art Newman told of the aftermath of this scene in the Buick garage. The four men, three of whom Newman named as "Blackie" Armes, Ray Walker, and Everett Smith, were naturally angry. When Charlie gave his word that the victim would send the $1,000 later, they stalked out muttering of violence. Needless to say, they were never paid. To complicate matters even further, they decided that Pruett really had paid Birger but that the money was not forwarded as promised and had been kept by Birger as his negotiator's fee. Whatever the truth of that facet of the diamond incident, Pruett was out at least $500 and no small amount of mental anguish.

This curious tale has a final twist. Pruett later came to believe that Birger himself had engineered the robbery with the idea of profiting from the result—and the banker believed he did. The very mention of the matter would raise the old fellow's blood pressure, laughed Arlie O. Boswell, who knew him well in later years. If any verification is needed for this theory, that encyclopedia of underworld chicanery unwittingly supplies it. According to Art Newman, rumor had it that Orb Treadway had "lined up the robbery" before his untimely death in Herrin. If so, Birger almost certainly helped in the planning, for he and Treadway were very close friends.

Beneath the manicured lawn of Harrisburg's Sunset Hill, oblivious to the Main Street yarns of his pal's trickery, lies J. Milo Pruett. As they have for fifty years, tales about him and his diamond continue. Colored with each telling, they correctly depict the curious, hand-in-glove relationship between a gangster and a community leader, but they do nothing to explain the gang war.

Other reasons given for that "war" include that Birger wanted the Sheltons to smuggle in some of his relatives by way of Florida and that they refused to do so and that the Sheltons were peeved because Birger didn't take a greater part in the Masonic Temple shootout—and vice versa. But the most convincing explanation came from a fellow who claimed to have once been Birger's collector. The falling out began, he said, over a dispute about the slot machine returns.

Arlie O. Boswell, for another, said he had always heard that the trouble had started with the slots. Certainly in a position to know, Freddie Wooten, in an interview with the *Post-Dispatch*'s Roy Alexander, said that Carl Shelton had learned from one of the collectors of Birger's twin set of account books.

But it was left to the fellow using the pseudonym "Ralph Johnson" to provide the name of that tattling collector and to detail the first of the minor tremors that signaled a split in the organization. "Johnson" would seem to be the ideal choice to describe the sequence of events that led to the conflict, for, by his own account, he was the first collector of the proceeds for the Shelton-Birger machines.

In November of 1925, Birger suggested a partnership between the Sheltons and himself whereby they would place slot machines in the more promising Williamson County roadhouses. The Sheltons agreed, providing Birger supplied the capital. In return, they would buy the needed protection from the local authorities. Of the proceeds, fifty percent was to go to the owner of the roadhouse, while the remaining fifty percent was to be divided among themselves. Birger was to be the treasurer.

On December 18, 1925, all machines previously controlled by either party were placed under joint control. And for $30 a week plus expenses, "Johnson" set about the not-unpleasant task of collecting the returns.

That first month the business partners had for their combined share $867 (half of the total take). A shutdown order was issued from Boswell's office on February 13, but that lasted only a short time. Long enough, though, for Birger to decide that "Johnson's salary of $120 a week plus expenses was too high. In stepped John Howard, whose salary was to be $100 a week plus expenses.

During Howard's five-week stint, a profit of $1,700 was realized, but the treasurer only forwarded $300 of this to the Sheltons, according to "Johnson." Possibly Carl would never have known of the missing $550 his partner owed (according to Wooten the sum was $410) if Birger had not fired Howard, replacing him with Ward "Casey" Jones, a former coal miner from Herrin. Carl bided his time—for a time. This interlude, no doubt, saw the dogfight that led to the shootout in the area behind the cabin.

That his tip to Carl Shelton would trigger a gang war in which many of his friends would die probably did not occur to Howard.

In any event, the Dorrisville man was denied a role in the coming conflict, thanks to an incident at Harco in the predawn of August 16, 1926.

A crap game was running in the back part of McCormick's Poolroom. After Howard had slapped him during an argument, "Sod" Gaddis left the room—returning about twenty minutes later with a shotgun under his arm. Immediately, Howard took a position behind some of the by now concerned gamblers and began firing at his would-be assailant. Their own welfare foremost in their minds, some of the men persuaded Howard to stop shooting. Still cradling his shotgun, Gaddis then reduced the tension by making his exit, followed by John Howard also calling it a night. Hardly was he out the door, however, when a shotgun blast was heard. Running outside, the poolroom crowd found Howard, pistol in hand, lying dead from a charge that had torn through his left side, under his arm.

In his diary entry for August 16, Alpheus Gustin observes that one "Babydoll" Flick was in his office with a petition for a contribution to John's widow. Some of the money may have been used to ship the body by rail from Eldorado to Providence, Kentucky, for burial. "Hardrock" Davis may have contributed to the widow's fund, but it is doubtful. Gaddis gave himself up, as Sheriff Small predicted he would. He was released after a coroner's jury ruled that Howard had died at the hands of parties unknown.

# 16
# Shotgun Shot Between the Eyes

Several events that occurred in the late summer and fall of 1926 point to the kindling of the fire that would soon break into an all-out gang war. Warrants for searching the Palace Hotel, where the Sheltons were believed to have a cache of guns, were secured, and Marshall McCormick, the mayor of Herrin, placed a call to Adjutant General Carlos Black in Springfield requesting that he send two of his officers to Herrin to participate in an important raid. Shortly before noon on August 27, Lt. Col. Robert W. Davis of Carbondale and Major Kenneth Bucannon of Urbana were in Herrin. Within an hour after their arrival, they, along with Mayor McCormick, the entire Herrin police force, and several special deputies (among them Dr. Carl Baker, a local physician) were ready to begin.

Why he had been ordered to stay over from the "night trick" was a mystery to George Wright until he and the other members of the force arrived at the hotel entrance. As luck would have it, the weary policeman was the first to enter the foyer at the foot of the stairs.

"I expected to be shot the minute I stepped in," Wright said years later.

Much to his relief on that long-ago day, no automatic barked, no machine gun chattered as he stepped through the door. Gun in hand and still half expecting a bullet to find him, he climbed the stairs.

In a bedroom, they found gang members Monroe "Blackie" Armes, Pat Pulliam, and Eddie Crompton, along with "all sorts of guns," including, Wright remembered, one sawed-off shotgun. Not only was there no shooting, there was also no argument. An exercise in etiquette on both sides, the raid was pronounced a success and a bright feather in Mayor McCormick's wide-brimmed hat. That night, however, Carl and Bernie Shelton and their pals Ray Walker and Floyd "Jardown" Armes demanded that Chief of Police George Griffiths return their weapons. When the message was relayed to McCormick, the mayor answered with a resounding no.

Crompton was released the night of the raid. Armes and Pulliam were released the following day.

Sometime later, Wright was sitting in a police car parked in front of the city hall, when a man got in and sat down beside him. Said the stranger, "I'm Charlie Birger. I guess you're wondering why I'm here." Wright assured him he was.

It seems that one of his men had a pistol taken from him by one of the Sheltons, and now that a number of their guns were in police custody, he wondered if it might be returned. Insisting that he was only a hired hand, Wright advised Birger to check elsewhere. Satisfied for the moment, the gangster bade him good day and got out of the car. "As far as being in a temper, he was just as calm as you are now," Wright said to me as we sat in a car parked near the site of the old Palace Hotel in Herrin.

The night of September 12, 1926, Mr. and Mrs. Pat Pulliam and their friend "Wild Bill" Holland were leaving Grover's Place, a roadhouse near Herrin, when bullets tore through their roadster. Although seriously wounded, Pulliam drove the car to the Herrin Hospital. The luck that accompanied him and his wife that night did not extend to Holland. Upon hearing the news of his death, Earl Shelton eulogized the victim (reputed to have been his brother Carl's bodyguard) as "the main support of his widowed mother and sister—a dear little mild-mannered chap."

Another who mourned the death of "Wild Bill" was his friend George Wright. Just off his stint on the "night trick," Wright was home in bed when someone knocked:

It was Art Mann, one of the night men. He said, "George, get up. Bill Holland's been killed. He's in the car down there in front of the hospital, and Pat Pulliam and his wife have been shot." Bill was in that car and he was sitting on the right side. Pat had been driving the car and Mrs. Pulliam had been sitting in between them. He [Bill] was sitting there, his eyeballs were out on his cheeks. He'd been shot in the back of his head—I suppose with a shotgun with slugs. I walked around on that side and opened the door—back in those days cars had running boards—and a thumb fell out on the running board. It was off of him. Later Pat said to me—he was in the emergency room and they had already put his wife to bed—"George, go down there and go through Bill's pockets. He has $50 and his old mother will need that." I didn't go through his pockets to get the $50, but stayed there until the undertaker arrived with the ambulance. I told him about it and he went through the pockets and found one little old dime. Somebody had rolled him after they shot him.

While Holland's killing remains a mystery, officially at least, a possible solution was provided by a former Birger gangster in a letter to this writer. The careful reader will notice that his account does not match George Wright's exactly. So be it. To quote:

"Wild Bill" was killed by Birger. It happened during a raid by the Birger gang on a roadhouse between Johnston City and Herrin. The Sheltons were known to be there at the time of the raid, and those that could, got away, fled—except for "Wild Bill" and Pat Pulliam and his wife—also shot in the gun battle. I was not a witness, but quoting those who were, Charlie came up behind "Wild Bill" and said, "Turn around, you son of a bitch, so you can see who's killing you."

Two days later, an ambulance was traveling from Herrin to Benton. In front was the driver, Joe Nolen, and his father, E. B. Nolen. Lying on a cot in the back under the watchful eye of his mother and his longtime friend "Strawberry" Wells was the wounded Pat Pulliam. Ed Russell, another friend, followed in his automobile. A third car was driven by the patient's father, Fred Pulliam. In the fourth and last automobile were Pat's wife and his father-in-law, Bert Steward.

When the tiny caravan reached Johnston City, Fred Pulliam remembered that he had forgotten the X rays, and he turned back toward Herrin. For reasons unexplained, Mrs. Pulliam and her father also decided to return to Herrin.

All was well until the ambulance neared the Benton Cemetery, south of town. Roaring up from the south came a car carrying five or six well-armed men, one of whom shouted for the driver to stop. When Nolen refused, the car pulled out in front. Again came the order, and this time the driver had no choice but to pull over. While the two Nolens and Wells were taken at gunpoint across the road and guarded, two of the gangsters, one bearing a machine gun, the other a pistol, entered the ambulance. Mrs. Pulliam screamed. As well as she could, this woman of rare pluck tried to shield her son's body with her own, taking as she did a number of blows across the hands and arms. Pressing his weapon to her side, the man with the machine gun ordered her out of the way, to which she replied that she would die before allowing herself to be pulled away.

This time as before, the luck of Pat Pulliam held. He took a couple of blows to the head. Those that were more an afterthought than an attempt to kill him perhaps were a reminder that while doling out rare acts of charity, the Birger gang felt obliged to set a price, in this instance a strong headache. It should be mentioned that while the beating was in progress, a number of drivers passed by, but no one was foolish enough to stop.

Details of Pulliam's second brush with death were hardly out of print when fresh atrocities crowded the front pages of southern Illinois newspapers. One concerned the body found in the ashes of an abandoned farmhouse in the Pulley's Mill area south of Marion on the night of September 17, 1926. Later, the remains would be identified as those of Lyle "Shag" Worsham, a native of West Frankfort and an acquaintance of both factions.

The following day, yet another body, this one badly decomposed, was found in a timbered hog lot north of Shawneetown. This well-dressed man of forty or so had been shot between the eyes with what appeared to be a shotgun slug. On his chest stood an empty shotgun shell, and folded in the watch pocket of his trousers was half of a five dollar bill. "He was shotgun shot between the eyes and the awfullest smelling man I ever smelled," said Bill Bunch, who was police chief at Old Shawneetown at the time of the interview. "You could smell him a mile away. Buzzards had done eat his eyes and part of his nose off."

When word reached Williamson County that another body had been located, Arlie O. Boswell and one or two others drove over to see if they could provide identification, but they were unsuccessful. Still, because the Birger gang was often seen in Shawneetown, it was generally assumed that the victim was killed either by the Birger or the Shelton gang.

Interestingly enough, Connie Ritter was in charge of the roadhouse near the hog lot where the body was found, and as proprietor, he lifted many a glass of home brew with the locals, among them Bill Bunch. Ritter certainly wasn't above suspicion. The same could be said of Helen Holbrook, who was called to testify before the coroner's jury. There is even a story—one that became almost a tradition—that the body in question had lain atop her Richeson mansion for sometime prior to its transfer to the wooded lot. Neither killer nor victim was ever properly identified, although the writer did hear that the latter's nickname was "Smoky."

Two and a half weeks later, Art Newman and his wife, Bessie, were driving west from Harrisburg toward Shady Rest, when a two-and-a-half-ton truck came rumbling toward them. Protruding from the circular steel tank on the back was an assembly of weapons, all of them well aimed toward the couple.

In the ensuing gunfire, twenty-five bullets tore through the car, but only Bessie was wounded and she only slightly. Swerving the car back toward Harrisburg, that city of refuge for Birger and his friends, Art Newman easily outpaced the lumbering vehicle with its murderous crew. Covering those few miles back to Harrisburg and safety, the clever gambler, soon to be Birger's right-hand man, had plenty to ponder.

# 17
# Art Newman and Connie Ritter

U NTIL THE ATTACK, NEWMAN HAD NOT BEEN PARTICULARLY close to Birger, although he had supplied him with whiskey from time to time. Both had lived in Macoupin County (Newman in Gillespie and Birger in Staunton), but it may be that Newman was telling the truth when he said the two were introduced to each other in East St. Louis by their mutual friend, Carl Shelton.

At the time of this alleged introduction, Art Newman was the owner and proprietor of the Arlington Hotel, a noted hangout in East St. Louis for small-time crooks and prostitutes and an ideal spot for plying one's trade as gambler and bootlegger. Working as a night clerk at the Arlington was Freddie Wooten, who had labored with Newman years before in the coal mines near Gillespie, or so he claimed. Like his boss, Wooten was equally agile with a deck of cards or a pair of dice, and he was far more articulate in conversation. In fact, he was considerably brighter than most men of his stripe, according to a former Birger gangster who knew him well.

Fresh from the "sticks" of Wayne County came three down-and-outers named Carl, Earl, and Bernie Shelton. Newman took pity on the trio, providing them with bed and board and even loaning them money to get started in their bootlegging operation. Eventually Earl would haul booze up from Florida for his brothers to sell at their saloon on 19th Street and Market Avenue in East St. Louis. Newman fails to mention that all three of the Sheltons were well acquainted with St. Louis and East St. Louis long before he met them.

Anyway, all was cozy at the Arlington until Bessie got tired of the freeloaders and their bumpkin ways. Particularly galling to her was their habit of cleaning their weapons in the lobby. Her husband could and did overlook that—as well as the stolen tires they crammed into his garage—but being a family man, he, at last, had to accede to his wife's wishes. The Sheltons had to go, and they went—across the street to the Savoy.

Despite this rift, their friendship remained more or less intact until three days after their mutual enemy, S. Glenn Young, was shot and killed by their mutual friend, Ora Thomas, moments before Thomas was mortally wounded. On the day of Thomas's burial, January 27, someone robbed the mail messenger at Collinsville of $15,000. Convinced that his former tenants were responsible for the crime, Newman asserted that the real reason the Sheltons wanted to attend the Thomas funeral in Herrin was to provide themselves an alibi. Unfortunately, the brothers and Newman arrived too late for the funeral, although they did meet the party returning from the cemetery. One of the mourners advised them to return posthaste to East St. Louis via the back roads, because by now Young's friends in the Ku Klux Klan would have blocked the more widely traveled route. It was advice not to be taken lightly, and they took it, arriving in East St. Louis that night.

Once back in familiar territory, Newman, without thinking, walked into one of the back rooms of the Shelton saloon. There he saw Carl and some other men seated around a table, the top of which was heaped with money. "See you later, Art," Carl said in a none too friendly tone.

At that point, the friendship between the two men really began to fall apart, Newman said. So much so, in fact, that about two months later, a fellow by the name of Charlie Gordon was induced to pick a quarrel with him, a quarrel Carl hoped would be the death of the sharp little East St. Louis gambler, bootlegger, and hotel proprietor. As it turned out, Gordon was the one who got killed.

Following his acquittal for Gordon's murder in 1925 on grounds of self-defense, Art Newman sold the Arlington and for more than a year "worked" out of Memphis, running booze and rattling the dice. Traversing almost the entire South, this tireless fellow chased the dollar bill with marked success, yet yearned to return to East St. Louis—and did.

Unfortunately, his former pals had neither forgotten nor forgiven. They had, in fact, started a rumor that he had robbed and dynamited a moonshine still in Madison County, Illinois. Now he had not only to scan the alleys for Shelton thugs but also to keep a weather eye open for irate moonshiners. Poised as he was between the two possibilities, Newman felt the only sensible thing to do was pull up stakes and join Charlie Birger, who was lately warring with the unpredictable brothers.

Wooten, who had made the mistake of siding with his old work mate the night of Gordon's killing, had reason to believe that he, too, would suffer the wrath of the Sheltons, so for his own protection, he also joined the Birgers. Like Newman, he quickly became one of the top men in the gang.

Shortly after arriving in Harrisburg, Newman, accompanied by Birger, chanced to meet Helen Holbrook on the street. Hardly had they parted when Carl Shelton's phone rang in East St. Louis. Having received Helen's astonishing message about the company Newman was now keeping, Shelton placed three calls to Birger's home. His darkest fears were confirmed by the "no comment" from the other end of the line.

Carl Shelton's own comment came the next day when he and his men sighted in on Newman and his wife west of Harrisburg. It is not clear if they actually were looking for Newman or simply happened upon their former benefactor while prowling for other game, such as the "boys" who had routed them from "Grover's Place" the night Bill Holland was killed.

Prior to their sighting the Newmans, the Sheltons and their truck passed through Marion, causing some citizens to mistake the unwieldy vehicle for a gasoline truck; others were alert enough to notice the guns protruding from the sides. Following the attempt on the Newmans, the truck returned to Marion, then turned north toward Johnston City. North of town, the Sheltons searched Lester Thetford's roadhouse, then drove to the County Line roadhouse between Johnston City and West Frankfort and proceeded to shoot up the place, an event that was only fitting since Charlie Birger was co-owner of the joint. (His partner was Roy Shaw, one of the men at Halfway the night "Whitey" Doering was killed.)

If the Sheltons were out for blood that afternoon, they were markedly unsuccessful. If, on the other hand, they sought to impress the citizenry with their war implements, their success was beyond measure. Following their exhibition, the Marion streets were noticeably lacking in pedestrians. Even the next night very few attended the Orpheum Theatre—it was usually packed.

On Jordan's Curve, east of Shady Rest, one of the factions set up a roadblock. Flashlights scanned each suspicious vehicle for members of the other side. Of particular interest to the gangsters was an ambulance that was reported to be traveling toward Marion. Since they believed that a situation similar to the one involving Pat Pulliam was about to unfold, the men conducted a thorough search but found nothing. Because of the location, it is generally assumed that the Birger gang was responsible for the roadblock.

Among those inconvenienced by this outrage was the "Blonde Bombshell," who was on her way to work at Shady Rest. Her driver was so frightened that he refused to drive further and be scrutinized. As a result, she had to walk the rest of the way, over a plowed field.

Meanwhile, back in Marion, the owner of a small coffee shop located near the jail was warned by officials to close early, the rumor being that certain of the Shelton gang had been sleeping in the jail. Poised for the first confirmation of that rumor were three carloads of Birger gangsters who were parked near the jail and who waited there without success for most of the night.

Birger's own war machine took shape in "Uncle Tom" Cain's repair shop located at 509 South Granger in Harrisburg. The car, a Lincoln, was stripped down to the chassis, and the upper part of the frame was armor plated. No one, not even the most goggle-eyed child of twelve, was more interested in "Uncle Tom" Cain's progress than three of the gang, all of whom were heroes to the youngsters gathered around. Almost every day, Freddie Wooten and Art Newman stopped by to check on the progress. Often they were accompanied by an uncommonly handsome fellow they called Connie.

Conrad Ritter came from Orient, a Franklin County coal town where his mother and sister ran a store and where his good looks and dancing ability "wowed" the girls, much to the chagrin of the local fellows. In the Miner's Hall, he sometimes played the piano and sang "Ja Da, Ja Da, Jing Jing Jing." In a word, he was gregarious, the sort of friendly fellow that fellow Mason Arlie O. Boswell could appreciate and understand.

The two up-and-coming young men had become friends during the time that Ritter ran a shoe store in Marion. After he went broke, he told Boswell that Charlie Birger had offered him the job as business manager for the Birger operation, a position that was not dangerous in the least, the gang leader had assured him. As one of the elite, he would be removed from the sordid details, such as midnight raids and flying bullets, but near at hand to the wine, women, and song that the Shady Rest environment so amply provided. The sales pitch had won him over, yet here he was in Harrisburg rubbing shoulders with two quite discernible gangsters while anxiously awaiting the completion of an armor-plated car. Had he blinked and missed something? Connie Ritter came from good stock, but he had this one problem: He was an absolute "bonehead."

The pledge that Cain and other Harrisburg residents found so heartening came in a message of Birger's that was read over radio station WEBQ (We Entertain Beyond Question), Harrisburg, during the height of the gang war. Later it appeared in the *Daily Register* and read, in part:

> The break between the Birger and Shelton factions came a few weeks ago when Charley Birger would not permit his friends in Harrisburg to be robbed by members of the [Shelton] gang. He appeared in time to stop a hold-up and robbery, and that was the start of the breach between the two factions. This breach became more bitter as the days passed on, and until now it has reached the stage where a meeting of the two gangs means a death battle. The breach was made the more severe last week when Mr. and Mrs. Art Newman of East St. Louis, who were the guests of Mr. and Mrs. Birger, were fired upon by the enemy gang. In the shooting, Mrs. Newman was slightly injured, but is now recovering.
>
> A big payroll robbery and several other robberies planned to have been staged in Harrisburg during the past two years have been

prevented by Birger. . . . People on the highways are in no danger because a gangster's bullet in this instance will be aimed at an enemy gangster.

In this announcement meant to pacify the public, Birger failed to mention that he and his cohorts sometimes robbed poker games in nearby towns. One night Freddie Wooten, Art Newman, Birger, and two others decided to hold up a game in West Frankfort. Because one of the gang had once lived there, he was handed a machine gun and told to guard the cars.

That same night, following their successful haul in West Frankfort proper, the men held up another poker game, this one out toward Orient 2 Mine. This time the man from West Frankfort was told to guard the door and to let no one escape. When a woman tried to make her exit, he grabbed her money before shoving her back inside.

On some of their forays, they may have stolen slot machines. At least, Charlie's neighbor Delbert Balabas was surprised to see slots stacked in Birger's kitchen after Charlie had invited him over to do some work. Using one of his best drills, Balabas proceeded to bore out each of the locks until the coins came pouring out. Birger dumped the proceeds in a heap on the kitchen table. As his neighbor was about to leave, drill in hand, the affable Birger scooped up a handful of coins as payment for the labor. Later, Balabas discovered he had made two cents less than five dollars, a princely sum for a half-hour's work.

To adequately protect Harrisburg, "his home and where he was educating his children," Birger claimed he needed an armored car, something imposing enough to plant fear in the hearts of hardened criminals and efficient enough to back it up with bullets. In time, this piece of unwieldy armament would be abandoned, but for now, as the Sheltons had impressed the citizenry of Marion, so Birger felt duty bound to display his might to the folks at Harrisburg. One ex-gang member recalled riding on top, machine gun in lap, as the mighty car toured the Square. They wanted to impress the law, he said, and no doubt they did.

As broadcast over the radio and carried in print, Birger's assurance that his neighbors could rest easy under his protecting arm did nothing, of course, for the unfortunate many who found themselves outside the city limits. And for those who operated outside the law, he had another quite ominous message, one conveyed by his underlings or sent humming across telephone wires: All bootleg joints were to be closed for the duration of the "war." It seems Birger believed that the various roadhouses scattered throughout Williamson County and elsewhere in southern Illinois made ideal fortresses for Shelton gunmen. Perhaps so, but his almost comic-opera attempt to inject a semblance of fair play into the deadly and quite ugly free-for-all was earmarked for failure.

One roadhouse operator who thought and said so was Joe Adams. Despite his 280 pounds, Adams was anything but lethargic, being also a Stutz dealer in West City and, not least, the mayor of that Benton "suburb" long noted for its defiance of the Volstead Act. The town was ridden with bootleggers and dice men. With the passing of Noble Weaver, leader of the Franklin County underworld, the booze vendors did as they pleased, and Joe Adams was no exception. Having his brother Gus for neighbor and ally, Joe felt capable of defying Birger or anyone else who attempted to impose restrictions.

It is known that the personable Gus did at first try to dissuade his brother from getting deeply involved in the gang war, which was really a blood feud not so different from the vendettas that plagued the hills and hollows of Kentucky and West Virginia in times past. Now it was too late for cool reason. While their friendship with the Sheltons contributed to this cocksure attitude, at least on Joe's part, it also automatically assured them of Birger's enmity. Joe's bullheadedness made their position even more untenable.

Take a moment to pity Joe Adams. Many years earlier, his father, Jack Adams, had his heart set on shooting the young man his daughter was determined to marry. To save the bridegroom on his wedding day, Joe shot and killed his own father. Gus would have nothing to do with his brother for years, and only with the growing conflict did Gus and Joe reconcile.

One day T. Mills Moore saw Joe Adams standing on the Benton Square and asked what he was doing. "I'm just standing here," replied the mayor of West City. He then threw back his coat to reveal a machine gun.

Joe did have sense enough to realize that to spite Birger was to invite trouble. Accordingly, he sent an invitation to the Sheltons down at Herrin to move their operation to West City, where men of their cunning were appreciated and where Marshall McCormick could no longer harass them. Adams was, after all, the nearest thing to a "wheel" that the little town had, he was not reluctant to add. With enough men and guns at their disposal, they could drive that "Russian Jew" Charlie Birger into the earth where he belonged. Sweet words, these, to Carl and Earl and Bernie Shelton, to Ray Walker, and to Monroe "Blackie" Armes.

Tradition has it that the Sheltons brought with them their famous steel tank and that they left it in Joe Adams's garage for repairs. Another account states that the tank was merely dumped in a field nearby, an indication that it, too, had contributed more to showmanship than to actual battle. Whatever the tank's contribution to the chaos of the moment, its very presence in West City made Birger furious. That it was reportedly sitting in Joe Adams's garage sent him into a murderous rage. He called up Joe and stated his case: Get me that tank or be killed. Joe refused to comply with this simple demand.

During the autumn of 1926, the overweight mayor and the gangster described by W. A. S. Douglas as bearing a strong resemblance to Tom Mix in his younger days enjoyed several telephone conversations that were notable for impolite dialogue. Art Newman, the unlikely and often untrustworthy chronicler of gangland goings-on, recalled those chats during an interview with a reporter from the *St. Louis Post-Dispatch:*

> *Adams:* "Why don't you come out of that cornfield and fight?"
> *Birger:* "You lousy fathead, why don't you leave that garage of yours and come over to my cornfield and do your fighting here?"

As leaves brightened to yellow and red and nights turned cool, the curious business of staying alive was much on the minds of Birger and his men. To guarantee their continued existence, they needed more machine guns. On the advice of "Honest John" Renfro, a former resident of Hardin County, a carload of the gangsters drove to Rosiclare on Saturday night, October 16, for the purpose of stealing the machine guns that were kept in the office of the

Rosiclare Spar Mining Company. At the outskirts of town, they asked directions of Joe Hurford who, along with his wife, Edith, was on his way to town to attend a movie. Because the men were well dressed, very polite, and driving a car much finer than his own Model T, Hurford assumed they were mine officials and volunteered to guide them to the mine.

Inside, the men tore the wires loose from the engine room and ordered the guard, Ed Smith, to lead the way to the guns stored in the main office. Smith hesitated, saying that the place was locked. With some prompting, he managed to locate the keys. Soon the guns were in the hands of the gangsters and traveling north.

The week of October 17 was one of relative calm despite this valuable addition to the gang's arsenal. But on October 25, Birger and his men felt compelled to visit Joe Adams and demand that he turn over to them the celebrated tank belonging to the Sheltons. That visit, later to be recalled in a courtroom, was closely followed by two murders.

Early in the morning of October 26, the upright body of William Burnett "High Pockets" McQuay was found on a dirt road about three miles east of Herrin. The frost-covered car in which he was sitting was bullet pocked, as was "High Pockets." Local residents reported hearing the unmistakable rattle of machine gunfire but decided not to investigate until the following day. A member of the Birger gang, McQuay was said to be on his way from his West Frankfort residence to visit his parents, Mr. and Mrs. Orville McQuay, in Herrin, when he was overtaken.

A few months later, Art Newman laid the blame on the Sheltons, recalling how they had pursued the young man and his girlfriend from the Hippodrome at Herrin and how "High" was informed by his girl's brother, himself a Shelton crony, that the gang was still on his trail. Leaving the girl at her home, McQuay once again took to the road, but three miles east of town his luck ran out. So said Newman.

The murder was never solved, nor does it appear that the authorities made any great effort to determine the killers' identities. Within the Birger gang, however, it was thought that Connie Ritter and Fred "Butch" Thomasson had done the shooting. A former member of that gang wrote:

I do not know for sure who killed "High Pockets" McQuay. It was rumored, however, that the killers were Fred "Butch" Thomasson and Connie Ritter. In hearing them at one time discussing the murder of Lyle "Shag" Worsham, they mentioned the demise of "High Pockets," inferring that it was they who had wiped him out.

That Birger gang members had indeed killed McQuay at Birger's behest is buttressed by an entry in Alpheus Gustin's diary dated October 1, 1927: "Mrs. Ray Shamsky—nephew—Mrs. Chas Birger—up Am after Ins. Policy to McQuay. Papers delivered to Ray Shamsky."

Later in the day, a young black named Alvin Woods—the same Alvin Woods who often entertained with his saxophone at Shady Rest—"discovered" a hand protruding from the water that flowed beneath a bridge east of Equality in Gallatin County. The body in the North Fork of the Saline River was thought to be that of Ward "Casey" Jones, a machine gun man for the Birger crowd.

Charlie Birger, Art Newman, and Connie Ritter (and possibly Freddie Wooten) drove to Equality later that day, ostensibly to determine if the Sheltons had killed their pal "Casey." To the youngsters looking on, the well-dressed gangsters emerging from their fine car presented quite a sight. Newman and Ritter were of special interest because of their machine guns.

Birger instructed the undertaker, A. K. Moore, to give their fallen comrade a splendid funeral, complete with flowers and frills, at his expense. He also invited Moore and Sam Bunker, a local businessman, to accompany the gang to Shawneetown, where they planned to swear out a warrant against those who had so brutally murdered poor "Casey." The county judge refused to act. (Later, Connie Ritter would be successful in getting Judge W. T. Smyth to issue warrants against Gus Adams and two other men, but the charges proved groundless.)

Returning to Equality empty-handed, Birger saw what he at first thought was a car with only one headlight parked off the highway just west of Junction. But it turned out to be a motorcycle.

"I told you that son of a bitch was following us," the gang leader said, adding as the others brought forth their machine guns, "We ought to go right back and kill the son of a bitch now."

In all the excitement, they forgot to tell Bunker and Moore who the motorcyclist was or why he was following them.

Ward "Casey" Jones was buried in Moore's own plot in a cemetery in Equality. The undertaker's son, Ted, wore the dead man's bullet-holed leather jacket to school for some time, to the envy and delight of his classmates.

# 18
# Death in Drag

THE PRESS MADE MUCH OF THESE CLOSELY SPACED KILLINGS and the shooting up and burning of Birger's county line roadhouses between Johnston City and West Frankfort on the early morning of October 28. Located on the highway just south of the Franklin-Williamson county line, this trio of houses connected by a hallway was approached in the pre-dawn hours by perhaps a dozen men with guns. They began firing into the bar room of the first building and into the dance hall of the third. The structure sandwiched between the two, its function unspecified, was likewise shelled. Several volleys later, the shooting faded away, and someone shouted that anyone still capable of doing so was to step forth with hands raised. Not surprisingly, no response was forthcoming, but as it turned out, the houses had been abandoned some days earlier. Then came the pouring of gasoline and the inevitable striking of matches. A small shack of a dwelling that housed the lighting plant was also set afire.

At the time, it was felt that the Sheltons must have been responsible. Not so, according to a fellow who witnessed the shooting. Despite the more than half a century between the 1920s and the late 1970s, he felt that to reveal the names of the raiders would serve no useful purpose and might even get someone hurt. But he did say that it was a vigilante action carried out by local residents

and that the Sheltons had no part in it. Was the Birger gang causing any trouble for the neighbors? To the contrary, he said, they
were always courteous, but their presence was a stain on the community and a drawing card for enemy gangsters.

The Birger gang, meanwhile, concentrated on the elimination
of their rivals. Top priority was given to Carl Shelton, who was
designated "Number One." Because of his rough and tumble ways,
brother Bernie was ranked "Number Two"; that left "Number
Three" to Earl, a "big, fat slob," in Art Newman's estimation.
This numerical rating was used by the gang during telephone conversations, to confuse any eavesdropping operator.

To erase "Number One," the four top men of the gang, Birger,
Newman, Wooten, and Ritter, talked one of Carl's former girl-
friends into registering at a hotel in East St. Louis. From there she
called Carl, who promised to look her up. When Carl somehow
learned that Birger and some of his men were stationed nearby, he
failed to appear.

A second opportunity came a short time later when Newman
chanced to see Carl and some of his pals at a drug store in East St.
Louis. Some of the fellows had rifles, however, a situation that
prompted Art to speed back to his hotel room and fetch his machine gun. Alas, when he returned, the men were gone. It was all
very discouraging.

Other attempts were made with the same results. But Art and
Charlie and Freddie and Connie were practical fellows at heart. If
we can't polish off "Number one," they reasoned, then try for
"Number Two." If he is not available at the moment, aim for
"Number Three."

Here they were in luck, for at that particular moment, Earl
Shelton happened to be recuperating in St. Mary's Hospital in East
St. Louis. Accordingly, the deadly duo of Newman and Wooten set
about reducing by one the number of their enemies.

Both being small in stature, Art and Freddie hit upon the clever
scheme of disguising themselves as women. Since he had to wait
in the car, the rouged and powdered Newman left off wearing
women's shoes but otherwise was dressed in a style befitting any
middle-aged matron lucky enough to be wearing a "small fur cap
retailing for $1,200." Freddie, who was designated to go inside,

outdid his glamorous partner. As Newman told the reporters from the *St. Louis Post-Dispatch:*

> Freddie, he was dressed a lot classier. He had a Hudson seal fur coat, a black turban, silk dress, and woman's shoes and stockings. He only wears a number 4 shoe. He had a good clean shave and he was painted up so you'd never recognize him.
>
> "And you remember, Art," interrupted Freddie, "I wore a fur neckpiece, or choker or whatever you call it, but I had to take it off, because I figured there might be some shooting to do and I knew if my rod got tangled in that thing I'd probably kill myself. We had a lot of fun getting dressed up that night."

Art pulled up in front of the hospital and out minced Freddie. Using his softest voice, the diminutive gangster asked the Sister at the desk where one might find a Mr. Earl Shelton. When she actually told him, Freddie nearly fell out of his makeup. "That big boob was booked there under his own name," he recalled incredulously. Clearly, "Big Earl" was not ranked third for nothing.

So much for the reconnaissance. Now for the dirty work. Since nothing is quite so lethal as a razor-sharp hunting knife drawn firmly across one's jugular vein, it was agreed that in this manner Earl was to make his exit. To speed him on his way, they had engaged the services of a "hired killer" who happened to be their old pal Rado Millich. The following night their plan was to go into effect.

But that same night, St. Louis detectives nabbed Art, Freddie, Bess Newman, and the "hired killer" himself. Millich was promptly returned to Menard for breaking parole, Freddie was fined $100 for carrying a concealed weapons, and the Newmans were held as suspects.

Finding no charge to pin on Newman, the St. Louis Police Department wired Williamson County officials. They were told that they had a warrant charging him with the killings of Harry Walker and Everett Smith. Realizing that it would not do to be sent back to Williamson County at this point—the Sheltons were likely to overpower his guards and do worse to him—the wily gambler intimated to post office inspectors that he had inside information as to who pulled the 1925 Collinsville mail robbery. (As luck would have it, Birger had already confided to reporters that the Sheltons had, indeed, committed the robbery.)

A few days later, Newman was escorted to Springfield, where he testified before a federal grand jury, then in special session, naming the Sheltons as the perpetrators of that particular crime. Indictments resulted. A free man, Newman then went to Chicago and from there slipped back into Williamson County, where the dragon known as financial woe was beginning to peer over his particular horizon.

With his joints closed, Birger, too, was in a pinch. His army of boys and older, hardened criminals had to be fed. He later said that his meat bill alone ran to between $130 and $140 a month. In normal times, these and other expenses could have been written off as overhead, but normal times had faded into the recent past.

Newman estimated that he personally lost $25,000 in cold cash. The greater amount that would have been his—had not the gambling all but dried up—was, if not astronomical, at least too painful to contemplate.

Still, the overriding concern was preventing rival gangsters from pumping daylight into one's vitals. That required luck and discipline. Luck, being the province of the angels, Birger concentrated on the discipline. Part of the "shock troops," composed of older, more tested men, patrolled the highways and back roads in search of the Sheltons and their cohorts. In the daytime, while the veterans slept, the younger men guarded Shady Rest.

As one of the organization's top four, Freddie Wooten was in an ideal position to report on the daily schedule of the "shock troops": "Matinee from two to five every afternoon—target practice. Evening performances—road patrols with roadhouses to be histed [sic] and searched for Shelton gangsters, and maybe fights to be found. Our beauty sleep usually began just around sunrise."

Apparently Leo Simmons forgot to read the newspapers prior to the night he drove from Carbondale to Golconda and decided to stop by the cabin for a glass or two of hospitality. Instead, he found a frightened bartender, as well as two rough-looking characters, both of whom shoved up against him so hard he could not move. Indicating he had a gun, one of the men motioned Simmons to get in the car and be gone. He did leave, but so did the other two men. They followed him all the way to Harrisburg and even a short distance down Route 34. Simmons said he never went back to Shady Rest again.

Only a kid at the time, Logan Cox had vivid memories of the gangsters in their fortress:

> I was a member of a quartet that was formed at our school at Crab Orchard, and we had been invited to sing at a pie supper at Carrier Mills. Driving east past Shady Rest [we saw] some men with guns in front of Shady Rest close to the building. As we passed by—both ways—they dropped to their knees and followed our car with their guns pointed.

Somewhat of a military man throughout his career as a bootlegger and gangster, Birger tried to enforce his edicts on his men, a motley crew by most accounts, as he earlier had on the roadhouse operators. In both cases, he was unsuccessful, despite Wooten's schedule as given previously, largely because he was dealing with people who were refugees from society, individualists with a bent toward criminality. An example of one of the gang's unmilitary behavior was experienced by Willard St. John, a frequent customer at the barbecue stand:

> My brother and I helped build the Illinois Central Railroad east of Shady Rest. Hot and weary in our work clothes and clodhoppers, we would stop at the barbecue stand after work to wet our whistles with a cold glass or two of beer.
>
> That particular afternoon Art Newman was behind the counter. I don't know what was the matter with Art, but his eyes seemed glassy like he was on dope, or drunk or something. Anyway, there I was drinking my beer when Newman spoke up. "You can dance, can't you?" he said.
>
> "Nah," I replied, "I can't dance."
>
> "Yeah, I think you can," he said. That son of a gun pulled out a sawed-off shotgun from under the counter and laid it right in my face. Like I say, I don't know what was wrong with Art, but I saw he meant business and I went to dancing. Every time I'd let up a little, he'd just raise that gun. I figure I was at it five minutes or more.

Well, as luck would have it, Charlie Birger came in about that time. Boy, I'm telling you what, he ate Art Newman up.

"Oh, I was just having some fun out of him," Art said.

"That's a hell of a poor way of having fun," Birger replied.

After that Charlie went to the cash register and emptied his pockets of watches and everything. I don't know where he got them or whether someone had been on a raid or what. The next thing I heard was "Come here a minute, St. John." There was an old icebox in the back and in it was a long watermelon. When Charlie cut it, that big heart rolled out. He sliced me a piece of that heart. But all the time he was cussing Art Newman. I think he even ran him off down there at the cabin where they had the women and everything. Charlie got so mad I was afraid he was going to shoot him.

Sometime later, St. John stopped again at the barbecue stand, only to find a boy crying. Since they were alone, he asked the lad, who was only about sixteen or seventeen, what the problem was. After saying that he was in "one heck of a shape," the young fellow told a chilling tale.

Out of Missouri, he had gone as a harvest hand shucking corn for farmers. Harvest done and on his way home he managed to stop by Birger's place, and finding the atmosphere congenial, he stayed. One day, though, he made the mistake of telling Birger he was finally ready to leave.

After leading him to a wooded area, Charlie sat the boy down and began to talk to him. His voice not so different from a father's when reasoning with a son, Birger said he was going to do something he very much hated. When the youngster asked what that might be, the middle-aged gangster looked him full in the face and said quietly, "Shoot your head off." He quickly explained that the lad knew too much, had seen too much ever to leave alive. If he tried to escape, Birger added, he would be followed and found. Though the boy cried and begged Birger to let him go, promising never to say a word about what he had seen, the answer remained the same.

"Whether he slipped off or Birger finally killed him, I don't know," St. John added. "But that boy disappeared, and I never did know where he went to." It's just a story told in autumn by a stranger long ago.

Another tale bearing the whiff of the surreal concerns the

farmer who heard a knock on his door around midnight. The stranger at the door said his automobile was stuck in the mud near a certain graveyard and asked if the farmer would pull him out? The man hitched up his team.

After some effort the deed was accomplished, following which Charlie Birger paid the man $100. He also warned him never to tell a soul. The next day the sleepy farmer went to the cemetery and found what seemed to be fresh digging in an old grave site. The visit at midnight and the discovery afterwards he kept to himself until shortly before his own death many years later, or so the story goes.

# 19
# Aerial Bombing

IF THE IMPRESSION IS GIVEN THAT THE TWILIGHT OF INDIAN SUM-
mer had a mellowing effect on hostilities, that Newman had
nothing better to do than force a young man to dance on the
sawdust floor with his heavy work shoes, that somehow the wind-
ing down of 1926 had brought out the best in the worst—a shaft
of sunlight in the dark, so to speak—an incident that occurred the
night of November 5 quickly put that rumor to rest. That night
two or three cars drove into the tough little coal-mining town of
Colp, located a few miles west of Herrin and even fewer miles
north of Carterville. Whether followers of Birger or Shelton gangsters—as most accounts suggest—the men within those vehicles
had no use for the youthful gambler Johnny Milroy. One version
has it that Milroy was forced to grovel in the street before a hoodlum behind a tripod-mounted machine gun opened fire.

Outraged that such a thing should happen in his town, Mayor
Jeff Stone soon arrived with his police chief, a man named Keith.
The mayor was shot as he stepped from the car. Sure to suffer a
like fate, Keith bolted. Fire flashed as he ran, but only once was he
hit, that once in the hand. He ran, it is said, until he reached Carterville, where a Dr. Foster treated the wound. No, said the police
chief the next day, he did not recognize his assailants. Similar de-
nials came from almost everyone who had witnessed the shootings. Said one man to a reporter for the United Press: "We didn't

140

see anything at all. If we were to admit that we did, we'd never see anything again."

When the coroner's jury was finally called into session (Boswell had ordered the first session postponed so that additional witnesses might be located), the tension prevailed. Not enough evidence was presented to warrant indictments, however, and the old refrain of "death at the hands of parties unknown" droned forth again.

Why Milroy was killed is not clear, but according to newspaper speculation, each side had its reasons for killing Stone: Birger, because the mayor had not supported the Republican ticket in the recent (November 2) election in Williamson County as he had requested, and Shelton, because earlier that year Stone had killed then Chief of Police John Freeman, a friend of the Shelton crowd. As usual, the coroner's jury had exonerated the recently elected mayor.

Still other accusations were to follow, including those of Rado Millich, who would credit the killings to Harry Thomasson and two other of Birger's hangers-on. (Many years later, this writer had occasion to talk to one of the men Millich had accused of the crime. The old man shook his head, claiming he had never even heard of Jeff Stone, although he had heard of "Apie" Milroy.)

Hours before the killings, the *Carterville Herald*, a weekly journal appearing each Friday, reported what must have seemed to the editor a newsworthy item:

Monday night [November 1], two of the Sheltons were in Carterville with some 8 or 10 men. They dropped in at the Carterville Cafe for a short time. They were in two large cars, according to one who saw and noticed them. Just what their mission was is not known.

They may have had a number of things in mind. The story is told that on the night of the killings, a boy in his late teens who was something of a wizard on the slot machines, was hiding in the beer cooler at Pete Salmo's, a bootleg joint in Colp. His winnings from the Shelton-owned machines had been considerable, and to make matters worse, the Birger gang had escorted him from joint to joint, taking for their trouble a hefty cut in the earnings. The story goes that when word reached the Sheltons that the boy wonder was in town, they drove to the mining camp. Failing to find the lad, they concentrated their fire upon Milroy and Stone instead.

I asked the one-time slot machine prodigy to verify the account of his hiding out that bloody night. He didn't deny it but was reluctant to add details.

Straying from the killings of Milroy and Stone, it might be mentioned that the account of the boy wonder has a near match in another story, this one told by a former pool hustler who once worked for Birger at the latter's pool hall in Harco. In this instance, as in the other, it is clear that the gang leader had a keen appreciation of talent, especially when it promised a solid financial return.

For the privilege of playing "all night for nothing," the Harco boy had only to rack the balls for the other players. When the opportunity presented itself, his other job was to win prearranged matches with the other pool hustlers but always with the cooperation of his boss. Their system was simple: When Charlie walked to the door, the budding hustler would let his opponent win, but when his silent partner kept away from the door, the game was for keeps.

Men would come from Chicago, he says (although St. Louis seems more likely) to play and compete against him. One night his share of the winnings was $1,500 or one tenth of the total. Needless to say, the remaining $13,500 went to Birger.

But to get back to the events that happened that fall of 1926, around 2:00 A.M. on November 10, a homemade bomb was tossed from an automobile speeding past the barbecue stand at Shady Rest. Instead of destroying the stand, as the bomber intended, the explosion merely shattered the windows of a nearby farmhouse.

At almost exactly the same hour, two days later, Joe Adams's home in West City was machine-gunned. Again, no one was injured.

In retaliation, Joe's friends, the Sheltons, decided to carry the battle one rung higher. Hours after West City was rudely awakened, a single-engine airplane circled Shady Rest. In the cabin at the time were Connie Ritter and Steve George. Presumably,

George wanted to use the big bird for target practice, but Ritter managed to restrain him, as he thought it might be a government plane. The airplane circled higher, possibly to be out of range of any gunfire from below. From an altitude of about four hundred feet, three bundles were dropped. One of these exploded near the hardroad, by one account killing a bulldog and an eagle. The other two bombs failed to explode. Circling back to survey the damage, the bombardiers were fired upon by Ritter himself. The half dozen or so shots he sent on their way were of little consequence, for the plane disappeared to the east, seemingly untouched.

That his foes would resort to such unorthodox measures had never occurred to Birger. Before, he had been concerned that rival gunmen might hide behind the trees, so down went the trees, leaving his masterpiece of revelry a target from the air. This once his persistent enemies had been clever, but the small pair of dice he kept in his pocket for luck was still potent, since the bombs were mostly duds.

Each of the three bombs consisted of a bottle of nitroglycerine surrounded by sticks of dynamite. For some time, Birger had known that the Sheltons had the powerful explosives, or so he told W. A. S. Douglas, a writer from the east. If only he had realized "that the glycerin was on the fritz," he and the boys could have fought it out with the rival gang. His pencil racing over the pad, Douglas volunteered that perhaps it wasn't too late, after all. Oh, but it was, came the reply, because by now the skulking cowards were back in East St. Louis. But Joe Adams was still in West City.

One week after the airplane attack, the home of West City's mayor was damaged by a bomb blast. No one was injured.

The following day, the explosion that rocked West City brought, among numerous sightseers, a young woman who worked for the *Benton Evening News* and her fellow worker and fiancé, William Bey. On a whim that cold day, the couple had walked to the Adams home from the Benton Square. Recalled Rhoda Bey: "When we walked up on the front porch, the front door was lying down in the living room. Mrs. Adams said, 'Well, Rhoda, shut the door after you. You're letting all the heat out.' And she was laughing like it had been a joke."

Joe, on the other hand, failed to see the humor of the situation.

He was pacing the front porch with a machine gun on his arm. When the young lady suggested that he vacate the country for his own protection, Adams replied, "All I want is a shot at one of the SOBs."

He certainly had plenty to shoot with, as Rhoda soon discovered for herself. "I didn't know that anybody kept that many guns outside an armory. One part of the dining room was stacked full of guns," she recalled.

Still, for all his sophisticated weaponry, Joe Adams was incredibly naive. While Adams paced with weapon in hand, praying for a shot at handsome Charlie, his enemy was plotting not only Adams's demise but also that of another rival closer to home, one Virgil Hunsaker, a bootlegger in west Harrisburg.

The revelers at Flo Stone's place drank moonshine and cavorted. Suddenly "Madame" Flo heard the familiar racket of machine gunfire, as did her customers, a "rough crowd" according to one fellow who was there. Located on Route 13 just west of Harrisburg, this brothel and roadhouse that Flo managed for Birger was much too easy a target for passing gunmen. One young man who happened to be seated with some of the young people on a couch in the front room observed that the bullets were thudding into the lower part of the couch, just missing everyone's legs. Running toward the back door, the fleeing customer paused in midflight just long enough to snatch one of the two jars of moonshine setting on the kitchen table.

Crouched by a window upstairs, Flo's son Clyde saw it all. As soon as the gunmen made a pass and disappeared toward Harrisburg, Clyde ran downstairs. Before the clock's second hand could turn full circle, he was driving hard toward Shady Rest to deliver the bad news to Birger and his men. He figured the gunmen who shot up his mother's place would take a U-turn at the Dorris Heights detour and there swing back west for another round of hot lead and mayhem. To tarry on the highway would ensure him a blizzard of bullets.

Meanwhile, in Harrisburg, George Cummins and two of his drinking pals had bought a couple of half pints at a "pig stand," a small shack of a building where candy bars, soft drinks, and tobacco served to divert attention from the whisky sold there. The young men then went to a restaurant and bought a coke before wandering into an alley for some serious drinking. Suddenly head-lights shined upon them. More than fifty years later Cummins re-called that night:

> There were two cars, a Lincoln sedan and a Lincoln Coupe. . . . I passed the bottle around and I was taking a swig and I felt some-thing or another hit me in the side. I recognized the guy that had the gun—looked like a sawed-off shotgun. It was Bert Owens, from Dorrisville, who was in Birger's gang. I didn't call his name and he didn't call mine. I didn't want him to recognize me. Couldn't tell nothing about that bunch. So they started asking us if we knew who shot up Florence Stone's place at the west of town. We told them we didn't know anything about it.

Once Cummins persuaded the men he and his friends had only been drinking in the alley, they were questioned about any cars they might have seen driving past. "After they asked us three or four questions, they went back over to Birger's place," Cummins added.

A short time later, Cummins and friends again encountered these same gangsters, though in another part of town. Apparently the search was still on for the thugs who had shot up Flo's place; at least Cummins felt the three of them were being watched too closely, and to escape further scrutiny, they went into a pool hall, where they slipped out a side door into the night.

When the amateur detectives from Shady Rest concluded they had found the guilty party at last, Birger's response was resound-ing. The dynamite blast that wrecked the home of bootlegger Virgil Hunsaker at about 4:00 A.M. on November 25 jarred Har-risburg's west end. Some residents were even knocked to the floor. That was only round one.

Several hours later, at 6:45 P.M., Hunsaker, Louis Robinson, and Millard Vinson were driving west of Harrisburg on their way back to town via a detour, when Hunsaker noticed a car following them. He thought little about it until the car, a Chrysler, drew near and the passengers began firing. Passing, they poured another volley into Hunsaker's hapless Oakland coupe. Hunsaker and the others scurried for cover for their lives. The bootlegger, as it turned out, took a bullet through his neck, another through his right side, and still another in his arm. Robinson was shot in both feet. Luckiest of the three was Vinson, who was taken to jail.

With only a slight foot wound to remind him of the recent excitement, the man, though drunk, had some advice for outgoing Sheriff Small. "John," he said, "if you don't stop these fellows who are carrying guns around your county, somebody is going to get hurt."

Despite his condition, the fellow's observation was sound, although it would have carried more weight if a loaded Thompson submachine gun, a .30-.30 rifle, and a .38 Colt Special had not been recovered from what was left of the Oakland coupe.

During the shooting, Charlie Birger was busy making himself visible in front of the Orpheum Theatre while the crowd within watched Anita Stewart and Lionel Belmont in *Never the Twain Shall Meet*. When somebody—perhaps theatre manager Steve Farrar—told Charlie about the shooting, the gangster decided to go home. After all, his alibi was good—far better, in fact, than the marksmanship of some of his men.

Alibis were always a big thing with Charlie. One man recalled how Birger and/or members of his gang would sometimes park on the west side of Harrisburg Square, before slowly and deliberately strolling around the Square. When such a performance occurred, others on the street assumed a holdup or a murder was happening elsewhere.

Whether Virgil Hunsaker acted on his own or at the behest of Carl Shelton was a question the people in Harrisburg asked in the days following the explosion and shootings—or until other events, no less dramatic, soon put such asking to rest. His misfortunes having earned him a small place in the *New York Times*, Hunsaker finally recovered, only to find that he was once again an obscure bootlegger. Not so lucky was his sworn enemy Charlie Birger.

November 1926, the month in which the warring gangs gave the United States its first aerial bombing, ended with a spectacular robbery of the Bond County State Bank at Pocahontas, Illinois. While two men waited outside in a "closed automobile," three companions hurried into the bank, lined up the patrons, and proceeded to help themselves to the money in the cages. The day before, employees of the Pocahontas Mining Company had been paid in vouchers. The money with which these vouchers were to be redeemed had been shipped to the bank, and more than half of the miners had already received their pay. Even so, the robbers managed to gather up $5,000 for their trouble.

As the holdup men fled, the townsmen raised their rifles and fired repeatedly. But as far as they could see, they only shot out a window in the escape car.

That night, Dr. J. C. Lightner of Harrisburg heard a knock at his front door. Before him stood his friend Charlie Birger and some of his men, one of whom had been shot in the leg. For attending to the wound, Dr. Lightner was given a new $100 bill, a small part of the Bond County take.

It was his understanding that part of the proceeds also went to the City National Bank of Harrisburg, where Birger did most of his banking. Two of the officials of the bank, he added, were aware of the money's origins. Recently, when reference was made to the incident, one of the ex-gang members denied Lightner's allegation, claiming that wine, women, and song had consumed every penny.

Again and again, the bank robbery at Pocahontas would crop up in confessions, in court transcripts, and in various allegations. And like the Masonic Temple riots, the repercussions would be far reaching.

# 20
# The Death of Joe Adams

JOE ADAMS HAD BEEN UP MOST OF THE NIGHT GUARDING HIS home and badly needed sleep that Sunday afternoon of December 12. But he was awakened by his wife, Beulah, who said that two young men were at the door with a message from Carl Shelton. When Joe Adams got to the door, he did not recognize either of the two fellows, one of whom wore a sheepskin coat. He was handed a note, and as he read it, the man in the sheepskin coat let the barrel of his revolver slide down his sleeve until the handle of the gun was in his hand. He fired. At the same time, his companion also began firing.

"My God, they've shot me," cried Adams as he fell. His assailants ran to the Chrysler parked a short distance west of the house, jumped in, and sped toward the west, according to eyewitnesses. A half hour later, Joe Adams was dead.

Arlie O. Boswell and Maurice Potter were having their supper at the B. B. Tea Room in Marion when Charlie Birger arrived. When the gangster asked Boswell who had been killed at West City, the state's attorney replied that he wasn't aware of any killing but that he would phone Franklin County Sheriff James Pritchard and find out. Together the two men went upstairs to Boswell's office to make the call. From the other end of the line, Jim Pritchard said that Joe Adams had been shot to death.

Pritchard and Franklin County State's Attorney Roy Martin thought they knew who had Adams killed, as did Gus Adams and Joe's widow, Beulah. At the coroner's inquest the following night, Mrs. Adams appeared to have no doubt about the matter. Many times Birger had called to threaten her husband, she said. Once, hearing the all too familiar voice on the telephone, she had asked, "Won't we do?" referring to herself and the two children. Taken aback, the caller protested that women and children had nothing to fear from the guns of the Birger gang. Ever thoughtful of the welfare of others, Charlie even suggested that she take out some insurance on her husband's life.

Alonzo Norris and his family lived across the street from Birger. The day after Adams was murdered Mrs. Norris concluded some "meanness" had occurred the night before because the cars parked at Birger's house seemed unusually muddy and guns were stacked on the lawn. Later that day she learned of the Adams killing.

A reporter from the *International News Service* placed a call to Birger's home with the inevitable question, "Who killed Joe Adams?" With just a touch of indignation, the gangster replied, "I don't know who killed Adams, but I'm certainly glad Adams was killed. Everyone comes to me to ask who did this and that. What am I, a detective for southern Illinois? What the hell does anybody care who killed Adams?"

The state's attorney and sheriff of Franklin County very much cared, but they had no evidence. In the minutes before his death, Adams had told his wife that he could not recognize his assailants. Their daughter, Arian, who had chased the men toward their automobile, indicated to reporters that Birger himself might have been one of the men.

More credence was placed in a statement by Gus Adams, and upon his testimony that he might know who wrote the note that Joe Adams was reading when he was shot, the inquest was postponed until the following night. At that time, it became clear that Gus's one-man investigation had ended where it began, in speculation. Still, the note remained close at hand, intriguing as ever.

Having little else to go on, Roy Martin studied the scrap of paper. There was little in the wording to offer much hope:

East St. Louis, Ill.

Jan

Friend Joe: -

If you can use these boys please do it.

They are broke and need work. I know their father.

C. S.

Only the day before the Adams murder, Carl Shelton was freed on $60,000 bond at Peoria, where he had been held as a suspect in the robbery of a mail messenger in Collinsville in 1924. Four days later, he was arrested in St. Louis. After several hours of intense questioning by the St. Louis police and particularly by police chief Gerk, the southern Illinois gang leader reportedly cried into his handkerchief. (Art Newman was later to capitalize on the incident by referring to Carl as a crybaby.)

Actually, he had a lot to cry about. His interrogation by the police, in fact, had resulted from his placing himself in their custody after receiving a call from the East St. Louis police saying that Birger and one of his men were driving up to St. Louis to kill him. Seeking refuge, the affable bootlegger had found only harassment and salt for fresh wounds. He was fingerprinted, then ordered out of town.

The following day brought Shelton even more troubles. He was arrested by the government and charged with having driven a stolen car into Madison County. His bond was set at $5,000. As a final insult, the local authorities again arrested him for questioning about the counterfeit $20 bills circulating in East St. Louis. All this bother and embarrassment came when he could have avoided it all by going to Franklin County, where his name still commanded respect. Certainly, he should have attended Joe Adams's wake. Humiliating as it was, his time in St. Louis was not completely misspent, however. According to Art Newman's account, published a short time later, Birger had dispatched two of his lesser-known gang members to the mayor's wake in the unlikely event that Carl did appear.

Peace was denied the sinner, but the righteous fared no better. While Carl Shelton was recovering from his first round of questioning under police chief Gerk's fiery eye, a minister of the gospel was in the process of having his car stolen in Marion. Wednesday night prayer meeting at the Warder Street Baptist Church found Reverend J. W. McKinney interspersing his rendition of the gospel with a heated denunciation of the local authorities, and in particular, Arlie O. Boswell. In all likelihood, the congregation liked their minister's style, for they had just bought him a brand new four-door red Chevrolet coupe. That night during the services, a thief turned the keys in the car in a promising direction and drove away in the vehicle.

The next morning, as was his custom, Boswell stopped by his favorite barbershop for a shave. He was not particularly surprised to hear from one of the patrons that his "funeral had been preached" the night before by Reverend McKinney. Fresh from his barber's daily services, the state's attorney stopped next at the sheriff's office, as he usually did each morning, to learn "who had been killed that night and all about it . . . [so] . . . I knew what I had to do." On this particular morning, a man with his back to the door was, in Boswell's words, "raising hell." "Good morning, Reverend McKinney. You seem to be excited about something," said Boswell. And the following conversation ensued:

*McKinney:* "Excited! Why shouldn't I be? A poor man like me having my new automobile stolen and the officers doing nothing about it!"
*Boswell:* "Brand new car, huh? Will you cooperate with me on this?"
*McKinney:* "I'll do anything to get my car back."
*Boswell:* "Anything?" [There was a pause.] "O.K., you be here at nine o'clock."

At nine or shortly thereafter, the two men were motoring east. "Where are we going?" the minister asked as they drove through Crab Orchard.

"Oh, we might end up in Harrisburg or some other seaport," came the reply. Actually, their destination was near at hand.

"Oh, my God! Oh, my God!" exclaimed McKinney as they pulled in at the barbecue stand. "This is Birger's—"

"Yeah."

"Well," sputtered McKinney, "I can't be seen here!"

"Well, if you can't, how do you think I can?" was the attorney's reply.

He failed to mention, of course, that he, Judge Hartwell, and Charlie Birger had met a short time earlier with Illinois Supreme Court Justice W. W. Duncan in Duncan's office in Marion. As gruff as he was shrewd, Duncan had informed Birger that he wanted an end to the murders and car thefts and other crimes that were plaguing Williamson County. In answer to his charges, Birger very coolly said that while he knew nothing of the crimes referred to, he would do everything in his power to help solve them. All they had to do was ask. Although no one in the room believed a word he said, the fact that he was so pleasant and reasonable was encouraging. Moreover, Boswell felt that if this supersalesman of a gangster could help solve this particular crime without implicating himself, he would do so, if only for the favorable publicity. The state's attorney also believed they would find the stolen coupe at Shady Rest.

As they got out of the car, a man stepped from the barbecue stand. Boswell asked him if Birger was around.

"Smart aleck," replied Ray Hyland, better known as "Izzy the Jew." "You know better than to come out here and ask about Mr. Birger. Now get going."

By way of answer, Boswell sent a well-directed right to "Izzy's" jaw and sent the East St. Louis gangster sprawling. Dazed though he was, Hyland was still alert enough to reach for his pistol, but when he did so, Boswell stomped hard on his gun arm, breaking it, he later was told. Still game, Hyland started to reach for his other gun with his left hand, only to hear the man standing over him promise to rearrange his countenance if he did so. Hyland acquiesced, and both of his guns were placed in Reverend McKinney's hands for safekeeping.

When Hyland got up, Boswell said, "I'm sorry I didn't introduce myself. I'm Arlie O. Boswell, the state's attorney. You tell Birger for me that I want that car by 3:00 this afternoon. It must not be stripped, nor do I want to be informed that it was burned up. I want it in toto."

In their quick tour of the premises, the visitors saw but did not enter the pit where the cocks and dogs fought. "I wasn't that big a damned fool," said Boswell.

As they drove back to Marion, Reverend McKinney seemed lost in thought. "You scared me to death," he said at last, adding, "That man could have killed you."

"Oh, no," Boswell beamed, "You don't know me like some people. I've always said, give me the first lick and I'm not afraid of any son of a bitch that ever lived."

That afternoon at 2:30 P.M., a call came from Sheriff Holcomb up at Mt. Vernon. A car had been located at Ina, Illinois, the sheriff said, a red Chevrolet that had been registered in the name of a Reverend J. W. McKinney of Marion. Grateful for the good news, Boswell telephoned Birger in Harrisburg to thank him for his cooperation. Birger wasn't having any of it. "What car?" he said.

Sure enough, the next morning an anonymous call came through. One of the hangers-on out at Shady Rest was pegged as the fellow who had turned the key that triggered the whole mess. He was picked up and brought in. In talking with the suspect, Boswell discerned that behind the young man's stutter was the kind of brilliance rarely found among petty thieves and gunmen. Said Boswell:

I would go in that jail and talk to this guy and would I get anything? No, just the impression that he came from a very wonderful family. I used every device that I had ever read about or dreamed about or anything else to find out who in the hell he really was. Nothing!

Williamson County had humored car thieves long enough. For this culprit, in all likelihood, would be the "salting away" behind the clanging cell door—and for local owners of automobiles, sounder sleep at night. But, being a seasoned poker player, the state's attorney decided to bluff a little.

"Incidentally, have you heard from your mother or sister lately?" he yawned.

"Wha..wh..aa..tt.., you kn..kn..kn..know who I am?"

"I know who you are. Why would you want to do that to your mother and sister?" (Aside, to me fifty years later, Boswell declared, "Hell, I didn't know if he had a mother or a sister!") "Your mother is coming out. Do you want your sister to come too?"

That did it. A son of one of California's leading architects, the young man had left Stanford University because his speech defect had made him a laughing stock on campus, or so he thought. This impediment, he felt, was also embarrassing his sister who had only recently been elected university queen. Convinced by newspaper accounts that the Birger gang of southern Illinois was the ideal refuge for such social misfits as thieves, murderers, and stutterers, the young man had journeyed east to notorious Shady Rest. There he had set about proving himself by stealing a car. To his great dismay, however, he soon discovered that the other social misfits were as quick to jeer at his defect as were his former classmates— perhaps quicker. They certainly did so with less wit.

"Of course, he wasn't a gangster any more than me or you. I dismissed the case," said Boswell, plainly satisfied with his decision. For years, he received a Christmas card from the former car thief, now an architect on the West Coast.

Someone had given Sheriff Coleman a tip that several gunmen had been seen in a "house" and bootlegging joint in Herrin that was operated by Jackie Williams, who was also known as Allie Pedro. The morning of December 27 saw the sheriff and his deputies setting out to confirm this rumor, and in the process, they managed to capture "four gunmen, four pistols, and two stolen cars." That day, the *Marion Daily Republican* identified the four being held in the local jail, as "Ray Hyland of Chicago, James Madison of Missouri, and George Brown and Clarence Williams of Kentucky." Ray Rone was picked up later.

Brief though the account was, it contained many inaccuracies: Ray Hyland was from East St. Louis; and Oren Coleman had merely mistaken "Alton B. Parker"—Danny Brown—for his brother, George. "Parker" and Williams hailed from the coal-mining region of Williamson and Franklin counties, rather than the Bluegrass state. Lack of evidence against Williams caused the charges against him to be dropped. For weeks, however, "Jimmy Madison" remained in the Marion jail, his true identity unknown.

That afternoon a coroner's inquest was in session at Benton for the fourth time in connection with the Joe Adams murder. This time the jury found that Adams had died as a result of "gunshot wounds inflicted at the hands of persons to the jurors unknown, and we recommend that Charles Birger be held as an accessory before the fact of such killing." A warrant was issued and Sheriff Pritchard set about serving it.

The scene thereupon shifted to Marion. With Coleman's morning raid fresh on his mind, Arlie O. Boswell did a bit of boasting just before leaving that night to attend the Illinois Association of States Attorney's annual convention in Chicago. "I can safely say," he declared, "that there has been more actual work done in the way of conducting liquor raids and apprehending criminals during the last two weeks by the sheriff's office than was done previously in the last two years."

Still in the future was the most ambitious raid of all, a joint effort by Sheriffs Coleman and Pritchard, and it would occur the following night while Boswell was hearing himself praised in Chicago by the Director of the Illinois Crime Survey, Arthur J. Lashley. In retrospect, Boswell felt he was not told of the raid because the two officers did not trust him. They believed his ties with the Birger gang were far too strong.

Warrant in hand, Jim Pritchard, along with some deputies, drove to Marion on the afternoon of December 29. At the office of Supreme Court Justice W. W. Duncan, he met with Oren Coleman. A plan was devised for the arrest of Charlie Birger.

As daylight turned to dark, one carload of Williamson County deputies, among them Special Deputy Homer Butler, then the city editor of the *Marion Daily Republican*, drove to a snow embankment just east of the barbecue stand. The rest of the six-car caravan drove to Harrisburg with the warrant. If all went according to plan, Birger would be arrested at his home (presumably by Saline County Sheriff "Lige" Turner, who had previously been notified of the approaching delegation.) Turner and his deputies would help escort the prisoner to the Saline-Williamson county line, there turning him over to Coleman and Pritchard. The final few miles would end, according to this scenario, with Jim Pritchard turning the key on the door of Birger's cell at the Benton jail.

As it turned out, the four men parked near Shady Rest waiting for the arresting officers and their prisoner to appear had no word from the others, and they became tired of waiting in the cold. The regular deputies wore bulletproof vests, but Butler, the newspaperman, had only a rifle and a cartridge belt.

Finally, one of the deputies walked to a farmhouse to place a call to Sheriff Turner. Much to his dismay, he learned that the plan had been a total failure and, worse, that Coleman, who had accompanied Pritchard to Harrisburg, was probably back in Marion by that time. Although a sterling officer in many ways, Coleman was about as personable as a wounded rattlesnake, when he put his mind to it, so said his enemies—and probably some of his own men under their frozen breath. Trudging back to the car and its shivering occupants, the deputy made no effort to hide his disgust. After all, they had been there two hours.

Stationed as they were between the very real cold and a possible confrontation with gangsters, the four men had every right to condemn their sheriff's lack of common courtesy. Blame for the failure of the plan itself was, in days following, largely credited to Lige Turner, who was friendly with if not a friend of Birger. Commenting later to a reporter, the gang leader said he had learned of the warrant early Tuesday—or several hours before the expedition began. Having been forewarned of unwelcome visitors, it had been an easy matter for him to be "rabbit hunting" that night.

In the days to come, it became clear to anyone who might read a newspaper or occupy space on a street corner that Birger's arrest was not imminent, nor did Turner improve matters by announcing, "I ain't putting out nothing." Zeroing in on what it considered an astonishing utterance, the *Marion Daily Republican* included the sheriff's offhand remark in a list of "Famous War Cries." The list included such time-tested gems as "On to Richmond" and "Turn the Rascals out." Less inclined to sarcasm, Jim Pritchard merely wished aloud that the proper authorities would act.

Pritchard's anger, shared by Coleman and others, was not dampened by Birger's insistence that he was too busy just now to submit to arrest. After all, we must remember that the new year was close at hand, and the word was out that Birger had a $500 wager with a friend that Carl Shelton would not see 1927. Known for his generous nature, Birger is said to have promised the money to anyone who could help him win the bet.

# 21
# "Jar like an Explosion"

ON THE NIGHT OF JANUARY 8, 1927, STATE HIGHWAY PATROL-man Lory Price drove to Shady Rest after watching a movie in Marion. In the few minutes he was there, Price talked with Steve George, who insisted on introducing him to his wife. She was knitting in the east room. Near the fireplace in that same room was a man in his mid-twenties who appeared to be drinking. Perhaps because the caretaker made no move to introduce him, the patrolman had the impression that the man was no friend of Steve's. One account had it that the gold-toothed Bulgarian told Price the fellow might be shot if he didn't leave soon.

In the west room, lying on an army cot, was a younger man whom Steve called Clarence. Although he was supposed to help guard the place, the boy, Steve concluded, was "playing hell doing it."

"I left and came toward Marion," Price said later, "stopping at Paul Corder's barbecue stand. I was there when I heard a jar like an explosion. I left pretty soon and went home. It was 11:20 when I got home."

The "jar like an explosion" that he dismissed so easily at the time had destroyed the cabin in which he had chatted with George a few minutes earlier. Around the same time, another explosion destroyed the power plant. A couple who lived nearby saw the flash from the fire and herded their children into the basement. A neighbor of theirs, J. R. Richey, told reporter Elva Jones that around eleven o'clock he had heard six or seven shots and that about ten minutes later there was a blast, accompanied by a flash. Running to look out, he saw another flash that seemed to come from the window of the cabin's east room.

A party of foxhunters in the woods nearby also heard the shots and explosions. Dousing their own small bonfire, these men managed to hide in the woods until almost dawn. The *Marion Daily Republican* gave a sardonic, almost humorous, account of the incident, but for one of the men, Charles Christian, those cold morning hours offered no lighthearted recollections. A former friend of Birger, he was shaken but continued to hunt at night.

All the witnesses who testified at the coroner's inquest, held at the Ozment Funeral Home in Marion on January 12, recalled seeing a REO truck parked west of the cabin the morning after the incident. Nearby was a pool of blood. One of them, Lory Price, thought the body found in the west room might have been dragged from the pool of blood and "thrown through the front door."

Four bodies were found. As with the body found south of Marion in the abandoned farmhouse a few months earlier, identification was difficult, although it was assumed almost from the first that Steve George and his wife were among the victims. In Steve's case, a belt buckle with the initials "S. G." was uncovered. His gold teeth also helped in his identification.

Because he had heard Steve call one of the occupants Clarence that night and because this particular fellow sounded like Ray Rone, Price assumed that Clarence Rone was among the victims, and said as much to Ray, who was in the Marion jail at the time. Because a storm had knocked down the power lines, Ray could not immediately call Herrin to determine whether his brother was dead or alive.

It was also believed at first that Jimmy Sims from Harrisburg was one of the four, but Sims turned up a short time later and said that he had been at the cabin shortly before the explosion. Accompanying him out there was Bert Owens, also of Harrisburg, who had remained. Because Owens did not reappear in days to come, his aged father, Elijah Owens, testifying at the final inquest held on January 26, expressed his belief that Bert was dead. The remaining body was finally identified as that of eighteen-year-old Santos Elmo Thomasson of West Frankfort. Any possibility that the body might have been that of Clarence Rone was erased when Rone was arrested in a Herrin poolroom on January 29.

When he read in the newspaper that one of the bodies was that of Elmo Thomasson, Leo Simmons remembered that day in Golconda when Elmo was talking to himself as he walked. He was holding a shotgun by the barrel, and with each step he hit the stock against the sidewalk. More astonishing yet, the troubled youngster kept muttering to himself that he was going to kill somebody. Simmons did not catch the name.

The murder victim was one of six orphaned brothers, the father having died in 1915, the mother in 1919. Overdose of laudanum was given as the cause of the father's death, although it was rumored that Yuell Thomasson had been shot in the forehead. One very old woman remembered seeing his body laid out in the coffin. She believed part of his forelock covered the bullet hole.

The ashes of Elmo Thomasson were placed in a baby's casket and shipped by rail to Reevesville, in Johnson County, where his grandmother lived. It was bitterly cold the day his tiny casket was lowered into the earth of the hilltop cemetery overlooking the hamlet. Near Elmo's grave stood his father's tombstone.

After two sessions, the coroner's jury finally reached their verdict that four people had met death by fire at Shady Rest. They did not guarantee positive identification, nor did they attempt to assess blame.

The public blamed the Sheltons, and Oren Coleman tended to agree—at first. They had, after all, tried to bomb the place from the air, and several times their guns had riddled the barbecue stand, causing the patrons within to "hit the sawdust," and prompting Birger to line the walls with sheets of steel. One of those patrons was Willard St. John:

One night I stopped there on the way home—always did every time I'd go in late at night. I was sitting there drinking a beer when Birger said, "If I was you, St. John, I believe I'd drink up and pull out. I got word through the grapevine that the Shelton boys are going to come by and shoot this place up." I said, "I'm already drunk up," and I left about half of that beer. When I got up where I turned off to go home [Dykersburg], those boys come by and shot that son of a gun. The next day I went by there. They'd shot every window out.

By word of mouth, the story spread that the Sheltons and/or members of their gang had driven a truck complete with gasoline tank into the woods near the cabin. Down a convenient ravine flowed the gasoline toward the log structure, soaking it at the foundation. A tossed match sent Charlie's dream into oblivion, as bullets had done for those within. The few who had reason to doubt this version were not talking—except for Lory Price.

At the first inquest, Price had given a spare account, but off the record he was heard to remark that while driving back to Marion that night, he had seen Charlie Birger, Art Newman, and Connie Ritter driving toward the cabin. This curious bit of information might have been part of the record had Price been able to testify at the second inquest.

Meanwhile, Birger had learned that Price was holding regular conversations with "Jimmy Madison" in the Marion jail. For reasons known to the gang leader, this was not an encouraging sign. Apparently, word got back to the patrolman that he was in disfavor with his old pal, Charlie. According to Joe Schafer, Price begged Oren Coleman for protection. A man noticeably lacking in personal warmth, Coleman did nothing to ease the patrolman's fears. At the urging of Arlie O. Boswell, however, he did insist that Price keep his distance from "Jimmy Madison."

The speed cop's darkest fears were not unwarranted. A gregarious man, he was often seen at Birger's place, drinking a beer and talking with the boys. There and elsewhere, he would perform wheelies on his four cylinder Harley-Davidson motorcycle for the entertainment of the mostly young onlookers. In the summer of 1926, after directing traffic at the "Hardroad League" baseball games at West Frankfort or Marion or Harrisburg, he would tell umpire Charlie Walker, "I'll see you out there." "There," of course, meant Shady Rest.

"He was always out there getting him a home brew because

they didn't charge him," Walker said. Apparently they didn't charge him in a lot of places, because former Birger man, Riley Simmons, said he saw Price "in a hundred different night clubs" around the area.

He had had his "beat" on Route 13 between Harrisburg and Carbondale since early November 1923, when the highway was nearing completion. Because of his open, easy manner, Lory Price had many friends. Some of them had elected him Commander of the American Legion in Marion in 1926. (Arlie O. Boswell had been his predecessor.) Only because the Germans had captured him was Price denied a Distinguished Service Medal following the war. An Oddfellow, a Mason, an ex-coal miner, and everyone's friend, this stringbean of a Kentuckian expected to be a father soon. Boyish at thirty-six, Lory Price seemed to have everything going for him. But did he?

"Looking like a question mark riding his motorcycle," as one fellow described him, Price came in for much of the criticism that hounded Arlie O. Boswell—namely, that he was too often seen in the company of gangsters. Boswell's stock response that "you don't get your information from Sunday school superintendents" would have served the patrolman as well. Furthermore, Price could defend his questionable associations by citing his record. In 1926 alone, he had recovered nineteen stolen cars. Only by "hanging out" with Birger and members of his gang could he have achieved such results.

The problem was, though, that simply by being there, he had access to information denied such straitlaced upholders of the law as Oren Coleman and Jim Pritchard. The darker possibility, that he was actually aligned with the Birger gang in the stolen car racket, as Art Newman later testified, would naturally have made his position all the more tenuous. Asked why he had committed certain crimes, a man who had once served as Birger's bodyguard replied, "Because I had one foot in the grave." Had he been asked, Lory Price could have answered the same.

Eleven days after the Shady Rest explosions and killings, six days after his testimony, Lory Price was missing. Also missing was his wife, Ethel, a schoolteacher who was on leave during her pregnancy. Their disappearance did not become known until the patrolman's stepfather, John DuFour, who lived nearby and fed the couple's chickens when they were away, discovered that the telephone lines to their house had been cut.

Missing too were the Charlie Christians. Finding their alarm clock still ticking and food still on the table, concerned neighbors feared the worst. So, also, did Arlie O. Boswell. Friend and fox-hunting companion of Charlie Christian, Boswell had been hunting with him one night near the ruins of Shady Rest when the tipoff came from a man unknown to Boswell that both men were marked for death by the Birger crowd. Because of his official position in the county, Boswell couldn't flee, but Christian could and did. At the time, however, many believed that the Prices and the Christians had been abducted at or about the same time. Not until Christian appeared years later in his law office, in Michigan, did Arlie O. Boswell know for sure that his old friend was still alive.

In some of the worst weather in years, Coleman and his deputies searched for the Prices throughout the county. The rain and sleet that marked the third week in January was followed by an ice storm.

Tempers, strained by the inclement weather, were not much improved by the superficial search made by the state authorities to find the couple, after leads in Williamson County petered out. The *Marion Weekly Leader* demanded that the state offer a substantial reward. State Representative Wallace Bandy of Marion introduced a resolution in the Illinois House calling for such a reward. The resolution was approved quickly and unanimously. Something about this latest outrage had angered and sickened the public, as the killings of Ward Jones, "Highpockets" McQuay, and the others had not. They wanted results. But as January ended, they were treated instead to another example of Birger's arrogance, this time in a Quincy, Illinois, courtroom.

Accompanied by two federal men and Art Newman, Birger passed through Marion the morning of January 31 en route to Quincy where the Collinsville mail robbery trial was to begin that afternoon. Originally Springfield had been given the honor, but the authorities finally decided that the Quincy federal building with its single stairway would be easier to guard. Also, the streets in the capitol afforded an easier escape route should friends of the Sheltons attempt a rescue in the event of a guilty verdict. That both the factions were there in force was a rumor believed by almost everyone—and especially by the men guarding their two prize witnesses, Birger and Newman.

Such fears were not unfounded. Returning to their room on the third floor of the post office building about 1:00 A.M., February 1, in the company of seven detectives, Art and Bessie Newman were fired upon from a building across the street.

Wild though the two shots were, they at least should have shaken the dapper little gambler, but when Newman took the witness stand later that morning, a broad smile shone from his face. Clearly pleased to be of help to the government, and at the same time to strike a blow against his former pals, he told how Carl Shelton had asked if he "wanted in on a good thing." That "good thing" was the Collinsville mail robbery.

On the morning of January 27, 1925, Newman stated, a telephone call came from Carl. They had just "pulled" the Collinsville job and needed an alibi. Ora Thomas was being buried that day, and Carl thought it might be a good idea to drive down to Herrin to pay their last respects to an old friend and fellow anti-Klansman. At the same time, they would neatly provide themselves with an alibi. Newman testified that he drove Carl and Earl Shelton and their attorney, Joe McGlynn, to Williamson County. Since they arrived too late to attend Thomas's funeral, they paid a visit to their friend Delos Duty, in Marion. They also stopped at the Marion jail to see two other friends, Sheriff George Galligan and his deputy, Hezzie Byrn. Following the visit, Newman said, he drove the two brothers and their attorney back to East St. Louis. He testified that three weeks later, the proceeds from the robbery were divided in Charlie Birger's home in Harrisburg. Newman related his tale with such relish that Judge Louis Fitz-Henry at one point had to admonish him to quit smiling.

After Art Newman completed his account that afternoon, Harvey Dungey took the stand. The rumrunner from Marion testified that at about 6:00 A.M., January 27, 1925, while driving a taxicab in Collinsville, he had seen Carl and Bernie Shelton near the town. Because he alone could place the two near the scene of the robbery, his testimony was especially important.

The last of the state's witnesses to take the stand was Charlie Birger. In his closing argument, Defense Attorney Harold J. Bandy

gave a brief description of Birger's demeanor that day: "You saw
Birger swagger into this room, stick his thumbs in his vest, and
sneer at Carl Shelton from the witness chair. You saw the glint of
vengeance in his eyes and the joy he took in testifying against
these men."

Aside from these theatrics (which began with a "Howdy, Sheltons" as he passed his three former pals on his way to the witness
stand), the main thrust of Birger's testimony was that $3,600 of
the $21,000 taken in the robbery had been divided in his dining
room by Carl Shelton and Charlie Briggs, another of the alleged
robbers. At the time, Birger stated, Carl told him that Bernie was
the driver of the getaway car.

In addition to Delos Duty and Joe McGlynn, defense attorneys
Harold J. Bandy and Edmund Burke called to the stand William
Oversee, the manager of the East St. Louis Taxi Cab Company, for
which Dungey claimed he had worked the morning of January 27.
Oversee testified that while the Marion man had worked for him
in 1925, he had not done so in January, as Dungey had claimed.

Mrs. Pat Pulliam said that at Shady Rest, Birger and Newman
told her and her husband that they would "get the Sheltons on
that Collinsville job." Thinking better of their careless remarks,
the two shot and wounded the Pulliams and killed their friend
"Wild Bill" Holland a few nights later near Herrin, she added.

In sharp contrast to the arrogant behavior of his two former
friends and associates, Carl Shelton seemed more a banker or a
successful businessman than a famous gangster, as he took the
stand. Following questions by his own defense counsel, in answer
to which he denied all allegations made by the other side, Carl
Shelton was cross-examined by United States District Attorney
Walter M. Provine. He asked him to state his occupation at the
present time. Studying his shoes for a moment, Carl answered quietly, "Collection agency." The ensuing laughter prompted Judge
Fitz-Henry to pound his gavel for order.

In their closing arguments on February 3, the defense attorneys
referred to Birger as "the Emperor of Harrisburg" and to the
eager Newman as "the new light in American literature." They
stressed the bias of each man and their character or lack of it. For
his part, in referring to two of the Shelton brothers' alibi witnesses—Joe McGlynn and Delos Duty—the U.S. district attorney

said, "After hearing some of the lawyers testify in this case, I think their licenses to practice in Illinois should be revoked."

During a break in the trial, Carl Shelton happened to see Art Newman near the elevator. For a moment, their eyes met. Then Shelton stepped over to the cigar counter, leaving Newman and his guards waiting for the elevator to arrive.

"Did you see them eyes of his?" Newman asked his stoic guardians. "That's the way he looks before he shoots and kills people."

Learning of these remarks after Newman and the others had stepped onto the elevator, Shelton swore a little before breaking into a smile. "You know," he said, "that little devil is clever. He can almost read your mind."

On the morning of February 5, Judge Fitz-Henry sentenced Carl, Earl, and Bernie Shelton to twenty-five years in Leavenworth Penitentiary. In the custody of six deputy U.S. marshals, the brothers arrived at the prison at 10:00 A.M. the next morning, which happened to be a Sunday. After their street clothes were exchanged for prison garb, they were escorted to their cells. The next day, deputy warden Fred Zorbst assigned the inmates to their new jobs "in the stone-cutting department."

Without problems of his own, Birger might have celebrated the trial's outcome. However, the presence of Jim Pritchard in the courtroom clouded his enjoyment of the proceedings. The Franklin County sheriff had been prevented from serving his warrant only because the federal men, in whose custody Birger remained throughout the trial, held the gangster on a $1,000 bond in a conspiracy case then being pressed against the Sheltons. (None too pleased with the "cold reception" given him by Birger's custodians, Pritchard was, nevertheless, informed that upon Birger's release after the trial, he would be notified. When that time came, he was not notified.)

By the time the verdict was announced, Newman was on a train heading for Long Beach, California. In the train station prior to Newman's departure, a reporter had seen him pretending to read a newspaper, but he was actually holding up a mirror to see who might be lurking in the shadows.

At the close of the trial, Birger was taken to Springfield and there released on the $1,000 bond. When he returned to Harrisburg, it seemed everyone was discussing the recent death of Helen

Holbrook in St. Petersburg, Florida. The coroner's jury there had called it suicide, but the rumor was that she had been silenced to prevent her testifying at the Shelton brothers' trial. Harrisburg remembered Helen as a buxom beauty who had enjoyed the company of gangsters, as had Lory Price.

Birger, *far left*, and the Newmans, *far right*, in the courtroom. Hyland, his head turned away from the camera, sits at the end of the table.

Birger at his trial

The jury. Front row, *left to right*: Clyde Downes, Paul Knight, Marion Warren, William Hendricks, Milo Hopper, and Harry Simpson. Back row, *left to right*: Louis Gunn, Charles Francis, Dow Fisher, Dave Whittledge, Marion Weeks, and John Krug.

Art and Bessie Newman

Ray Hyland, *front*, and Art Newman

Birger and his family. *Left to right:* Bernice, Minnie, Charline, and Charlie; *far right,* Rachel Shamsky.

Art Newman

Connie Ritter

Harry Thomasson

Clarence Rone

Ray Hyland

Bessie Newman

Beulah Adams

Nealy I. Glenn, assistant state's attorney
of Franklin County

Roy Martin, state's attorney of Franklin County

Judge Charles Miller

H. R. Dial, attorney for Ray Hyland

W. F. Dillon, attorney for Art Newman

Birger's attorneys. *Left to right*: Charles Karch, Forrest Goodfellow, Scerial Thompson, and Robert E. Smith.

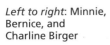

*Left to right*: Minnie, Bernice, and Charline Birger

Scerial Thompson, *left*, and Birger

Jim Pritchard, sheriff of Franklin County

The hanging of Rado Millich

Rado Millich on the scaffold

Millich awaiting execution

*Left to right*: Sheriff Coleman, his deputies Brady Jenkins and Joe Schafer, Sheriff Petrie, Sheriff Pritchard barely visible behind the hooded Millich, and Phil Hanna

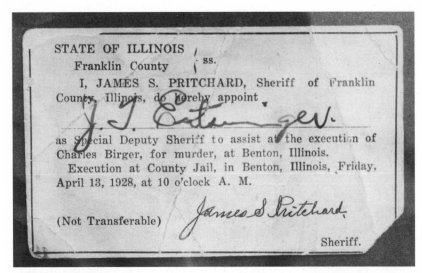

STATE OF ILLINOIS } ss.
Franklin County

I, JAMES S. PRITCHARD, Sheriff of Franklin County, Illinois, do hereby appoint

J. T. Ettinger.

as Special Deputy Sheriff to assist at the execution of Charles Birger, for murder, at Benton, Illinois.

Execution at County Jail, in Benton, Illinois, Friday, April 13, 1928, at 10 o'clock A. M.

(Not Transferable)                 James S. Pritchard,
                                                        Sheriff.

A pass to Birger's hanging

The crowd of people, many in trees, that attended Birger's hanging

Birger's casket underneath the gallows

Birger and Rabbi Mazur turning the corner to ascend the scaffold; Sheriff Flannigan, *left*, and Jim Pritchard looking on

Birger going up the stairs of the scaffold

Birger on the scaffold

Tying Birger's legs

*Left to right*: Sheriff Flannigan (large man with hat in hand), Sheriff Pritchard (in dark suit), Birger, and Phil Hanna (adjusting rope); Sheriff Coleman, hand upraised, standing at the top of the stairs; Rabbi Mazur reading from the Bible

Immediately after Birger's hanging

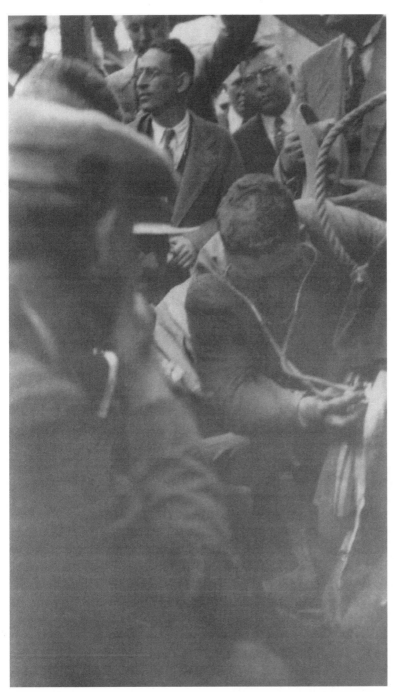

Birger's limp body

Birger's body being checked for any signs of life

Arlie O. Boswell,1976

Birger's tombstone in University City, Missouri

# 22
# A Man Who Knew Too Much

AT ABOUT 11:00 A.M. ON FEBRUARY 5, THE SAME DAY JUDGE Fitz-Henry sentenced the three Shelton brothers to the rocks of Leavenworth, Joe Waldman, a farmer and stock buyer living near Dubois in Washington County, was checking his wheat field after a recent sleet storm. In some weeds near the highway, he saw a man's body. Turning the corpse over, he noticed a badge with the number seventy-eight. From newspaper accounts that had mentioned the badge number, Waldman knew he had found Lory Price. Harold E. Wolfe, a Belleville stockbroker, recalled in a letter to the *Illinois Magazine*:

> I can see it yet, the partly exposed body of a man wearing the uniform of an Illinois highway patrolman, lying there in the snow. His star was still on his uniform, mute evidence of the authority that had been his until that fateful night, weeks before, when he had been "invited" to go for what proved to be his last ride. A heavy snow had fallen the night he disappeared, and it had been followed by others and by a spell of real cold weather. The snow had formed a pronounced drift or heap over the body, and the low temperature had kept it from melting until now, when a few warm days melted enough to disclose the tragedy the drift had concealed. It was not a pleasant sight—made more gruesome by the fact that some animals had gnawed part of the flesh from the exposed hand and arm. The hand and arm of Lory Price.

167

At about eleven o'clock one night early in February, Rudy Walker of Eldorado heard a knock on his door. As he flicked the light switch, Walker heard a man say, "Don't turn that light on." Cradled in the man's arm was a machine gun, and by his side stood a young woman, formerly of Eldorado. Charlie Birger said he needed a place to hide for the night now that Sheriff Turner was finally looking for him.

"I'll put you up here, Charlie, but how long are you going to stay?" his friend asked.

"I'll leave sometime tomorrow night, but I don't know where I'll go from here," Birger replied. And he added, "In the morning when you get up, knock at our door and I'll get up, but we won't raise the blinds nowhere in the house. We'll have to stay here all day."

"I got up the next morning," Walker said, "and knocked at his door. 'Are you ready for breakfast?' It was about nine o'clock. I'd done got the kids off to school. He told me to go to Turner and tell him that he would be willing to give himself up if he could take his machine gun to jail with him, because he didn't want the Shelton gang to take a potshot at him."

When Walker delivered the message as he promised, Turner asked where Charlie could be found. "I said, 'I don't know. He was at my house last night. He left sometime during the night.' Turner said, 'If you find out where he is, you let me know.'"

On the afternoon of February 8, Lory Price was eulogized by Reverend A. E. Prince at the First Baptist Church in Marion and later buried with full military honors in Maplewood Cemetery north of town. That same afternoon, Charlie Birger was arrested at his home by Sheriffs Turner and Pritchard and placed in the Saline County jail. There was an understanding between the two officers at that time that the prisoner would remain in his cell that night and be released the next morning into the custody of Sheriff Pritchard, who would then deliver him to the jail at Benton.

Taking no chances, Jim Pritchard drove into Marion Wednesday morning, February 10, in one of three automobiles, each of which was crowded with armed deputies. Coleman, his deputies, and the Marion chief of police, and even Coroner George Bell, joined the caravan at Marion. In short order, it was rattling toward Harrisburg.

That this expedition was merely Act II in a comedy of errors became evident at the Saline County line, where Pritchard was informed that Lige Turner had gone to Springfield to attend a hard-roads meeting. Before leaving, though, the Saline County sheriff had instructed his deputies that none of the prisoners were to be released during his absence.

Fearful that the cold excursion of December 27 was about to be repeated, the two sheriffs and their men, nevertheless, went to the Saline County jail. Only Pritchard himself, however, stepped in to see the much-publicized prisoner. He returned with both good and bad news. That Birger remained in his cell where he belonged was encouraging; that his machine gun remained with him was not. The Saline County deputies, Pritchard said, freely admitted giving Birger the weapon, citing their fear of the man in their "custody" and the possible wrath of his enemies on the outside. It seemed Pritchard and Coleman had given up, at least for the day, when they returned to their respective counties. Just before noon, however, Pritchard was back in Harrisburg awaiting developments.

That afternoon, through his secretary, George Sutton, Governor Len Small announced that unless riotous conditions warranted the presence of the state militia, he would not act in the Saline County matter and added that it was the responsibility of the local authorities to separate their "prisoner" from his machine gun. Back at the jail in Harrisburg, the fellow causing all the fuss realized by now that his free-wheeling existence was about over. That day he sold two tracts of his Saline County farmland to his sister, Rachel, "for $1 and other . . . considerations."

Accompanied by three Saline County deputies and his attorney, Scerial Thompson, Charlie Birger appeared before Circuit Judge Julius C. Kern at Mt. Vernon late the following day. Thompson had thought it possible that in the *habeas corpus* proceeding, his client might be released under bond, thus foregoing a stint in the Franklin County jail. Instead, after a session lasting approximately ten minutes, Judge Kern ordered that the prisoner now be placed in the custody of Sheriff Pritchard.

Birger was driven to the Benton jail, where he showered and

received a change of clothes. While he was becoming adjusted to his new surroundings, up the street Judge Charles Miller set his bond at $42,500—$40,000 for Adams's murder and $2,500 for assault to commit the murder of Pat Pulliam. Jim Pritchard's long day had ended well.

With the Sheltons in prison and with Birger in jail and his gang scattered, the authorities were busy trying to solve the crimes committed during the recent gang war. In the Adams affair, Roy Martin had the killers' note—and two names. The latter were supplied by a fellow who had recognized the two youths and divulged their identity to a trusted friend. The information was passed along to another person who got the word to Martin. Talking with the eyewitness, Martin had his hearsay information confirmed. Harry and Elmo Thomasson were the killers.

Roy Martin had read, of course, that Elmo Thomasson had been identified as one of the victims of the Shady Rest shootings and fire, but where was Harry? For all Martin knew, he was dead, also, or perhaps hiding out in another state. He may have read with passing interest the accounts of the attempted jailbreak of four prisoners at the Marion jail the night of January 29. Common sense and uncommon courage did not enable the middle-aged lawyer to see that Harry was almost literally at his fingertips.

Equally slow, and apparently as nonproductive, was the search for the murderer of Lory Price. On February 7, the day the Sheltons began serving their terms at Leavenworth, the Price inquest was held in the Washington County courthouse at Nashville. From 9:30 A.M. until noon, at which time the inquest was continued until the following Saturday, the six-man jury heard the testimony of Joe Waldman, Sergeant John O. Keefe of DuQuoin—who had positively identified the body—and others.

As had been the case for the last hour of the previous setting, the inquest of February 12 was closed to the public. These special precautions, it was felt, would encourage the testimony of those who might fear reprisals, since Price himself was a classic example of a man who knew too much.

While the patrolman's killing was discussed behind closed doors, the search for his wife continued. After Price's body had been discovered in Washington County, that area became the focal point of the search, as Williamson County had been previously. In time, the search would be broadened to include Pope and Hardin counties, with their abandoned mines and extensive forests. A joyless endeavor it was, this wading through the underbrush, poking through ruins for the body of a lady schoolteacher, and a very young one at that.

Meanwhile, Roy Martin had another break. At some point, possibly as early as mid-February, he learned that the "Jimmy Madison" in the Marion jail was actually Harry Thomasson. Without letting the prisoner know he was being observed, Martin and Beulah Adams visited the jail. There, Joe Adams's widow identified the prisoner as one of her husband's killers.

# 23
# "Black Hand" Letter

**D**URING THE FIRST WEEK OF MARCH, THOMASSON WAS ONE OF
several defendants in two trials. In the first, Thomasson, Danny
Brown, Ray Rone, and Ray Hyland were tried for the robbery
of Marshall Stewart at a roadhouse near Colp the night of December 27. The result was a hung jury.

Of the four, only Hyland was excluded as a defendant in the
second trial. In this trial, his friends were charged with robbing an
old man, Joe Murray of Weaver, the night of December 20. This
time, the jury voted to convict. In sentencing them on March 4,
Judge D. T. Hartwell delivered a scathing denunciation of the defendants' activities. In addition to sentencing the men to from ten
years to life imprisonment, Hartwell ordered that each defendant
be locked in solitary confinement for his first seventy-two hours in
prison and upon each anniversary of the crime to be again locked
in solitary for twenty-four hours. Because he claimed to be only
nineteen—Judge Hartwell thought him older and said so—Harry
Thomasson was to be sent to the Pontiac Reformatory until he
turned twenty-one, at which time he would join his companions
at Menard. The other two were to begin serving their sentences
there immediately.

When news of the verdict reached Birger, he surely winced.
Above all, he wanted Harry Thomasson out of jail and free so

that, if need be, the lad could be silenced. Bernice Birger had served as one of Thomasson's alibi witnesses at the trial, testifying that on the night of the robbery, Harry had been at their home in Harrisburg. Well, she remembered the date, said pretty Bernice, because Harry had brought a box of candy for Minnie and Charline.

One month after entering the jail, Birger was released on bonds totaling $42,500. Those who signed his bonds were Bernice Birger, Andrew Salus (Birger's next door neighbor), and Steve Stefancie of Harrisburg; Mr. and Mrs. Thomas Bell of Johnston City; Mr. and Mrs. Joe Kuca of West Frankfort; Horace Neeley and H. L. Summers of Marion; Thomas Parten of East St. Louis; and Mrs. Jacob (Rachel) Shamsky of St. Louis. The first signer—for $35,000—was Birger himself.

Free though he was of the bars and of the galling presence of Jim Pritchard, the graying gang leader was nonetheless far from carefree. As if Harry Thomasson's incarceration were not cause enough for grief, Birger read that Jack "Dopehead" Crews had been arrested in Akron, Ohio, by Chief John L. Stack of the Illinois State Highway Patrol. One of the many hangers-on at Shady Rest, Crews was thought to have been the "stranger" whose presence so disturbed Steve George on the night of January 8—the one George had incautiously threatened to kill if he did not quickly leave the place, according to Lory Price. Thanks to information supplied by Connie Ritter, first reports had listed Crews as one of the victims of the Shady Rest tragedy. Clearly the man was in a position to know too much, and apparently he was talking.

With Washington County temporarily center stage, Williamson County was not exactly fading into the background. On the night of March 16, Arlie O. Boswell returned home after buying ice cream downtown in Marion and was closing his garage door when a shot from the shadows tore through his right side just above the hip. Stunned though he was, Boswell managed to get off three shots at a fleeing figure. More painful than serious, the wound put him in the hospital at West Frankfort for a few days. Later, when he was back at his home but still in bed, he—as usual—was mystified as to who was trying to kill him. The closest thing to a clue was a "Black Hand" letter received the day of the shooting; it read: "You know Price knew too much. He didn't know half as much as you do. Ten years to life don't mean much to you."

As stated in the *Marion Daily Republican*, the "ten years to life" could have referred to the sentences handed down to Brown, Rone, and Thomasson, but the connection was never proven and the shooting, like so many others, was never solved.

Now that its most famous citizen was back in circulation, Saline County also had its share of excitement. As usual, the event took place in the dark. Early in the predawn of March 22, less than a week after the attempt on Boswell's life, "Machine Gun Charlie" noticed four men splashing gasoline on the east side of his Harrisburg home. Before the firebugs got a chance to light a match and illuminate the west end of Harrisburg, Birger emptied the contents of two revolvers at the men, sending them fleeing toward their automobile.

Then, before they could make good their escape, he brought out his faithful machine gun, possibly the same one that had made Sheriff Turner something of a laughingstock, and proceeded to perforate both men and their car, with better luck with the latter. Still, one of the crew who had been left behind unobserved by the irate gang leader walked to a restaurant uptown and hired a cab driver to take him back to Franklin County. It was reported that his hand was almost severed.

That same night saw the burning of a roadhouse south of West Frankfort. Picking through the ruins the next morning, authorities found a still and nineteen barrels of mash. Anyone who thought that the removal of the Sheltons would provide a period of calm had sadly misjudged the character of "Egypt."

For his part, Birger was worried more about what Crews might reveal than about another attempt at arson. Stack's announcement on March 18 that more arrests in the Price case would occur the following week only increased his fears. Taking into account his precarious position, the gang leader had nothing to lose and only time to gain by talking with Stack himself.

The close call of the night before prompted Charlie to take a room in a hotel in Harrisburg, and it was there that he, Connie Ritter, and possibly Scerial Thompson, Birger's attorney, met with Stack and five of his men. Crews, Birger explained, was a former employee at Shady Rest who enjoyed his work so much that he begged to become a bona fide gang member but had been denied the "honor." Merely for revenge, he continued, Crews might be framing him and his men. For two hours, Stack and his investigators listened patiently as Birger's plausible but somehow unconvincing account was put forth. Then they left for Carbondale.

On the day following this conference, Sheriff Coleman, whose reputation for being closemouthed around reporters was richly deserved, was in Danville with a prisoner, probably a bootlegger. Someone introduced him to one of the federal court commissioners. Off his guard for once, Coleman observed that he knew who killed Lory Price and was pretty sure that he knew who killed Mrs. Price. Intrigued, the commissioner made the mistake of admitting that he was also a newspaper reporter who would like to know more. Except for a long and studied glare, Coleman made no response.

For Birger and for Newman, who was working as a night watchman in Long Beach, California, it was a time of "wait and see." The date for the Adams trial had not yet been announced. The inquest into the death of Lory Price was not yet completed.

It had been Roy Martin's plan to let Harry Thomasson get to know life in the Pontiac Reformatory for several weeks before springing on him the extent of his own information. The presentation of this information was as important as the timing was. To enhance his performance, he decided to take along John Rogers, one of the three *Post-Dispatch* reporters who had extracted from Newman, Wooten, and Ritter a telling, if not always accurate, account of gang activities. Together Rogers and Martin had to convince Harry that they knew everything. Once this had been accomplished, they had to further impress upon the young man the idea that by confessing, he would not automatically be placing the rope around his own neck. Were he to plead guilty, it was most likely that Judge Miller would sentence him to life imprisonment, which meant that he could be paroled in twenty years. If he did not cooperate and they could prove him guilty, he might very well be hanged despite his youth.

Although their argument was impressive, Martin and Rogers had additional assistance in winning over the young criminal.

Thomasson's own suspicions were as black as the cinders of Shady Rest. When Elmo and the others were murdered and burned in the cabin, the public seemed to think that the Sheltons were responsible. But knowing the Birger gang as he did, Harry had for weeks pondered the possibility that Birger (or Newman) had ordered and perhaps participated in the killings. Since he was in jail at the time of the tragedy, his information was only secondhand, but one informant was especially convincing. He also knew who had the most to gain from Elmo's death, and it wasn't Carl Shelton.

When his two visitors put forth their account of Joe Adams's killing, Harry responded by giving one of his own. Both versions were essentially the same. In return for his confession, Rogers promised not to release the story until after Harry appeared before Judge Charles Miller to plead guilty to the murder.

Somehow Birger learned of Martin's visit. He was worried. He called Harry's brother Ray in West Frankfort and told him to come to Harrisburg for a talk. At his home, Birger gave the young man $24 for expenses and told him to go to Pontiac to warn Harry that Martin should be told nothing. "Tell him to take care of the inside and I'll take care of the outside. If he don't keep his mouth shut, he'll get the same as I do, and they'll probably hang both of us." Ray Thomasson testified later that at the time, he wasn't even aware of his brother's involvement in Adams's killing. He did as he was told, but the trip came too late.

At the final session of the Price inquest on April 9, Dr. Paul B. Rabbenneck, the coroner, stated that while an open verdict had been reached, evidence gathered in their investigation would likely be presented to the grand jury, which was scheduled to meet the following week. There was certainly nothing in this terse announcement to bring cheer to Charlie Birger, but one thing stood out: No one had been charged. A few days later, the *St. Louis Post-Dispatch*, the paper Birger had sold as a boy, did its best to keep him on his toes by announcing that he and certain of his gang would soon be charged with the abduction and murder of the Prices. The allegation stunned the accused as well as Stack and his investigators.

In Marion, the day after the story broke, John Stack vehemently denied the truth of that statement. Obviously, he said, if they had evidence that Birger had committed the crime, he would be under arrest at that very moment. The sad fact was that they did have some leads but nothing that would hold. Reading this in their evening newspapers, the tradesmen, the miners, and the farmers could only shake their heads and wonder if crimes in southern Illinois were ever solved.

# 24
# Birger Unsatisfied

F—IN MORE THAN A MONTH'S FREEDOM ON BOND—BIRGER HAD
dreams of continuing his existence as before, they were dashed
on April 29, when he was arrested and placed in the Benton jail.
His second setback that day was the announcement by Shelton attorneys Harold J. Bandy and Edmund Burke that during a three-
hour conversation with a "conscience stricken" Harvey Dungey
in Springfield the day before, they had learned that Dungey had
not seen either Carl or Bernie Shelton just prior to the Collinsville
robbery. He had lied on the witness stand, Dungey said, because
Birger and Newman had threatened to kill him if he didn't. Even
as he had walked down from the third floor quarters where the
witnesses were kept under guard to the courtroom itself on the
second floor, he had debated with himself whether or not to testify, but the image of the two machine guns Birger kept close by
had been the deciding factor.

Countering with a charge of his own, Birger said Dungey had
been promised $10,000 by the Sheltons to recant his testimony.
Birger further charged that Dungey now led a gang of his own,
that they headquartered at Dungey's Dew Drop Inn near West
Frankfort, and that it was this gang that had tried to burn the
Birger house a few weeks earlier.

Helpful though it was in winning the Sheltons a new trial and
their freedom, Dungey's affidavit was not particularly damaging

to Birger, but the day following his arrest came what must have seemed his finishing blow. At Benton, in Judge Charles Miller's courtroom, Harry Thomasson confessed that he and his brother Elmo had killed Joe Adams at the behest of Birger and Newman. Following his confession, Thomasson was sentenced to life imprisonment.

His story—as related to the newspapers—was that on the night of December 11, 1926, the two Thomassons had driven to Shady Rest in a stolen Ford roadster. Between the hours of 9:00 and 10:00 P.M., Art Newman called them into the west room of the cabin. Present also in the room were Charlie Birger and Connie Ritter. After the door was closed behind them, Harry and Elmo were seated, and Birger informed them that he had a job he wanted them to do the following day. Some indication of the nature of that "job" came when Newman asked Harry if he had ever killed anyone. The young gangster replied, "No, Art, I never had enough against anyone to kill him."

As though he had not heard, Birger said, "We picked you two boys to kill Joe Adams."

"Nothing to it," said Newman quickly, adding that they would be provided with an automobile, a driver, and two pistols and that a letter purportedly from Carl Shelton was to be presented to Adams. The Thomasson brothers' stolen Ford was first considered for the getaway car, but Birger decided a Chrysler would serve better, adding that it should be burned at the first opportunity following the killing.

After Hyland was called in, Birger turned to him and said, "Jew, we want you to drive the Chrysler car tomorrow to kill Joe Adams." On the basis of Newman's crack that "Izzy the Jew" lacked the guts for such a task, Hyland replied, "I don't know, Charlie. I'll think it over."

Harry insisted he had to care for some livestock and that Elmo, too, had errands to run. Not about to let them both leave, Birger said Harry could do his feeding, but Elmo must stay. Before leaving, however, Harry was told that if he did not return, someone would be sent for him. His chores finished, Harry arrived about 2:00 A.M. at the residence of Bessie Rhodes in Benton, where he boarded with his girlfriend, Pearl Phelps. His brothers, Elmo and Pinckney, lived with them.

Around eleven o'clock that morning, Elmo and Ray Hyland arrived, picked up Harry and Pinckney, and then drove on to Marion, where Pinckney got out. The others drove on to Shady Rest, arriving there about 1:00 P.M.. In the basement, they found Newman, Ritter, and some others. After following Newman and Ritter to an upstairs room, the two brothers were soon joined by Ray Hyland, who was carrying a .45.

"This ought to do it, hadn't it?" he asked. Newman said it would, but—being a big-time gangster—he ordered Hyland to take the pistol to the basement, split the bullets, and rub the grooves with garlic. While Hyland was applying this final remedy, Ritter was trying to disguise his handwriting while writing the note.

After Hyland came back with the pistol and its prize bullets, Newman smelled the latter, nodded, and said, "That ought to get him. If one of them ever hits him, he'll never get well." The .45 was handed to Harry. Elmo already had a .38.

After the deed was accomplished, Newman continued, they would all meet at the junction of Routes 2 and 14 west of Christopher and from there drive south to "Big Kate" Williams's place at Dowell. They would end up, he said, in Harrisburg.

There remained only the toast—and then another. Each of the Thomassons and Hyland downed two glasses of whiskey. The occasion may well have called for the pure stuff, the "Egyptian corn" extolled by journalist W. A. S. Douglas as a drink capable of "making a man or boy ready and willing to step up to a man-eating tiger and attempt to pull its toenails." The soon-to-be killers needed every drop and then some.

The empty glasses were then set aside. Art and Bessie Newman, Connie Ritter, and his "moll" Ollie Potts, left in a closed Chrysler. Hyland's car, similar to Newman's except for the mud spatters on it, followed. Their destination was an auto repair shop north of Marion. When they got there, Newman and Ritter bought gasoline and a fan belt for the muddied Chrysler. While the fan belt was being fitted into place, Newman again reminded the three of the point of the rendezvous and, almost as an afterthought, urged Hyland to drive carefully. Many miles would be covered before the day's end, if all went according to plan.

Newman and his companions drove back toward Marion, caught Route 13 at the intersection, and drove west. Meanwhile, the apprentice killers and their driver were soon into Franklin County, heading toward West City.

East of the Adams home, the car slowed to a stop, and the boys got out. Slowly, Hyland drove on to a block west of the house and parked the car. In his court appearance, Thomasson gave a terse but telling account of the killing:

> When we reached West City, Elmo and I went to Adams's house, leaving Hyland sitting in the car. We knocked on the door and then Adams came. Elmo handed him the note, and while he was reading it, I shot him twice with the revolver which I had hidden up my sleeve. Elmo then shot him once. We then ran back to the car where Hyland was waiting and drove away.

Eighteen miles west of Benton they arrived, as planned, at the junction of Routes 2 and 14 at Mulkeytown, but they did not find Newman. They drove north two miles, then turned around. At Dowell, three miles south of Mulkeytown, they pulled in at the roadhouse of "Big Kate" Williams, and there, waiting to greet and congratulate them, were the Newmans, Ritter, and Ollie Potts.

After various weapons were taken into the roadhouse, including the two machine guns, the two cars were driven into a garage. As if the small arsenal already at hand was not sufficient, either Newman or Ritter handed Elmo a high-powered rifle and told him to use it if the wrong people dropped by. Armed to the teeth, Hyland and the Thomassons were to wait until Birger arrived that evening with further instructions. They would be taken care of, Newman said, as he and his party were preparing to leave. "Big Kate" was even then preparing them a warm meal, compliments of Connie and him. Enjoy, he urged them, but don't relax. Not yet.

After the meal was finished and the dishes cleared away, who should walk in but Harvey Dungey, Clarence Rone, and a beaming Charlie Birger. "You sure did a neat job," he said. "That is one son of a bitch we won't have to worry about anymore." Pleased though he was, Birger was still not satisfied, because Carl Shelton continued to elude the undertaker.

Driving north, the party of six turned east at Mulkeytown, and upon reaching Christopher, they turned around, retraced their route, and ended up spending two hours in a roadhouse at Ward. A team of sorts, they were celebrating a victory.

Then once again, they were on the road, driving to Carbondale and from there back to Marion. At Marion, Birger asked bus driver Owen Berry if Carl Shelton had arrived from St. Louis. He had not been aboard, the driver said. While in town, Birger and Dungey talked with Arlie O. Boswell. They also had a talk with Lory Price.

When they arrived at the cabin around midnight, the Newmans and Ritter were already there. "We got that dough-bellied son of a bitch, didn't we?" Birger crowed.

"Yes, that was a clever trick to do," Newman added. The actual performers of that "clever trick" were paid $50 each, and no doubt a few more glasses were raised to these heroes of the hour.

Birger, Teddy Nurocke (a roadhouse operator from Franklin County), and the Thomassons drove on to Harrisburg, where, using the name of "James Madison," Harry signed the register at the Horning Hotel. Nurocke scribbled "John Winters" as an alias. It is probable that Elmo eventually spent the night at Birger's home. Around 2:00 A.M., Birger and his three guests went to an uptown cafe, where, as planned, the Newmans and Ollie Potts were waiting. The weary young murderer, Harry Thomasson, soon bade his friends good morning, and with his companion returned to the hotel.

Five days later, Freddie Wooten, Harry Thomasson, and Charlie Birger returned to Dowell in Birger's Buick coupe. The incriminating Chrysler was towed from the garage to a field southwest of town, and after the battery and heater were removed, the car was burned.

# 25
# "I'm Done"

WHEN WORD REACHED HIS CELL OF THOMASSON'S CONFESSION, Birger was reported to have wept. Whatever the truth of the matter, tears would have been appropriate, for the young man's matter-of-fact account of Joe Adams's killing was completing the wreckage that had begun when Harvey Dungey admitted he had perjured himself at the Shelton trial at Quincy. If extra salt was needed for these fresh wounds, Dungey, who was then being held in the Benton jail on charges of stealing an automobile, would happily oblige. For his part, Birger could still deny that he had ordered the kidnapping and killing of Lory and Ethel Price, and he did; but with the recent confessions and the promise of more to come, the public was beginning to think otherwise. A man with so much blood on his hands might have dipped them into many pools.

Until Stack and his investigators talked with Jack Crews, they, too, had probably thought the Sheltons responsible for the killing of Lory Price. The fact that Price's body was found between Williamson County and East St. Louis, where the Sheltons headquartered, lent some credence to those suspicions, but when Jack Crews told what he knew, the pendulum of suspicion swung hard the other way.

Across the country, one "John Rogers," a watchman at an oil refinery in Long Beach, was arrested on May 22 by the police of that city. It was soon learned that the name of the *St. Louis Post-Dispatch* reporter had been appropriated by a news maker of no less renown—Arthur Samuel Newman, formerly of Illinois.

Having failed in his attempt to saw out of the Long Beach jail, the diminutive gambler was finally extradited. Heading back to Illinois on a train, in the custody of Jim Pritchard and the real John Rogers, he not only admitted his role in the Adams killing but also confessed to his part in the Price murders. The body of Mrs. Price, Newman continued, was buried under debris at the bottom of an abandoned mine shaft located between Marion and Johnston City.

Newman was first taken to a cell on the first floor of the Benton jail, directly below Birger's quarters, but he was soon removed to Nashville, Illinois, where on June 11 he retold his horror story. On Birger's orders, he and Wooten had accompanied Birger to the home of Price near Marion and abducted the state patrolman. They drove him to Birger's home in Harrisburg and then back to the barbecue stand, or what remained of Shady Rest. There, during an argument, Birger shot Price but failed to kill him, Newman said.

In the meantime, Ethel Price was driven to an abandoned mine. After Connie Ritter and Ernest Blue shot her and threw her body into the shaft, they and the others in the car drove to the barbecue stand, arriving there just after Birger had shot Price.

Two carloads of gangsters spent almost the rest of the night searching for an ideal place to dump their victim, and finally they pulled alongside a weedy stretch of highway near Dubois in Washington County. As Lory Price pleaded for what remained of his life, he was carried into a field, where some of the fellows "finished" him.

About five hours after this devastating testimony, workers began removing the debris that Newman said the men had used to fill the shaft of the old Carterville District Mine. As the opening deepened, lines formed and buckets filled with tin cans and other debris were passed upward from hand to hand, dumped, and then passed back down again.

Inconspicuous in his slouch hat and overalls, Oren Coleman was one of several county officers laboring alongside the outraged citizens. Arlie O. Boswell was another official present who sometimes dug, sometimes passed buckets, and at intervals "traded off" to sample ice cream provided by the Marion Ice Cream and Ice Company.

As dusk became dark, lights were strung up—necklaces above a nightmare. Judging from those who stood quietly watching the men work in the depths of the pit, this might have been the mouth of hell, discovered at last on a late spring night by a large band of intensely curious men. But it was anger more than curiosity that drove these men to disclose the mine's terrible secret.

Whatever her husband's involvement with the Birger gang, Ethel Prudence Price was a classic example of an innocent bystander who was killed because she was a potential witness. Tempers were further sharpened by the widespread belief that the pretty school-teacher was pregnant at the time of her death. When neighbor went gunning for neighbor in the Klan war, when Mrs. S. Glenn Young was blinded by her husband's enemies, when gangsters or hangers-on were found murdered on lonely back roads or in the ruins of burned buildings, area residents shook their heads and questioned the sanity of the times. But this latest atrocity defied comprehension.

As the grim task of recovering the body continued, Franklin County authorities were completing the transfer of their best-known prisoner to the Sangamon County jail at Springfield. Only that morning, Birger and his attorneys had appeared in Judge Charles Miller's court for the purpose of requesting a change of venue. Harry Thomasson's allegations, the attorneys argued, had so poisoned public opinion against their client that a fair trial in the region was no longer possible. Judge Miller thought other-wise. The judge's ruling notwithstanding, it was clear to Sheriff Pritchard that, charged as the atmosphere was already, Newman's confession that afternoon made it necessary to move Birger and to move him quickly. They feared a lynching if he remained in Benton.

Throughout the night and into the next morning, the work at the mine continued, only to be stopped for a time by a rainstorm that began around 3:00 A.M.. While others wielded their coal buckets, Arlie O. Boswell, Deputy Arlie Sinks, and two other men set out from the Peabody 3 Mine and waded water up to their chins for almost a mile trying to find the bottom of the Carterville

District Mine. Within two hundred feet of their destination, water finally stopped them. Boswell recalled the incident:

> We started on foot and, of course, we got in water. We got water up to our shoes, then up to our knees, and where the rock had fallen from up at the top—we couldn't see, it was old slimy water—we'd stumble, just busting our shins all to pieces. We kept walking, and that water was cold as ice. They kept saying, "If we can just get over that hill—you hear that noise?—if we can just get over that hill we got it made." But the water began to go into our noses. That was the longest trip I ever took in all my life. That was the silliest thing I ever did in all my life.

On Sunday afternoon, June 12, the men achieved a depth of nearly thirty feet. Planks were nailed on telephone poles that had been laid across the opening earlier in the day. From this platform, the buckets could more easily be hoisted.

At about 3:00 A.M. on Monday, following another break caused by a storm, a large scoop shovel was put into operation. Again Arlie O. Boswell recalled: "Someone told me that the C. & E. I. Railroad had a dragline on a flat car, and they were quite sure they'd let me have it. We got in touch with them—it was at Mt. Vernon—and the dragline was brought down."

Using this piece of equipment, big chunks of concrete were hauled to the surface. After a piece of sheet iron was hoisted, the men saw in the pale yellow muck the well-preserved body of Ethel Price.

Later, streets near the Ozment Funeral Home in Marion were roped off to prevent curiosity seekers from crowding out friends and relatives who wished to view the body. Members of the American Legion Post of Marion served as pallbearers at the funeral; it was held the afternoon of June 14 at the First Baptist Church in Marion.

That same day, in Benton, Judge Charles Miller postponed setting the date of Birger's trial until the defendant was returned to Franklin County. "I'm done," Birger told reporters when he arrived in Springfield, and the disclosures of the next two days served only to confirm him in this belief.

That his trial had been postponed did offer some hope that the collective ire of outraged "Egyptians" might cool before his return to Franklin County, of course. Two days after arriving in Springfield, he was transferred to the jail at Bloomington.

The enmity that existed between Birger and Newman was apparent to fellow gangsters in January, if not earlier, but for reasons of self-preservation, the two chose not to make public their differences. Now, in the Belleville jail for his own protection, and having nothing to lose and possibly much to gain by severing his ties, Newman insisted that Birger lied when he denied his participation in the Price killings. Newman also intimated to reporters that revelations would follow that would shock southern Illinois to its already shaken depths. "Con man" and killer though he was, Art Newman had little of the reticence usually associated with gangsters, and his promise of future disclosures gladdened the hearts of reporters as it deepened the gloom of his former partner.

On the morning of June 21, shortly after Birger's return to Benton, Judge Miller set the trial date for July 6. Also present for the important announcement were Newman and Hyland.

Although Arlie O. Boswell read the news of the forthcoming trial with more than passing interest, his main concern was staying alive. On June 18, while driving to his home in Marion, he was again fired upon, but this time his assailant was wide of the mark—unless the mark was the state's attorney's nervous system. Preparing the prosecution's case against Eural Gowan and Rado Millich in the upcoming Jones trial was another pressing matter and one he pursued with his back to the wall whenever possible. Within the mainstreams, there were undercurrents.

Earlier that spring, before Harry Thomasson had unburdened himself before the eager ears of Roy Martin and John Rogers at Pontiac, Ray Hyland found himself in the Marion jail with little hope of being released. Although a jury had failed to return a guilty verdict against him and the others in the Marshall Stewart trial, he was being held on another robbery charge. In balmier times, Birger might have provided the bail, but the gang leader was either in jail or temporarily out on bail himself. Finding his situation more hopeless each day, the jaunty young man from East St. Louis let it be known that he wanted to talk to Arlie O.

Boswell, the man with whom he had fought at the barbecue stand, the man who had tried and failed to convict him on the robbery charge, and the man who would, in all probability, try again.

"I let him sweat there for a month, maybe two months," Boswell recalled. Relenting at last, he consented to be locked in with the prisoner, to learn what he had to say. For a consideration of a reduced sentence or probation or even to be out under bond, Hyland said he could help "salt away" any number of Birger gangsters. The best Boswell could promise him was a letter of recommendation to the warden at Menard, a handy document when parole became a possibility. Thinking the matter over, the prisoner decided small favors were better than none and began to talk.

"To my surprise," said Boswell, "the first thing he told me about was the 'Shag' Worsham affair." Secondhand though it was, Hyland insisted that his information was reliable, coming as it did from the gangsters who were there. Lyle "Shag" Worsham, who was suspected of being a Shelton informant, was abducted at Zeigler by Fred Thomasson and Harvey Dungey and taken to Shady Rest. There, Birger and Dungey wrangled over the young man's fate. Birger favored letting him live while Dungey insisted he needed killing. Apparently Dungey presented a convincing case, for Worsham was driven to an isolated area southwest of Marion and there told to run for his life, which he did. Seconds later that life ended in a clatter of machine gunfire.

The earthly remains of Lyle "Shag" Worsham would have lain in the weeds until the inevitable passerby stumbled upon him except that while looking for a likely place to turn the cars around, the men noticed the lights of a nearby farmhouse. Those inside the house had surely heard the shooting. Worse, they might have discerned the unmistakable chatter of machine guns, weapons most often associated with the Birger gang. Therefore the body was reloaded into an automobile and driven to Marion, where, at a filling station at the edge of town, Birger bought five gallons of gasoline. Driving south, they came at last to an abandoned farmhouse in the Pulley's Mill area near the Williamson-Johnson county line.

The ensuing conflagration did not entirely consume Worsham's body, but it did make positive identification almost impossible. Not until Boswell's conversation with Hyland did the circumstances of the killing become known outside the gangsters' own circle. The story itself would not appear in the newspapers until later that year.

While he was at it, Hyland provided useful information about the Ward Jones killing as told to him by other gang members. At first, Boswell rejected his story, but as other informants came forth, he began to believe that Hyland's account was essentially true. The test would come later in the year when Judge Hartwell gaveled the court to order for the Jones trial.

No one would be more attentive to that trial's outcome than Birger himself, the verdicts serving as a possible bellwether of his own treatment at the hands of a jury. As he was well aware, there were outstanding differences in the attitudes of the two counties concerning capital punishment. Williamson had seen several executions, the last being in 1921 when Setimi DeSantis was hanged. Franklin County, on the other hand, had yet to erect a scaffold. The graying man in his second-story cell could only hope that those who believed it never would do so were right.

# 26
# Oral and Eural Gowan

O N JUNE 30, 1927, IN MARION, THE JURY WAS FINALLY CHOSEN
to hear the evidence against and determine the fate of the two
men accused of killing Ward "Casey" Jones. A unit at last,
these twelve "good and lawful men" the following day heard Arlie
O. Boswell in his opening statement promise to prove that Ward
Jones had been shot at Shady Rest by Rado Millich and Eural
Gowan; that after being tortured and beaten, the victim was driven
to the North Fork Creek just east of Equality and there thrown
from the bridge. Two days later, a young, black man named Alvin
Woods "happened" to find the body.

The court-appointed attorney for Gowan, Judge R. T. Cook,
opened for the defense by stating that the evidence would show
his client took no part in the killing. Attorney J. H. Clayton, appointed by the court to represent Millich, agreed with his colleague that Gowan was guiltless and admitted that his own client
had, indeed, killed Jones, but only after the latter had commenced
firing at him with a machine gun.

Then began the parade of Shady Rest alumni. From the penitentiary at Menard came Danny Brown, one-time bartender at Shady
Rest and former cell mate of Millich. Brown stated that Eural
Gowan told him of an argument Jones and Millich had as to who
would be in charge of the cabin while Birger was away on business
in St. Louis.

190

This argument ended in gunfire and the wounding of Jones; Gowan then "finished" him with two bullets. He and Millich dragged the body down to the dog pit and wrapped it in an old army blanket. The following night, at Birger's orders, the earthly remains of Ward "Casey" Jones were loaded in a car and driven to a watery grave in Gallatin County.

Brown was followed to the stand by his friend Clarence Rone, one of the three who were originally indicted. Rone's case had been nol-prossed on June 29, after he agreed to turn state's evidence. At the time of the shooting, he said, he was at the barbecue stand. Later, as he and Gowan were walking to the cabin, he heard his companion say, "We killed 'Casey' Jones." Continued Rone:

I didn't believe him and he took me over there and I saw the blood. I saw a tree where Gowan told me a bullet had struck after passing through the body of Jones. He said he also saw where a bullet had nicked a concrete walk. Gowan said that they dragged Jones back to the cabin. Casey wasn't dead yet, and Gowan said he fired one or more shots into Jones and Rado fired another. Then he told me they took Jones down close to Equality in a Lincoln sedan. He said he drove the car, and that they were lucky not to have turned the car over when they collided with another machine on the way to Equality.

Ray Hyland testified that shortly after the shooting, the two defendants and Steve George arrived at Birger's home in Harrisburg, where Hyland was staying. Prior to the shooting, Millich told him, an argument broke out between Jones and himself. After Jones threatened him, guns were drawn but were put away. But when Jones went to the cabin to pack his clothes, Millich followed. Hyland continued: "Millich said they went down there to see that Ward did not take anything that didn't belong to him. They got in an argument there, he said, and they killed him."

Perhaps more than the others, these jurors were prepared to believe Harry Thomasson, if only because of his recent revelations concerning the Adams killing. He had told the truth once; they had no reason to believe he would not tell it again. Like the previous witnesses, he had not actually seen the shooting of Jones, having been in the barbecue stand at the time, but upon hearing the shots, he had run to where Jones lay face downward and dying. Above the groaning man stood Eural Gowan with Jones's machine gun in his hand. Rado Millich stood nearby. The last thing Thomasson said he saw as he and the others walked back to the barbecue stand was Gowan and Millich dragging the body behind the cabin. Then there were two more shots.

As dramatic and as damaging as anything the gangsters said was the testimony of Oral Gowan, the defendant's brother. He was plowing Birger's field at the time of the shots, and as he heard them, he dropped the reins and ran to the scene, where he found his brother Eural standing over the body.

Equality undertaker A. K. Moore had seen four wounds, any of which might have been fatal. One bullet in particular, he felt, might have passed through the victim's heart. Since Moore wasn't present when the body was first brought to his funeral home, greater detail was added by his assistant, Noel Flanders, who was there and who helped undress and wash the body. The seven actual bullet holes, Flanders said, indicated that of the four shots entering the body, only three had passed through. He was convinced that two different weapons were used and that the shots were fired from different directions. Neither he nor Moore, however, could confirm Boswell's allegation that Jones had been mutilated and tortured.

A good friend of the state's attorney, Deputy Joe Schafer, testified that on June 20, Millich told him that while in Harrisburg, he received a call from Jones, saying that a parole agent was waiting at the cabin to see him. By the time he got there, Millich said, the agent had already left, or so Jones told him. Millich said while walking down to the cabin, he began hearing shots and turned and saw Ward Jones firing at him with a machine gun. Schafer continued:

He said that he saw Bert Owens throw down his machine gun and run, while Jones kept firing at him. Millich said that Jones snapped a clip of twenty cartridges into a machine gun and fired at him. Then Millich told me he shot at Jones with a rifle, firing two shots. He said that on the last shot, Jones grabbed his side with his hand

and fell. Millich said that he was within three steps of the porch of the cabin when Jones began shooting at him. He said that Jones was about twenty-five yards away from him and that he fell where he stood.

During a conversation he had with Millich on June 29, also in the county jail, another deputy, Arlie Sinks, testified he was told the trouble really started with the death of Noble Weaver on April 13 at Herrin. As Weaver lay dying from a Klansman's bullet, he was "rolled" by none other than his fellow gangster Ward Jones, according to Millich. When word reached him of the charge, "Casey" began making trips to Benton to find and silence the homely fellow who was tarnishing his reputation. His efforts were to no avail, asserted Millich, because while Jones was skulking in the back alleys with pistol and ever-present machine gun, the target of his schemes was in St. Louis helping Art Newman sell liquor.

The prosecution's last witness, wintry-eyed Oren Coleman, took the stand Saturday morning, July 2. He testified that Eural Gowan told him he was a hundred yards away from where the shooting occurred, and when it was over, he walked over and saw Rado Millich and Bert Owens dragging Jones behind the cabin.

That afternoon, Ray Hyland again took the stand, this time for the defense. He testified that on the day of the shooting, he had driven Jones to Shady Rest from Harrisburg: "Jones was under the influence of dope. And he was nervous and angry. He had his pistol between his knees and said he was going to kill somebody. I told him to forget it. I took him to the cabin and left him to get his clothes and his car."

The next witness, Harvey Dungey, had motored out that day to borrow one of Birger's hunting dogs: "I was at the barbecue stand when Jones came in. He asked if Rado Millich had come out yet, and when somebody told him he hadn't, he threw a gun down on the table and said, 'I'm going to kill that "Hunkey" when he does.' I left before Millich got there."

Following a July 4 holiday that found the jurors at home with their families, court reconvened on July 5 with Harvey Dungey again on the witness stand. This time he claimed to have additional information concerning the nature of some of the previous testimony. Only the morning before, Dungey said, Harry Thomasson had admitted to swearing lies in Saturday's session at the prompting of "Ku Klux officers." Instead of being repaid the favor, he was now denied visits by his own relatives.

The motives and methods of Harry Thomasson were set aside, at least for the moment, while Rado Millich took the stand. Under Clayton's questioning, the defendant told of receiving a telephone call while in Harrisburg from Jones, who said a parole officer was out at the cabin looking for him. He stated that he borrowed a car from Bernice Birger and drove out, only to find the officer had gone—or so he was told by Jones. As he was leaving, he heard the familiar voice of Jones say, "Rado," and as he turned, he saw Ward Jones firing at him with a machine gun. He continued:

> I had a rifle in my hand and I fired at him four times. I don't know how many shots he fired. He had a 20-shot clip in the gun. A man can't count machine gun shots. I got in my car and drove to Harrisburg to give myself up to the law. I went to Birger's house, and Mrs. Birger said she would notify Charlie.

Millich also testified that previous to the shooting, Jones had made several threats against his life.

After getting the witness to state for the record that Eural Gowan had not shot Jones, Gowan's attorney was reminded by Millich that a certain question had been omitted. Rather than phrase it himself, Cook instructed the witness to speak directly to the jury. "Bert Owens was coming behind me with Jones," said Millich, in his broken English, "but when the shooting started, he dropped his gun and ran."

The final witness presented by the defense was Eural Gowan. Not yet twenty, an orphan since early youth, the slender Gowan seemed in both dress and demeanor more at home with a plow than a machine gun. Along with his brother Oral, he had tended a truck patch for Birger near Shady Rest, and between chores "ran off" home brew, all for a salary of $10 a week. Hearing shots near the cabin while he was "toting" a case of home brew to the barbecue stand, Gowan said he turned in time to see Ward Jones fall. After that, he never saw the man again. He said Steve George,

Millich, and himself were present. Neither Harry Thomasson nor Ernest Blue was there, as Thomasson had testified.

And concerning that testimony, Gowan said that the night before his appearance in court, he had heard a clearly disgusted Harry Thomasson mumbling aloud in another cell of the Marion jail: "He said it was funny to him that he would be brought down here to testify to a lot of —— lies and then get a dirty deal. He said something about his folks not getting to see him."

Under Boswell's cross-examination, Gowan denied telling Oren Coleman that Jones fell on the concrete in front of the cabin, or that he had pointed to the pool of blood from the fallen man near the cabin walk, or that after shooting Jones with a rifle, Millich laid the weapon down and finished the job with a revolver. But Boswell pressed hard:

"You drove Charlie Birger's Lincoln sedan with the body of Ward Jones in it, and helped dump the body into North Fork Creek near Equality, didn't you?"
"No, sir."
"Didn't you carry a pistol at the time Jones was killed?"
"No, sir."

Final witness for the defense was former jailer A. L. Bradley. He testified that Thomasson had used the alias "Jimmy Madison" while in the Marion jail months before.

To counter potentially damaging testimony that Thomasson had admitted to lying on the witness stand, the prosecution called Deputy Joe Schafer, Deputy Arlie Sinks, and the jailer G. W. "Wash" Sisney, all of whom stated that Thomasson had not recanted his story.

Final arguments began late on the afternoon of July 5. Directing his attack at the state's witnesses, Judge Cook declared, " . . . Hyland denied his story, Thomasson wants out. He admitted that he lied on the witness stand. How, gentlemen, would you convict a mangy, stumped-tail, three-legged dog on the testimony of these perjurers. If you would, God pity the dog."

Boswell smiled, but his own presentation was no less spirited. Coatless, his tie loosened, his voice brought to a calculated shout, he pointed to the defendants, branding them as members of "an infamous band of marauders, murderers, and rascals." Twelve men, two of them ministers, watched his right hand slice the air and listened:

> The evidence shows in this case that all the defendants were employees of Charlie Birger at the gang resort in the edge of Williamson County, that the deceased, Ward Jones, was also an employee of Birger; that on the day of the killing, Ward Jones went to the cabin of Charlie to get his clothes and while placing his clothes in his automobile, the defendant, Eural Gowan, walked up to the deceased and threw a pistol on him and forced him to throw up his hands; that Bert Owens, who is now dead, having been blown up in the cabin when it was destroyed along with three other persons, took the pistol of Jones from his scabbard and the defendant, Rado Millich, immediately stepped out from behind a car and shot Jones twice with a high-powered rifle. After he fell, he was taken by each foot by Millich and Gowan and dragged by the feet through the woods, a distance of about 85 yards, and thrown into a cock pit where he remained from about 2:00 in the afternoon until sometime the following night, when he was loaded in a car and driven to North Fork Creek, east of Equality in Gallatin County and thrown into the creek. The body was found about two days later.

At 12:03 P.M. the next day, following instructions from Judge Hartwell, the jury retired to begin its deliberations. Fifteen hours later, just before 3:00 A.M. on July 7, the jurors reached a verdict. Six hours later, Judge Hartwell opened the sealed envelope and read:

> We, the jury, find the defendant, Eural Gowan, guilty of murder in manner and form as found in the indictment, and fix his punishment at 25 years in the penitentiary. We, the jury, find the defendant, Rado Millich, guilty in manner and form as charged in the indictment, and fix his punishment at death.

The younger defendant appeared unmoved, but Millich swallowed hard; one of his legs began swinging back and forth. Not until he was led from the courtroom a short time later, however, did he comment on the sentence. "They didn't have no evidence like that," he said.

Clearly pleased with the verdict, Boswell sought out each member of the jury to shake his hand. Had Gowan received a stiffer sentence, he would have been more pleased, the state's attorney told a reporter for the *Marion Evening Post*, but quickly added that in a juror's shoes he might have voted the same.

# 27

# "We Have Beans, Beans, Beans"

T HE DAY BEFORE THE JONES TRIAL ENDED, A PACKED COURTROOM twenty miles to the north awaited the arrival of the sheriff and his three prisoners. Elbowing a walkway through the crowd on the courthouse lawn, Jim Pritchard escorted Ray Hyland, Art Newman, and Charles Birger up the stairway of the Benton courthouse. Pritchard, taking no chances on a rescue by the prisoners' friends or a short-circuiting of the legal process by their enemies, had special deputies along the route from the jail to the courthouse. Many of them were armed with .401 automatics. Within the courtroom, other guards watched the crowd closely.

Reporters scribbled as Birger embraced Bernice, Minnie, and Charline. Set against a backdrop of gangland atrocity, this tender scene made for far better reading than the argument of motions, the real business at hand.

Between word pictures of the defendants, the reporters duly noted that the defense attorneys moved that the indictments be quashed. The matter having been taken under advisement, Judge Charles Miller ruled against the motion. Birger's attorneys, Robert Smith, Forrest Goodfellow, Charles Karch, and Scerial Thompson, having failed there, on the morning of July 7 moved for a separate trial, as did Newman's attorney, W. F. Dillon. The effort was to no avail. Despite the fact that Birger and Newman no longer communicated with each other except by threat and counterthreat, they would be tried together along with Hyland.

Before court convened on Friday, July 8, newspapermen asked Birger his reaction to Newman's latest charge that he had planned the Pocahontas bank robbery. Glancing at his codefendant, who sat at the other end of the table, Birger replied, "Why, that guy's crazy. I didn't even know him then. Look at him sitting over there. Anybody can tell he's crazy."

Another of Newman's "crazy" accusations would concern the abduction and murder of Jimmy Stone, a young man from Poplar Bluff, Missouri, who disappeared from Harrisburg the night of November 30, 1925, and whose body was found in a ditch near Halfway the next day. To his breast was pinned a note: "He stole from his friends. KKK." Birger and Orb Treadway were the actual killers, according to Newman.

Newman said that after the murder, Birger or Treadway stuck a cigar in the victim's mouth, then proceeded to drive the corpse around Marion to impress fellow gangsters. (From his jail cell in Marion, Rado Millich told a tale eerily like Newman's, except for one detail. He said that Birger told him Ward Jones had done the actual killing.)

"You dirty, woman-killing son of a bitch," Birger snapped at the man who was causing him so much grief. "You ought to be ashamed to ask for a trial. You ought to ask the people to hang you."

Newman, who was seldom at a loss for adjectives of his own, replied with a subdued, "That's enough of that."

Despite efforts by one of his lawyers to smooth the matter over—they should thresh it out among themselves after the trial, the lawyer insisted—Birger managed to turn the blade one last time. "If Newman gets out, I want to hang," he stated. After this outburst, he cooled down long enough to have his picture taken with Bernice and his two daughters.

With the gaveling to order of the morning session, there began the tedious task of selecting a jury. Uppermost in Roy Martin's mind that morning and in the mornings and afternoons to follow was how each of these prospective jurors regarded the death penalty. Most said they could vote for it but only for the most heinous crimes. That pleased Martin, of course, but he was not so pleased to learn that many of these otherwise right-thinking gentlemen had already decided to their own satisfaction the guilt or innocence of the three defendants. These men were dismissed outright.

Court did not reconvene until Monday morning, July 11. That day four jurors were accepted. Drama was at a minimum in the sweltering courtroom, but even so, a vacant seat could be found only at rare intervals. As soon as one became available, the first in the waiting line at the foot of the stairs was ushered into the room. Having arrived on the scene before the morning rush, one clever youngster sold his seat for a dollar, a practice he continued throughout the trial. For the most part, the spectators came to stare at the defendants, especially Birger, one of "the two best dressed men in court," according to reporter W. A. S. Douglas, who covered the trial for the *Baltimore Sun*. His only sartorial rival was Judge Miller.

Birger, aware of the attention centered upon him, tried to appear nonchalant, as though the unfortunate predicament in which he now found himself was only a thing of the moment, a bother and nothing more. Occasionally, however, his onlookers, many of them smelling none too fresh, according to Douglas, would catch him glancing in Newman's direction. This was especially true when Thompson and Dillon were up and about. (Wisely, the two attorneys had placed their chairs between those of the two antagonists and were usually seated in them.)

When the jury was finally selected on July 14, the defendants appeared to relax somewhat. Hyland had actually seemed relaxed throughout the mind-numbing week. On one occasion, he had asked reporters which of the courtyard trees would be his gallows. In a lull before the testimony, a reporter asked Birger his opinion of jail food.

"We have beans, beans, beans," he replied in response to this rather pointless inquiry. Hyland, overhearing the exchange, could not resist adding a comment or two of his own: "We get beans three times a day all right, but they are cooked better than the Williamson County beans. This jail is paradise compared to the jail at Marion."

The reporters loved it, this whistling in the dark, but that afternoon, when Roy Martin began his opening statement, the tossed-off wisecracks died away. The time for levity had passed.

The state would prove beyond a doubt that the killing of Joe Adams was planned by Birger and Newman, said the Franklin County state's attorney, and it would further prove that the murderers, Harry and Elmo Thomasson, were driven to and from the scene of the crime by Ray Hyland. Most of the afternoon was given over to Martin's presentation.

After a bench conference between all the attorneys the next morning, Roy Martin was instructed to call his first witness. To the stand came Jim Pritchard. When shown a photograph of a house, the sheriff testified that the dwelling shown therein was that of the late Joe Adams.

Another sheriff, Oren Coleman of Williamson County, was asked to describe the ruins of Shady Rest as he had observed them on the morning following the fire. When asked what he found in those ruins, his answer was, "The charred remains of four human bodies."

Another witness, Pinckney Thomasson, age seventeen, said that he and his brothers, Elmo and Harry, were living in Benton with Harry's sweetheart, Pearl Phelps. He stated that on the night of December 11, Harry and Elmo were not there but that on next morning, Harry was back, having returned sometime late in the night. Around 9:00 A.M., Elmo and "Izzy the Jew" Hyland arrived and had breakfast. Later, the three Thomassons and Hyland drove to Marion, where the witness got out of the car. He did not see his brothers the rest of that day, nor did he know where they went.

The most illuminating account during that first day of testimony came from Waddell True of West City. A proprietor of a barbecue stand whose menu included home brew, True said he once had some unwelcome visitors who came inquiring about a tank that had been dumped off near his place of business by some men he had taken to be hardroad workers. On October 19, two cars had pulled in. One was a Hupmobile driven by Art Newman. Around eleven men, all armed with machine guns, shotguns, rifles, and revolvers, got out of the two cars. Charlie Birger, wasting no time on formalities, aimed his machine gun squarely at True's vitals and ordered him to lead the way to the tank. The witness lost no time in complying. Satisfied by what he had seen, the gang leader returned to the barbecue stand, where he introduced himself to the patrons—still held there at gunpoint—and then issued an ultimatum: If True didn't deliver that discarded bit of armor by the side of the road, West City would have one less business man.

That wasn't all. True was also told to deliver two messages, one to Joe Adams and the other to "the Franklin County law." The first was simply to inform "His Honor" that he was to be killed before the week was up—nothing subtle or between the lines. The second was to inform "the little old Franklin County law" that it was not big enough to keep him from keeping promise number one.

When the courier-to-be protested that he didn't, as a rule, talk to the law, Birger jabbed the end of his machine gun into True's midsection and said, "I tell you, you got to talk to the law." Given this added inducement, True said he would.

Although no one in the room laughed harder at the anecdote than Birger himself, his attorney, Bob Smith, failed to appreciate the humor. Jim Pritchard came down the aisle to maintain decorum. After horselaughs had settled into chuckles, foot shuffling, and silence, the testimony continued.

As one of many guards stationed at Adams's home, True was present when Adams received a telephone call from Birger. During the conversation, he heard Adams protest that he had done nothing to incur the gangster's wrath, adding, "We've got to get this fixed up."

Somehow this eavesdropping "special deputy" caught the reply. "I'll show you what you've done," Birger said. "We're coming up to get you, and we don't care how many guards you've got." That was not the first call, nor would it be the last.

The last witness of the day was Gus Adams, brother and next-door neighbor of the slain mayor. He was present, he said, when Birger, Newman, and several other armed men drove up one December day. Newman and Birger were in a Hupmobile, and the others followed in a Lincoln:

Joe and I were standing near the fence between my house and his. Birger came up to us, pointing a machine gun at Joe. He said, "I'm going to kill you, you son of a bitch." Then the other men pointed their guns at us. The only one I recognized among them was Rado Millich. Afterwards, in jail here, Hyland told me he was driving the Lincoln car that day.

After Joe Adams appealed to the sheriff, without success, he next called on his friends the Sheltons, who responded by sending a few of their men to guard the place. Their reputations, however, had preceded them, and they were soon sent on their way by deputy sheriff Joe Telford. Thus, this great target of a man had to rely on his friends—his "special deputies"—to guard the place and that only at intervals.

Gus Adams said his home was fired upon a few days after the visit, and the day after that his phone rang. On the other end of the line was a familiar voice with a note of elation in it.

"Where were you yesterday?" Birger asked.

"At home," came the terse reply.

"We came near getting you, didn't we? You tell that brother of yours we are going to kick him out."

And then there was the bomb blast that occurred about a month before his brother Joe was killed: "One morning, somebody threw a bomb into Joe's front yard from an automobile. The bomb made a hole in the yard, tore away part of the front porch, part of the side of the house, broke all the windows, and broke the windows out of the houses around here."

Following a two-day recess, court convened on Monday morning, July 18. In "monosyllables or short toneless sentences," Beulah Adams began her testimony, telling of a telephone conversation she had in November:

When I answered the ring, a voice said, "Here's a long distance call from Harrisburg." Then another voice said, "Is this Mrs. Adams?"

"Yes."

"It doesn't sound like you."

"It is, just the same."

"Is Joe there?"

"No. He's gone to Chicago."

"I don't see how that is. All the depots have been guarded."

"Who is this?"

"Wait a minute, I'll tell you. Do you have any insurance?"

"I have a little."

"This is Charlie Birger, and we're coming up there to kill him. Better take out all the insurance you can get."

Backtracking a bit, she remembered the caller's reply and the exchange that followed when she said Joe wasn't home:

*Birger:* "There won't be any use of us coming up there, will there?"
*Adams:* "Me and the children are here if you want us."
*Birger:* "We don't bother women and children. I should say not."

The only break in her composure came when she spoke of the killing itself, and even that was discerned only by reporters sitting at the press table. As she told the story, her lips trembled:

It was on the afternoon of December 12, 1926. Joe and I were in the bedroom. He was lying on the bed when two young men came to the front door. I went to the door, and the young men asked if Joe was at home. I said, "Won't I do?" They said that they were from Carl and that they wanted to see Joe in person.

I called Joe and he came to the door. They handed him a letter, and then they shot him. I think five or six shots were fired. Joe fell to the floor. He told me to get a doctor. A few minutes later he told me that he was dying.

After the shots were fired, the two young men ran off the porch, and my daughter, Arian, ran after them. I ran out in the yard and called her back. Before Joe died he told me he didn't know who shot him.

She later recognized Harry Thomasson as one of the killers, when she and Roy Martin saw him in the Marion jail.

Following the testimony of Arian Adams, who added no new information, two other witnesses completed the morning's roster. Both witnesses were brought down from the Pontiac Reformatory. Alva Wilson, nineteen, and David Garrison, twenty, both of Mt. Vernon, had been sentenced in January, along with others, for the holdup of a filling station at Albion. Prior to their capture, they were occasionally at Shady Rest. They happened to be in the barbecue stand on the night of December 8, when, according to Garrison, he and Wilson were approached by Birger, who asked if the pair would like to "make some easy money."

"Sure. What's doing?" Garrison replied.

"Go to West City and call a certain man to his front porch and shoot him." With the job completed, they would each be paid the princely sum of $50.

Garrison replied angrily, "What do you think I am, a goddamn fool?"

Of the others in the barbecue stand at the time, he could recognize only Newman and Hyland. Birger, he said, wore a cap and, under an overcoat, a gray suit.

While the morning's testimony was in progress at Benton, the courtroom in Marion was the scene of another gang-related drama. After overruling Millich's motion for a new trial, Judge Hartwell set October 21 as the date for the man's hanging. On his feet, listening intently, Millich asked to be heard, and his request was granted.

"I had no fair trial," he said. "The evidence was framed against me by Mr. Boswell. I never killed the man because I wanted to but because he [Jones] forced me to. I tell the truth."

Judge Hartwell did not agree. Alone and unarmed, he said, Ward Jones was preparing to leave the place when Millich gunned him down. As if the crime itself were not shocking enough, the Birger gang went to some trouble to focus the blame on their enemies, and to complete this travesty of human decency, Birger bought the flowers and a casket, all the while bragging that nothing was too good for one of his men.

Concluding his comments, Hartwell announced that Millich would be "hanged by the neck until dead" in the Marion jail yard, this despite a new law designating electrocution as the supreme punishment in Illinois. (Only for crimes committed after July 1, 1927, were their perpetrators entitled to this newfangled streamlined death.)

A familiar figure at the Jones trial was the ailing Clarence Rone. As testimony resumed in Benton on July 18, Rone was again detailing the criminal activities of the Birger gang. Speaking almost inaudibly, he said that the night before Adams's murder, he saw Birger, Ritter, Newman, the two Thomassons, and Hyland go into a room at the cabin. They stayed about two hours, and after the meeting, Harry Thomasson left. On the afternoon of December 12, the witness said that he, Birger, and Harvey Dungey visited Marion, where Birger talked to Lory Price and later to Arlie O. Boswell.

Last to testify that afternoon was Ray Thomasson, a salesman from West Frankfort and the brother of Harry Thomasson. While Harry was in jail at Marion, said the witness, Birger tried to get him to arrange his brother's bond. After Harry was sent to Pontiac, Birger somehow learned of Roy Martin's visit. Desperate, he told Ray to go to Pontiac and warn Harry that he must say nothing to Martin or anyone else. Ray Thomasson did as he was told, but it was already too late.

Even as his brother stepped down from the stand, Harry was in or on his way to Benton. He spent the night in the Martin home, where he was treated as hospitably as any visiting relative. He was especially taken with the cooking of Mrs. Martin's mother. Only a few years younger than the polite killer in their midst, the children of the state's attorney were agog, but at the same time, they felt sorry for Harry, knowing that his best years would be shadowed by the prison bars. While they all dined, a bodyguard with a machine gun sat in the living room, as he had done and would do throughout the trial. In an alley across from the house, a similarly armed guard sat in a car.

Smartly attired in the new suit of clothes Roy Martin had bought him, Harry Thomasson took the stand the morning of the nineteenth, there to retell the story of Adams's murder in graphic detail. Although the particulars were well known by now to anyone who had time to read a newspaper, hearing the words from the murderer's own lips was well worth the hard chairs, the stifling heat, and the interminable waiting in line. His testimony, which took up most of that morning, was attacked that afternoon by the defense attorneys, detail by damning detail. Their many-pronged assault was markedly unsuccessful.

That day, amid the questioning about the Adams killing, Harry was asked what he knew about the killing of his brother Elmo. His audience was stunned to hear him say that Bernice Birger had told him Charlie was responsible for the deaths of Elmo and the others that night at Shady Rest. For some reason, this astonishing remark was mentioned in few, if any, of the newspaper accounts.

The next morning at eleven o'clock, after other witnesses had confirmed details of Thomasson's testimony, Roy Martin announced that the state would rest its case. Court was adjourned until 1:30 P.M..

In that hour-and-a-half recess, Birger's attorneys first learned of Art Newman's refusal to cooperate with them in a joint defense—a setback, to be sure, but not a mortal blow. That would come later.

First to speak that afternoon was R. E. Smith. On the night of December 11, he said, when his client allegedly hired the Thomassons, Birger was not even at Shady Rest. And his motor trips the following day were solely for the purpose of "taking a bead" on Carl Shelton.

H. R. Dial admitted that Hyland drove the car. But he claimed that he did so unwittingly.

It was simply a coincidence that Art Newman met the Thomassons at Dowell following the killing, said W. F. Dillon. He added that his client was there only to deliver some gin.

Thin as these arguments were, the attorneys had, at least, provided a basis for doubt in the minds of the jurors. In doing so, however, they had reckoned without Art Newman, who had plans of his own, plans set in motion during his cross-country journey more than a month earlier. At the completion of opening statements, Newman asked for a private conference with his attorney. When Dillon emerged a short time later from the small room adjacent to the courtroom, he brought back the very bad news to his colleagues that on the train trip from California, his client had "told all" to John Rogers and Jim Pritchard. Furthermore, Rogers had promised to keep the story quiet for a time, that time being until Newman's day in court. The gangster calmly told his attorney that his testimony on the following day would include everything he knew about the Adams killing.

Shocked, outraged, and bewildered, Birger's attorneys knew their client could present an account at least as convincing as Newman's but only if he had time to prepare it. To that end, Charles Karch filed a motion for a continuance.

When Karch and his colleagues began to argue for a continuance the next morning, they were met with strident resistance from Roy Martin. After ruling for the prosecution, Judge Miller instructed the defense to call its first witness, presumably Birger himself. His lawyers, however, knew if he presented an alibi only to have it shattered by the testimony of a hostile codefendant, the result would be disastrous. For that reason, they agreed among themselves that Birger would not take the stand until after Newman testified. Dial announced the same for his client, Hyland. Now Newman could do his worst—and they fully expected it— but after conversing briefly with Dillon, Newman decided he would waive evidence until after the others had their say. A stunned courtroom heard his decision.

Again came the invitation to present evidence, and again the answers were the same. The trial had been tedious, but now time leaped ahead, leaving the three defendants somewhat dazed and suddenly near the end, whatever that might be—as invoked by Hyland's choicest quips, Newman's calculations, and Birger's darkest fears. On arguments alone, the case would go to the jury. Except for those arguments, the jurors' deliberations, and their verdict, the trial was over.

For fear that the defense might even waive their arguments, Assistant State's Attorney Nealy Glenn reviewed the prosecution's case in its entirety in his opening argument. He spoke for an hour and a half. At the conclusion of his presentation, during which he had paced before the jury box employing all the gestures at his disposal—including the shout, that tool so indispensable to lawyers, auctioneers, and certain ministers—he got his point across: "Think of it, gentlemen! Newman, 38 years old, and Birger, 45 years old, forcing two orphan boys, one 17 years old and one 19 years old, to go out and murder for them."

Raising up the image of Elmo Thomasson, "who had no mother, no father," and—in his allegiance to Birger—had allowed the gangster "to send his soul to hell," Glenn then asked what was the proper punishment for the three who were on trial. "Hang the conspirators by their necks until they are dead!" he demanded.

Less fiery than his predecessor, young Harrisburg attorney Scerial Thompson stressed the dubious quality of the testimonies of the state's witnesses, in particular that of Harry Thomasson

and Clarence Rone. His colleague, Forrest Goodfellow, re-empha-
sized the questionable nature of such testimony.

The morning of July 22 found H. R. Dial arguing against the
barbarity of hanging. His ringing appeal to the jurors' emotions
contrasted sharply with Charles Karch's plea for reason. Karch argued that it had not been proved that Birger was present at Shady
Rest the night the murder was plotted. Only two men had so far
connected him with the killing—Clarence Rone and Harry
Thomasson, both lifelong criminals. Thomasson, especially, was
not to be trusted, for not only was he a convicted robber and murderer, he had also admitted to living in sin with a girl his own age.

Feudist, friend of the Shelton brothers, and roadhouse operator,
Joe Adams was as much a symptom of the times as Charlie Birger.
Cataloging Joe's shortcomings brought to mind the story of the
passing of a drunken Irishman.

"What did he die of?" asked a neighbor.

"He died of a Tuesday," came the reply.

"What was the complaint?"

"Oh, there was no complaint. Everybody was satisfied."

Charles Karch thought it a funny story and very much to the
point. But the jurors were not amused.

The afternoon's fireworks were provided by W. F. Dillon, seventy-two, the oldest practicing lawyer in Franklin County. To be
sure, he said, the state's attorney would ask for the death penalty.
"He is going to dupe you gentlemen to sign a death warrant for
these men to hang them until they are dead, dead, dead, until their
tongues stick out of their mouths, and they hang suspended in the
air." (If it had been in his power to choke for a moment each of
the jurors, he would have done so to let them feel death itself in
its vast bitter and black—the death Roy Martin would plead that
the jurors deliver to three fellow human beings.)

"If you have to find these men guilty, give them some human
punishment so that when the end of time comes and the lightning
strikes, the hills crumble, and the fire rages, as the pearly gates
open, we may meet these men, take them by the hand, and say that
we have forgiven them." It was oratory from the 1890s, when machine guns were unheard of and automobiles were toys for the
very rich and very foolish. It was a stunning performance.

Last of the defense attorneys to speak was R. E. Smith, who in his allotted hour and a half pleaded with the jury to, first of all, disregard the testimony of Thomasson and Rone. Only on the word of these two former henchmen, one of them the actual murderer, was Birger implicated in the killing—and even then only in the planning. He pleaded for mercy, noting that hangings such as those in Williamson County had not reduced the crime rate. Would they shoot the defendant point blank where he sat? If not, could they in good conscience order Jim Pritchard to do essentially the same thing? Would they stain the honor of Franklin County for the first and last time by causing to be erected the gallows, that symbol of the Dark Ages?

The following morning, Roy Martin concluded the prosecution's case by urging the jurors not to be swayed by rhetoric. As for Thomasson's credibility, he was convinced the boy was telling the truth. But even without his testimony, the evidence was sufficient for conviction. He concluded:

> I see in your verdict the passing of the rule of the machine gun gang and the establishment of the rule of the law. I know you men will say that the gang war has no place in this part of the state of Illinois and that the gunman or gangster has no place in Franklin County. That's what we ask, gentlemen. Thank you.

The jury returned its verdict at about 1:15 P.M. the following day, a Sunday. Refusing to look the defendants in the eyes, the jurors entered the courtroom. Word had gone out, and the courtroom was almost filled. Judge Miller opened and read the sealed envelope that jury foreman Dow Fisher handed to him: Death for Birger. Life imprisonment for Newman and Hyland.

As Ray Hyland heard his sentence, he may have thought back to mid-November 1926. Three days each week he worked at American Steel in East St. Louis. On a night before one of his days off, he happened to meet a fellow who said he had a car to sell and asked if Ray would like to ride along the following day. Assured that they would be back in East St. Louis the next night, Hyland agreed. He thought that maybe it would be fun.

Only after they arrived at Birger's place at Shady Rest did he realize the car in question was stolen. He soon began working at the barbecue stand on the premises, although East St. Louis was still home. Not one for reading newspapers, he did not know Birger and the Sheltons were feuding, but he did remember having seen the Shelton brothers at Art Newman's hotel in East St. Louis. In a manner of speaking, Hyland was still along for the ride.

More than fifty years later he would recall the day he drove two brothers to the home of Joe Adams: "I didn't even know where I was at. We went into Benton in a roundabout way, and I'd only been in Benton once or twice, and they said, 'You go down to the corner, wait for us. We want to see a fellow.' And then I heard a shot. I figured it was something. They came running down the street, jumped in the car, and said 'Get out of here.' So, we did."

Ray Hyland would serve one week less than twenty-four years in the penitentiary. Fifty-one years after the crime that put him behind bars for so long, the elderly man once known as "Izzy the Jew" quipped, "I figured we'd be back in East St. Louis later that night, and it took me almost twenty-five years before I got back."

On July 27, Birger was formally sentenced to be hanged on October 14, between the hours of 10:00 A.M. and 2:00 P.M. Judge Miller announced the date after overruling a motion by Birger's attorneys for a new trial. They vowed to take their cases to the Supreme Court, if necessary.

Following his ruling, Judge Miller addressed the man standing before him. It was not his intention, he said, either to detract from the dignity of the court or to hurt Birger's feelings:

> However, your position is unique in the history of Illinois. You so far forgot yourself that you did many things and then set yourself up as superior to the law. You surrounded yourself with young men, and you were proud of the fact that when you appeared on the scene, the clarion blew to announce your arrival to your lieutenants. You became a character in the community in which you lived. The youth of the various counties assembled to watch your dexterity with your pistols. You had a glamour about you that youths tried to imitate.

The condemned man standing before him was a puzzle to Judge Miller. An acquaintance, he said, had often mentioned Birger's kindness toward her simply because he knew her uncle. Appealing to the gangster's best impulses, the judge asked him, for his children's sake, to "clear up" the many as yet unsolved crimes attributed to his gang. Concluding his remarks, he said that there was no way of knowing what effect his little speech might have, but that aside, Birger's end would be the gallows.

Birger's request to be heard was granted. Describing himself as a man hunted by his enemies, he said he had appealed to the Saline County sheriff (whether Small or Turner he did not indicate) and to the Williamson County state's attorney, Arlie O. Boswell, for protection but finally had to settle for three "Negro" guards of his own. Only by swapping cars with another man had he escaped death the time eight men in a Cadillac came looking for him.

"I laid out in the weeds for nights and days—for seven days and nights I didn't have my clothes off," he said.

He said that the real villains were the Newmans, both of whom he accused of causing Mrs. Price's death. As for Newman's contention that he had participated in the various crimes for fear of Birger's wrath had he acted otherwise, that was nonsense: "He was never scared of me or no other human. I was in Herrin one night and he took nine guns from sixty men, and he weaved in and out of the crowd like a bumblebee. I can prove that by twenty people." He also lashed out at John Rogers, the reporter who, with Newman, "has conspired and condemned me to the public."

Birger concluded his rambling remarks by saying he was now paying for his decision not to leave the country. "That is the mistake I made, and that is the mistake I am going to pay for."

There was another mistake for which Birger would pay dearly. For hired killers, he had used two young fellows who were known in the area.

# 28
# The Mystery Couple in the Ford Coupe

COLD AND CLOUDY, THE SUNDAY AFTERNOON OF DECEMBER 12, 1926, was the perfect time to see a movie; to do just that, Jesse Cremer, twenty-two, of West Frankfort, and his sweetheart, Jennie Murray, also of West Frankfort, drove to nearby Benton in his Ford coupe. Jennie wore a red mum on her coat. In an area known as Sugar Creek, just outside of their hometown, an "Airflow" Chrysler passed the couple. "It wasn't driving very fast, but I noticed someone had smeared mud all over the back window but then cleaned off a square place," Cremer recalled, "and I remarked to Jennie that it looked like they intended to make a peephole. The car continued on, and I soon dismissed it from my mind."

Arriving at the movie theater on the southeast corner of the Benton Square, the couple realized they had already seen the picture. Rather than turn around and go home, the driver suggested they journey further to West City, to see where Joe Adams's home had recently been fired upon.

Then (as now), the deeds of Birger were discussed and magnified. Anyone who read newspapers then knew that Adams, the corpulent mayor of West City, had allied himself with the rum-running Shelton brothers, Carl, Earl, and Bernie, and that by so doing, he had won the undying hatred of the Shelton's former friend but now devoted enemy, Charlie Birger.

Time was when Birger and the Sheltons together were warring

against the Ku Klux Klan, the Sheltons began to realize that Birger, friendly though he was to strangers, was not above holding out slot machine profits from business partners. Following several killings in the summer and autumn of 1926, the Birger-Shelton gang war made the headlines throughout the Midwest. Thanks to an armored car, a truck converted into a "tank," and even an airplane that dropped "bombs" on Birger's roadhouse, Shady Rest, the affray had a Keystone Kops atmosphere that was somewhat belied by too many gang-related murders. When Birger became convinced that Joe Adams was keeping the steel tank portion of the Shelton's armored truck in his garage, trouble was assured. Sensing this, a wiser man would have left the country; but, being as bullheaded as Birger, Adams chose to stay and take his chances. Besides, he might be lucky enough to catch Charlie in his gun sights.

Three or four blocks east of the Adams's home, Cremer passed a customer of the mercantile store where he worked. This man was on the south side of the street, walking west. Seeing a familiar face, the pedestrian threw up his hand in a wave. The fellow behind the wheel did the same. Again, this was a little thing, hardly worth mentioning.

Equally unimpressive were the two young men who stood on Adams's porch, talking to someone who stood inside the door, possibly Joe himself. The two "men," one seventeen and the other nineteen, wore khaki-colored, sheep-lined coats, a common item of winter gear in those days. Driving past as slowly as possible and keeping the car in low to prevent stalling, Cremer pointed out the house where the men were talking. No sooner had he done so than the sound of gunfire came from that direction. The figure inside fell.

The assailants turned and jumped off the porch. One of the gunmen stumbled, got up, and ran behind Cremer's car—which was still moving very slowly. Remarkably enough, Adams's young daughter, Arian, chased the two until her mother called her back.

Cremer recognized this fellow as Elmo Thomasson. Elmo's brother, Harry, staying to the south side of the street, actually outran the Ford coupe, and in so doing, also passed a fellow standing on the corner. Harry shot at the man's feet, then continued to run down the street, so fast that one could have "shot craps at his shirttail." Next, he crossed the street in front of Cremer, stepped in the middle of the street, and for one terrifying instant, pointed his pistol at the couple.

While Jennie ducked, Jesse, not knowing what else to do, threw up his hand to wave. Recognizing him, Harry did the same, then leaped aside and ran to the muddied Chrysler with the "peep-hole"—it was setting on the shoulder on the north side of the brick pavement. Behind the wheel was Ray Hyland, better known as "Izzy the Jew," a man Cremer had seen several times. After Elmo and Harry jumped in, the car took off at a high speed toward Christopher.

Still not knowing exactly what to do, Cremer continued to drive in low gear. Part of his problem, believe it or not, was the curtain on the window. With a broken spring, the curtain simply could not be opened. And that was too bad, because the young man behind the wheel, who had just looked down the barrel of a gun held by another young man scared half out of his wits, knew that Adams was supposed to have guards stationed around the house. These men, seeing a car with drawn curtains in daytime—just after the shooting—might decide to shower the occupants within with machine gunfire. However, that did not happen.

If not for the condition of the roads, he would have driven on to Christopher, from there to Zeigler, and then back to West Frankfort. Instead, a quarter of a mile to the west, he turned the car around and drove back the way they had come. Although by this time several cars were parked at the site of the shooting, not a police car could be seen among them. About thirty minutes after being shot, Adams was dead.

The eyewitness behind the wheel urged his fiancée not to tell anyone what they had seen. Ignoring his advice once back in familiar territory, she confided the news to a trusted neighbor. Under no circumstances, said this friend, was she to tell another soul outside her own family. This second warning coming so soon after the first made it very clear that her life and the life of her fiancé depended on their keeping the secret.

There was a catch, however. Cremer's face—and possibly his name—was known not only to the Thomassons but also to the pedestrian who had waved. It was this man, Cremer felt, who got word to State's Attorney Roy Martin that someone down at the mercantile store had possibly seen the whole thing. Because Cremer worked at the store, which was owned by a Mr. McGint, the man on the street assumed he had waved to one of McGint's sons. Being close friends, Scotty McGint and Cremer were often mistaken for brothers.

The next day, at the mercantile store, Roy Martin asked to talk with Scotty. As luck would have it, the young man had an iron-proof alibi. On the afternoon that Adams was killed, Scotty not only was in Harrisburg but also managed to get into a scuffle at one of the restaurants. There was nothing to it really, just enough to make the West Frankfort youth memorable to the proprietor.

With Scotty out of the picture, only Cremer remained for the state's attorney, Martin, to question, in his kindly but persistent way. "I lied like a dog," Cremer admitted nearly sixty years later.

Canny enough to know that he was lying, Martin listened to the cock-and-bull story about driving around in Johnston City that afternoon and not seeing one familiar face. Martin yawned. Later Cremer realized he should have brought in the name of a man later to be his brother-in-law, a true friend who would have backed up his yarn—no matter how implausible it may have seemed to a middle-aged state's attorney. Martin suggested he go home and think it over. They would definitely be in touch.

Oh, he thought about it, and the more he pondered the situation, the more he realized the danger he and Jennie were in. Seeking advice, he called his good friend T. Mills Moore, at that time chief cost clerk at New Orient 2 Mine. Well, Cremer knew that Moore was on good terms with Martin and that if anyone knew what to do his friend was the man.

Cremer and his brother drove to New Orient. After his friend confided the whole story, Moore advised that he "come clean" with Martin. He added that the state's attorney, being a man of his word, would see to it that Cremer's identity would not be revealed. The eyewitness was about to make the most important decision of his life.

T. Mills Moore told his uncle, attorney Frank Moore. Without actually divulging Cremer's name, Frank Moore dropped enough clues that the state's attorney could begin to apply pressure.

When Jesse Cremer finally "told all," Martin nearly "hit the ceiling." From the note alone—the one that Adams was handed by one of the Thomassons and that he was reading when the shooting occurred—the authorities should have guessed that the killers were brothers. Purportedly written by Carl Shelton but actually penned by Birger gangster Connie Ritter, the message read:

Friend Joe:
If you can use these boys please do it.
They are broke and need work. I know their father.
C. S.

What made it even more incredible, Cremer said, was that the Thomassons were the only pair of brothers who were known henchmen of Birger. In return for his information, a promise was made to the eyewitness that he would not be called to the stand should there be a trial.

As much for her own protection as for the need to work, Jennie got a job in Chicago. She stayed with a sister. However, her fiancé was still in West Frankfort—working at the mercantile store by day and staying home each night—and, thus, in danger. Twice, known Birger gangster Harvey Dungey and another questionable fellow stopped by the mercantile store. Their presence was so ominous that one of the store's employees got it in his head that they were planning a robbery. Knowing too well why they were there, Cremer managed to slip out of sight.

In time, Harry Thomasson's confession was splashed across the newspapers; a once-defiant Charlie Birger was finally behind bars. Then came the trial.

True to his word, Roy Martin never called Cremer to the stand, although on the first day of the trial he came very near to breaking his word. Yes, he remembered well their agreement, Martin said, but it might still become necessary for Cremer to give his testimony behind closed doors, for fear Birger's attorneys might try to get Thomasson's confession thrown out. Reluctantly, the eyewitness agreed.

Who should he see in the judge's chambers but Harry Thomasson, friendly as ever. Never mentioning the trouble he was in, the young gangster thought a moment, then said he remembered where they had last met. "It was in front of Joe Adams's house, and your girl had a big red flower on her coat."

"I thought you were going to take a shot at me when you pointed your pistol." Cremer replied.

"Yeah, but I saw who you were. I'd had a couple of drinks before we started to Benton."

At that point, Roy Martin entered the room, saying Cremer could leave—that they "were over the hill on Harry's part."

That same day Cremer saw Birger. Gone was the personality that had charmed numerous women and not a few newspaper reporters. In its place was the icy gaze of a killer whose freedom was at an end.

For Jesse Cremer and Jennie Murray, the nightmare was over. They were married in November 1927.

# 29
# The Sympathetic Hangman

ARLY IN AUGUST 1927, MASSAC COUNTY DEPUTIES LEARNED that certain members of the Birger gang had been seen at a "resort" near Brookport, Illinois. They relayed this information to Sheriff Coleman. On August 12, the Williamson County sheriff and a deputy drove to Metropolis. There they and the Massac County officers pooled their forces and drove to a patch of woods approximately six miles southeast of Metropolis and surrounded the fugitives' haunt.

The next morning, Coleman told the world essentially the story Hyland had given Boswell concerning the killing of Lyle "Shag" Worsham. The two prisoners, Fred "Butch" Thomasson and Joe Booher, alias Clarence Bryant, were charged with Worsham's murder, along with Harvey Dungey, who was then serving a ten-year sentence, in the Chester penitentiary, for murder.

For Coleman, the capture of Thomasson and Booher was a personal triumph. As early as June, he had heard the details of the killing from no less an authority than Art Newman—while the latter was in the Benton jail awaiting trial for the Adams murder. As recently as August 4, Eural Gowan had given his version. That was crucial because, unlike Newman, Gowan claimed he was present when the killing occurred. With the convictions of Rado Millich and Charlie Birger a matter of recent history, Oren Coleman had reason to believe one or more additional death sentences might be in the offing.

Nearly two months passed before the trio went on trial. For Arlie O. Boswell, it was something of a rest period, a time to bask in the triumph of the Jones trial. He, too, felt the upcoming case would be relatively easy to win, since the evidence was clearly on his side.

His sense of well-being was marred by another attempt on his life. With the exception of S. Glenn Young's massive concrete monument in the Herrin Cemetery, the state's attorney was very nearly the most popular target in the county. This time he was returning to his home in Marion from a meeting of the American Legion at Round Pond near Shawneetown. He had planned to follow some fellow legionnaires from Williamson County but lost them on Harrisburg Square. More than fifty years later, too well he remembered:

I guess they had a little speedier car. I never did catch up with them. Before I got to Crab Orchard, I noticed there was a car too close to me, but every time I'd speed up, they would speed up; every time I'd slow down, they'd slow down. I got scared as the devil. I thought once of pulling off at Crab Orchard, but when I came to Crab Orchard, nobody was open at that time of night. I decided, "Well, hell, I've outrun them this far and I'll outrun them yet." I started on through, and just as I got to the west, maybe a quarter of a mile out of Crab Orchard, this car came up along the side of me to pass. As I looked, it looked to me like a fellow was standing on the running board, and just as he got even with me, he began to shoot. I certainly went off to the ditch. They kept on going.

The window on my side was down, but the window on the other side was up. There wasn't but one bullet that went through the car and it went out the right hand side. Nobody understood how that bullet failed to hit me in the head unless at the time I could have ducked down. Anyway, my car came to a stop right up to a concrete abutment. Well, I was scared to death, and I didn't know what to do. And I started my motor and, by damn, it ran. So I waited—I knew they'd turn around and come back—although I felt they felt they'd killed me. They didn't come back, thank God, until another car I saw coming. So I pulled on the road and as it got to me, I rode right in front of the lights all the way into town. I went directly to the police station and reported it. Incidentally, I stayed all night in a hotel that night.

Looking back, Boswell blamed the Birger gangsters, although he never had proof to back his suspicions.

For Birger and Millich, the days and nights of August had the smell of jail about them. Another jailbird, Art Newman, was whisked mysteriously to Taylorville on August 25, where he testified before a grand jury. On August 30, he was returned to Menard.

Later it was learned that the Sheltons were to be tried in Taylorville for the robbery of the Kincaid bank in 1924 and that, as usual, Art Newman was presenting evidence against them. On September 27, four years to the day after the robbery, the brothers surrendered at Taylorville, only to be freed on bond. (The Shelton's subsequent conviction on January 7, 1928, was reversed by the Illinois Supreme Court after a witness recanted his testimony.)

Their other foe, Charlie Birger, had an October 15 execution date hanging over him. Announcement had been made on September 6 that attorney R. E. Smith would appear before supreme court judge Warren Duncan on the following day to ask for a stay of execution, but September 7 came and passed without such a request being made.

On October 5, Birger's lawyers filed a petition for a Writ of Error, with the Illinois Supreme Court, and on October 7, the Court granted a stay of execution. "Birger will not hang. I predict he will die a natural death," gushed Charles Karch when he heard the good news. Even though it was now a certainty that the hanging would not occur in 1927, Birger signed papers the following day for the adoption of Minnie and Charline by his sister, Rachel.

Living in Detroit and married again, the former Beatrice Birger was stunned by the news. From a newspaper account, she had learned that adoption proceedings were under way, and upon her husband's advice, she wired the judge in St. Louis informing him that she was Charline's real mother. Needless to say, her attempt to gain custody was unsuccessful.

Meanwhile, her former husband took some comfort from knowing that his onetime pal and now bitter enemy, Harvey Dungey, had been moved to the Marion jail from Menard on October 10, preparatory to his appearance as a defendant in the upcoming Worsham trial. That was small comfort, however, considering that Dungey's testimony would probably brand Birger as a cold-blooded killer or, worse, a weak leader swayed to unspeakable violence by members of his gang.

As October ticked away, one gang member thought often of the hangman. Despite efforts on his behalf by the Serbian consul in Chicago, Rado Millich still was scheduled to hang on October 21. Time—so slow and wearying when he worked in the mines at Benton and Zeigler—raced for the sad-eyed man with large ears. Before it was gone, he wanted his photograph taken. Heretofore, he had appeared in group shots of men firing at mythical enemies or was shown as one of many gathered around an armored car, doing his best at bravado. But Rado wanted a formal portrait, something to show the world he wasn't such a bad-looking fellow, even for a gangster. The more fortunate Eural Gowan, who would only forfeit his young manhood in prison, also wanted an image— in his case, of youth itself—permanently fixed in black and white. Dressed in their finest, the two were manacled and placed under a heavy guard, then marched to a local studio.

After the sitting, Millich asked how long they would have to wait for the results. When the photographer replied a little too casually that the prints would be ready in about a week, Millich insisted that he hurry, since he had only eleven days left to live. It was only after he was assured that the prints would be ready before October 21 that he allowed a smile to break through his otherwise sad countenance.

October 21 also disturbed the thoughts of Oren Coleman, who usually kept his ruminations to himself. Shaken to discover that as sheriff, he was also expected to be Millich's hangman, Coleman immediately began to look for someone to take his place. Boswell suggested Phil Hanna of Epworth, a gentleman farmer who was known throughout the Midwest as "the sympathetic hangman." The two officials wasted no time motoring to White County to secure Hanna's services. Boswell recalled that long-ago conversation in the hangman's home:

*Coleman:* "What is your price?"

*Hanna:* "I'm afraid, Mr. Coleman, that you can't pay the price."

*Coleman:* "Just what is your price?"

*Hanna:* "The price will not come from you, Mr. Coleman. It will come from the state's attorney here, Mr. Boswell." [A pause. He had their attention.]

*Hanna:* "The hanging, I believe, is to be at 10:00. Five minutes of ten, I will be in Boswell's office. Nobody else is to be there but Boswell. Setting on his desk will be a quart of Old Taylor whiskey and in another container will be a quart of water with ice. After the hanging, I will go directly to Boswell's office, and no one will be there but him, and still setting on that desk will be what is left of that quart of whiskey and fresh water and ice. After five minutes, he may invite to his office anyone he wants.

"Now you, Mr. Coleman, thirty minutes before the hanging, I will be at your jail. I will want you to take me into the cell of Mr. Millich, and I will talk to him until ten minutes before the hanging, when I will leave for the office of Mr. Boswell. I will return to the scaffold promptly at 10:00. If the victim desires to make any statements, he will make those statements, and that you will have to ascertain. And when he has completed his statements and you nod, I will put the black hood over his head and adjust the noose around his neck, and I will nod to you and you will spring the trap. Gentlemen, it has been good to talk to you. Good day, and I will see you October 21."

Was it some repressed blood lust that drove this middle-aged, seemingly gentle man to take the lives of convicted killers? Hardly. Thirty years earlier, young Phil Hanna had had the misfortune to see a man strangled to death as a result of a hangman's ineptitude. Since that time, he had become an authority on ropes and knots and other paraphernalia usually associated with death on the gallows. All this to ensure that the victim died quickly and painlessly.

The night of October 20 was a somber one in the Marion jail. To liven it up a bit, one of the prisoners turned, with his finger, the turntable of a broken-down record player, thereby flooding the closeness and dark with a scratching melody.

His wasted life almost finished, Rado Millich bade farewell to

his fellow prisoners. Among the recipients of the gangster's parting remarks were two youngsters who were spending the night in
jail for committing some minor offense. These two, in particular,
Rado admonished to "go straight," lest, like him, they someday
find themselves facing a last tomorrow.

It was a night for visiting. From Franklin County came a family
with whom Millich had boarded when he worked in a coal mine
at Zeigler. Also, some of his countrymen—whom he had known
before the gangster days—came to pay their respects. As well as
he could, Rado thanked each for stopping by. Less welcome was
Arlie O. Boswell, who earlier in the day had learned that a vindic-
tive Millich was spreading tales about his involvement in some of
the unsolved crimes of the Birger gang. Ill-timed and awkward
though the confrontation was sure to be, Boswell felt it important
that they talk.

"Rado," he said, "I hear that you are sore at me," thus under-
stating considerably the condemned man's grievances. Less than
clever at the best of times, Millich could only mumble that he was
being framed.

Was it true he was accusing him of ordering the Prices killed,
and of plotting with Birger to kill Sheriff Coleman, Boswell asked?

"You know I tell the truth," Millich replied.

Staring at him for a moment, the state's attorney asked the prisoner where he was when those crimes were committed and was
satisfied to hear him reply, "In the penitentiary."

The halting strains of the phonograph drifted through the midnight silence. Millich and the other prisoners played cards until
almost dawn.

The weather on the morning of October 21 provided no somber
backdrop to the execution soon to occur in the boarded-up area
beside the Marion jail. Better a chilling rain or a storm punctu-
ated with the roll of thunder than the beautiful harvest weather—
a sky like a vast blue glass bell and, beneath it, in fields that might
have been painted by N. C. Wyeth, pumpkins half the size of
washtubs. This was the time for young men to be in those fields
and for old men to read a mild or mean winter in the thickness of
the corn shucks. Yet here, just off the Marion Square, the meaning
of harvest was twisted, as young men and old gathered to watch a
man die. The "lucky" ones were admitted into the jail yard. One

of the young fellows had earlier asked Sheriff Coleman for a pass but, instead, had been handed a machine gun. He was now a guard.

Shortly before 10:00 A.M., Millich emerged from a side door of the jail. As his fellow prisoners watched from the barred windows of the two-story structure, he walked briskly toward the scaffold, mounting it two steps at a time. Standing on the trapdoor, he raised his manacled hands to the prisoners watching from the second story.

Also on the platform were Sheriff Coleman, Sheriff Pritchard, Sheriff Petrie of Belleville, Williamson County deputies Brady Jenkins and Joe Schafer, and the inevitable Phil Hanna. Among those witnessing the execution was Arlie O. Boswell, who watched as Petrie and Schafer tied the prisoner's arms and legs with leather straps. Once this procedure was completed, Boswell saw Coleman take a folded piece of paper from Millich's pocket, unfold it, and hand it to him. As well as he could, Millich read the typewritten letter:

Ladies and Gentlemen: I stand before you this morning for the last time. You no doubt wonder just how I feel. In these, my last few words, I want to say, as I have said ever since I was arrested on this charge, I killed Ward Jones in self-defense. People some day will know the truth, and they'll find out they killed an innocent man. I may not have been everything I should or could have been—I have done wrong, I know that—but when my last breath is breathed, I shall still be thinking and knowing and feeling I should never have been hung for killing Ward Jones.

None of you people would have hung for killing him. He was a machine gun man and had threatened to kill me. Ray Hyland told you people Jones was drunk that day and said he was going to get somebody. Harry Thomasson told Harvey Dungey at Chester he had come down here and swore a pack of lies because Boswell told him to, and he has offered to sign affidavits to that effect. My lawyers say they do all they can for me. Charlie Birger was to hang on October 15, but he's still alive. I was poor, and nobody cared anything about me. I never went to school a day in my life, but I know when they frame a fellow. I got out of prison on parole, but the mines were not working, and I had to get work any place I could, but I was not a gangster. . . .

After desperately trying to salvage one moment of glory from an existence bereft of grandeur or eloquence, Millich began tearing the letter into pieces, but he kept talking:

> I want to say to you people here that the man sending me to the gallows, Arlie O. Boswell, is the man who had Lory Price and wife killed, and some day you will know that I tell the truth. Also, that when Charlie Birger's cabin was burned, Charlie Birger himself was in the front line.

He handed the remnants of the letter to Coleman. "Thank you, go ahead," he said.

Over his head went the black hood. Phil Hanna adjusted the noose. At a signal from Hanna, Coleman tried to kick open the trapdoor.

"Sheriff Coleman kicked the trap," recalled Joe Schafer. "Just about that time, Rado went off balance, fell over in my hands, and I had to drop him through the trap, after he went down. It was a mess."

Interviewed about the incident five years later, Hanna would blame the "mess," as Schafer called it, less on Sheriff Coleman's ineptitude than on Millich's refusal to take the narcotic that was customarily made available to the condemned. Brave as he was, the man under the black hood fainted the moment before the trap door banged opened, plummeting him into Eternity.

However ineptly the trap was sprung, the jail seemed to shake with the sound, or so recalled a prisoner watching at the time. He also remembered Fred Thomasson holding his head in his hands as he cried aloud, "Oh, my God! Oh, my God!"

When reporters asked his reaction to Millich's parting remarks, Boswell quickly replied, "Why should I deny anything that a gangster or any condemned man might say?" Privately, however, he did not shrug off the matter so lightly, believing that Coleman had not only written the letter but also encouraged Millich to denounce him publicly.

From his cell in Benton, Birger defended Boswell, calling the charges the "last shot of a poor dumb fool at the man who had sent him to die." While he disagreed with much of what Millich had to say, both about Boswell and himself, he could find no fault with the man's "game" manner at the end. He had really never liked Millich, had distrusted him in the beginning, but now that the homely Montenegrin had faced death defiantly, he could only shake his head and hope that he would conduct himself as well at his own hanging.

# 30
# Lucky Boys

THE TRIAL OF HARVEY DUNGEY, JOE BOOHER, AND FRED THOMAS-
son for the murder of Lyle "Shag" Worsham began in Marion
on December 12, 1927. Representing Dungey was John Reid
of Marion. Hal Gallimore of Carterville represented Booher.
George Crichton of Herrin represented Thomasson. Both Gallimore and Crichton were court appointed.

As presented by the prosecution through its two eyewitnesses,
Clarence Rone and Eural Gowan, the story of the Worsham murder had a quality of senselessness that had come to typify murders
committed by the Birger gang. It had all begun, they said, when
Harvey Dungey began to suspect Lyle "Shag" Worsham of being too friendly with the Shelton faction. Taken by Dungey and
Thomasson from a resort in Zeigler, Worsham was driven to
Shady Rest, where he waited in Dungey's Hudson coach while the
gangsters debated his fate. At first, Birger did not believe the allegations, but Dungey was insistent, saying, "I'll show you whether
he is guilty or not." He, Booher, and Thomasson got into the
Hudson. Birger, Ritter, Steve George, Ward Jones, and others got
into a Lincoln.

They followed Dungey's car to an isolated area about five miles
south of Carterville. There, while the Lincoln's headlights glared
fully upon him, Worsham was told how he would die. If, by some
miracle, he were lucky enough to escape their gunfire and reach

the top of a certain low hill, his life would be spared. Having no choice in the matter, the young man started to run but was cut down by the machine guns of Ward Jones and Steve George. According to Rone, Jones then finished him with a .45 automatic.

The cars were driven about a mile south. They turned around. Here Birger said something to Dungey and his passengers. Back they drove to where the body lay. After it was placed in the Hudson, both cars were driven toward Marion. At the W. T. Watkins filling station at the outskirts of town, Birger bought a five-gallon can of gasoline. Again, the cars headed south, this time to the Pulley's Mill area near the Johnson County line. Searching for a likely spot in which to deposit their victim, the gangsters found an abandoned farmhouse filled with broomcorn. After Worsham's body was carried inside, Steve George poured gasoline on the premises, and when all were in the clear, Birger struck the match, then tossed it. Back they drove to Marion, their dark secret consumed by the roaring brightness.

Such was the tale told by the two gangsters. Although Rone and Gowan gave basically the same account, they did not fully agree on the identity of the men who rode in the second car. According to Gowan, Birger was accompanied by Steve George, Ward Jones, Connie Ritter, Clarence Rone, Bert Owens, and himself. Rone, however, included the foregoing (with the exception of Bert Owens) but added to the list Paul Stanley, Jimmy McQuay (he probably meant "Highpockets"), and Ted Nurocke. The discrepancy in the two accounts was not lost upon the defendants' attorneys.

All three defendants at the trial wore blue suits and had ready alibis. Booher, whose somewhat stockier build and "pleasant countenance" set him apart from his two codefendants, claimed that from September 17 until October 1, 1926, he was at his home in Indiana visiting a sister who had been injured in an automobile accident (Later, on the witness stand, several relatives would support Booher's alibi.)

Thin-faced Fred Thomasson testified that at the time of the murder, he was in bed in his farm home in Franklin County, suffering from an attack of appendicitis. (From Menard came his brother, Harry, to back him up.) Short, dark-complexioned Harvey Dungey insisted he was hunting and working at his father-in-law's farm at the time Worsham was abducted and murdered. (His mother-in-law testified that Harvey and her husband spent the day of September 17 cutting corn.)

As for witnesses Rone and Gowan, Dungey claimed they were waging a personal vendetta against him. Gowan was "sore" at him for not testifying at the Jones trial. (Answering this charge, the prosecution later would show that Dungey did, indeed, testify for Gowan at the trial.) And Clarence Rone had threatened him for revealing details of the Price murders. Dungey also suspected that the dynamiting of a building he had owned in West Frankfort was Rone's doing.

Dungey, who had made accusations against Boswell for some-time, was hoping to be cross-examined by the state's attorney in order to get a few of his charges into the record. When Boswell chose to forego the expected questioning, the defendant was heard to mutter, "That's what I suspected." The jury saw the smile on the state's attorney's face.

To counter Booher's claim that he was in Indiana during the time of the murder, the prosecution called a well-dressed young woman who operated the New Grand Hotel in West Frankfort. She brought with her to the stand the hotel register, a formidable volume containing the useful information that Joe Booher was a registered guest at the hotel on September 15, 18, and 27, 1926.

That no such evidence existed as to the whereabouts of the two on September 17 did not deter Boswell's assistant, C. Ray Smith, from suggesting—in reply to Fred Thomasson's protestation of illness—"That's the first time I ever heard the operation of killing a man with a gun called appendicitis." As for Dungey's alleged two-day trip to Hamilton County, "confirmed" by his mother-in-law, Smith said that the woman had perjured herself to prevent further shame to her grandchildren.

That relatives would lie to save the necks of their kinsmen was to be expected, threats of perjury aside. But during the five-day trial there came testimony from undertaker Bert Scobey, testimony that would have been unsettling to Boswell had it not seemed so absurd at the time. After examining the charred remains, Scobey said, he was convinced the body was that of a woman. The prose-cution would brand that a ridiculous inference, but the damage was done. Seizing on the remark, defense attorneys hammered into the jury the fact that a leading undertaker of Marion had put his reputation on the line by testifying that "Shag" Worsham could not have burned in the broom maker's barn.

"Hang them for this most diabolic murder in the history of Williamson County, or turn them loose," came Boswell's final argument. (His less than lengthy summation was due to a head cold and sore throat.) "Not that I want blood," he continued, "but these defendants have by their acts placed the rope around their necks. I am not asking you to take the lives of three men. I am not asking you to kill them. I am willing to take my part in the responsibility. I am only asking you to stand with me and Oren Coleman."

Three and a half hours later, the jury returned a verdict of not guilty. Entering the courtroom as Judge Hartwell announced the verdict, Boswell was more than stunned. "I never fainted but once," he said, "and that was when that jury returned the verdict of not guilty." It seemed clear to him that Scobey's testimony had been the key factor in the jury's decision.

In its editorial, "The Verdict," the *Marion Daily Republican* stated that the decision had "shocked the community more than anything that has happened in many months." Bitter that his efforts had come to naught, Sheriff Coleman refused comment, but his dour expression said it all. Boswell, who rarely refused comment on anything, said he no longer felt Williamson County was the place to try those accused of murdering the Prices and that by default, the case should go to Washington County. Both counties had returned indictments.

Word of the trio's acquittal brought a wistful comment from Birger. "Lucky boys," he said, "they sure got a break." When shown attorney Reid's closing statement comparing him with Pontius Pilate, Birger could not keep from smiling.

# 31
# "It's a Beautiful World"

CLOCKS TICKED AND SEASONS TURNED, BUT FOR CHARLES BIRGER, the iron bars enclosed what future remained for him. Hope had all but vanished after the Illinois Supreme Court denied his appeal for a new trial on February 24 and set April 13 as the date for his hanging. Less than a month after this decision was announced, his attorneys, Charles Karch and Scerial Thompson, withdrew from the defense, leaving R. E. Smith as Birger's sole attorney. As spokesman for the two, Karch said their former client showed an unwillingness to cooperate with them in efforts to get his sentence reduced to life imprisonment. He was unclear as to what those efforts were.

Following the Illinois Supreme Court's denial of yet another rehearing petition, Smith was successful in his request for an appearance before the Board of Pardons and Parole, in Springfield, the day before the scheduled hanging. The morning of April 12 found Smith and Martin making their respective pleas before the Board. Listening to each of them and following with his own appeal was Arlie O. Boswell, who had been driven to the hearing during the night by Birger's brother-in-law, Jake Shamsky.

The state's attorney pleaded that the condemned man's life be extended so that he might gather from him additional information concerning the Price murders. Furious at this interference,

Roy Martin charged, "This is more a friendship matter than an official matter," adding that his colleague to the south knew far too much already about the various crimes. At this point, the hearing very nearly turned into a fistfight. In a split decision, the Board voted against the stay.

Not yet defeated, Smith returned to Benton, arriving in time to file for a sanity hearing. Judge Miller granted his petition, much to the chagrin of Martin, who had himself hurried back to Franklin County to counter any last ditch effort to prolong Birger's life. With April 16 now set as the date of the hearing, Birger saw his life extended by at least three days. It was a wearying business, this staying alive, and he was later to say the hearing was Smith's idea. If so, it was not one of his better ones.

Rolling his eyes, swearing at hostile witnesses, tussling with Harry Weaver, one of Pritchard's deputies, Birger put on an embarrassing, unconvincing performance—one that added nothing to his legend. But in the midst of his disgrace came the testimony of another deputy, Charles Smith, a testimony that did touch up the legend a bit and that indicated that the wit long familiar to querying newspapermen had not yet abandoned the gang leader. The witness said on one occasion that Birger had requested burial in a Roman Catholic cemetery because that would be the last place the devil would think of looking for a Jew. Bob Smith wasn't laughing.

He was not much more impressed by their only witness, a barbecue stand operator from DuQuoin who had known Birger in Harrisburg and who had visited him two months earlier in the jail. Yes, said Orris McGlasson, he believed his old friend was crazy, because Charlie reminded him of patients he had known while working at the Anna State Hospital.

It took the jury only twelve minutes to find the defendant legally sane. Smith let it be known shortly thereafter that the long fight was over. "This is the end of the road," he said.

That night, Birger ripped off a strip of his blanket, tied one end to one of the horizontal bars in the cell and the other end around his neck. When the guards found him he was unconscious, but they quickly revived him. He requested that they keep the matter a secret. It was later revealed that two days earlier, he had taken arsenic. "I swallowed enough to kill three men, but I guess I took too much," he told the guards. He could hear the hammering of the scaffold.

From throughout the Midwest, newsmen arrived, hoping to get an exclusive interview with Birger in the hours before the hanging. Sheriff Pritchard told them that his prisoner had become disgusted with being constantly misquoted and wanted them "out of his sight." The sheriff added he intended to honor the man's wishes. From Epworth came Phil Hanna to test the trap and the rope, as he had done in his sixty previous hangings. While he worked, he could hear the prisoner raving—an unnerving experience for this gentle, middle-aged hangman.

No doubt chagrined at being denied access to the condemned, Elva Jones of the *Marion Evening Post* at least hoped that Birger would reveal to someone his inside information about certain crimes, including the shootings at the Masonic Temple in 1926, where, according to Jones, Birger shot Harland Ford from behind a car and where a wounded Noble Weaver begged for his life even as an unnamed man stepped from the temple and shot him, and shot him, and shot him again.

Despite his warning to newsmen, made through Pritchard, Birger consented to spend the night of April 18, his last, with Roy Alexander of the *St. Louis Post-Dispatch*. The young reporter heard a litany of past mistakes, broken occasionally by an anecdote. In particular, Birger talked of his former wife, Edna, who had traveled to Benton with her husband from their home in the northwest. Oh, she was a good one, he said, and by far the best of his wives, certainly the only one who cared enough to return for the hanging. Bea he had not seen in years, and even Bernice, so conspicuous at his trial—even she was gone. She worked in a factory somewhere near Chicago. Chances are he did not touch upon the unexpected visit by Winnie Mofield (the mother of his oldest daughter, Minnie) weeks earlier, a visit that had degenerated into a scene and a tearful exit by Winnie. In the end, there was only Edna, the big blonde who had loved him when he was only a penny-ante bootlegger on his way up, the one he hadn't had sense enough to keep.

He told of his being so caught up in a fervor on Armistice Day that he shot out the lights on the Harrisburg town square. One time he even shot up some canned goods in a store he ran.

As a gambler and bootlegger, he spent money as quickly as it came and had a grand time doing so—but he made enemies, too. Four times a coroner's jury ruled in his favor. Then came a dovetailing of circumstances that resulted in a number of senseless killings, and one of them now brought him within the shadow of the gallows.

He lamented the passing of his slain friend, Noble Weaver, former kingpin of Franklin County's underworld activities and, according to Birger, a totally fearless man. "All [Weaver] had to do was to tell Joe and Gus Adams to do a thing and they'd do it," he said, the implication being that Weaver's death following the Masonic Temple shootout at Herrin in 1926 had indirectly led to the murder of Joe Adams and thence to his own imminent demise.

"Just Another Day Wasted Away" droned from a phonograph in another cell as on and on he rambled, touching here a wry anecdote and there a very real truth. Once he had a friend who, while looking for a bargain in stale bread, had a tire worth $15 stolen from his car. The story of his life.

On a darker note, he held the local officials partly responsible for the atmosphere of lawlessness that had plagued southern Illinois and provided him with such opportunity, saying, "I can see it now, that it all came about because there was no law. The gangsters ran the country down here, just like they have for years. Sometimes I think they ought to give the country back to the Indians."

In the early hours of the morning, Bob Smith came for a last visit. For about half an hour, he listened as Birger talked. After their brief but poignant parting, the gangster confided that the sanity hearing had been Smith's idea and that he was ready to die on the 13th. When asked about his suicide attempts, Birger said he had prayed to God to stop his heart, but he now conceded he would have to die in the manner prescribed by law.

Throughout the night he seemed calm, although Alexander observed that in reminiscing, Birger's voice had a richer tone. Of his enemies he spoke without vindictiveness, recalling them as though participants in a drama where he played the starring role.

Daylight found him haggard, still talking. Though his voice remained even, it was clear from his foot movements and the tensing of his neck muscles that he was very nervous. And when Arlie O. Boswell came to talk to him later in the morning, Birger exploded. In Boswell's words:

> I walked in to where he was—and he had a bathrobe on and was walking up and down in his cell. I said, "Good morning, Charlie. How are you feeling?"
>
> He stopped just like he had been hit. He said, "How in the goddamned hell do you think you'd be feeling if you knew you had only thirty more minutes to live?"
>
> "Well," I said, "Charlie, I'm sorry. I didn't mean it that way at all. That's an expression that I always use. I'm sorry."

Except to say goodbye, this last visit was a wasted effort on Boswell's part, since Birger refused to give him the names and dates relating to the Price murders, with one exception. With death only minutes away, the gangster could not refrain from taking one last swing at the man he felt was helping send him to the gallows. "Art Newman is the man you want," he said.

While Boswell and Birger were saying goodbye, Sheriff Coleman and his deputies arrived from Williamson County. Because he had helped drop Rado Millich to his doom, Joe Schafer was asked to set the trap, and set it he did.

In the streets, on buildings, within the stockade, armed guards scanned the crowd. At approximately 9:45, Sheriff Pritchard led the condemned man down the jailhouse steps, around the corner to the scaffold erected beneath Birger's cell. Before mounting those thirteen steps, Birger did not fail to notice the wicker basket where soon his body would lie. One reporter wrote that he spat into it. True or not, the gesture would have been fitting, considering that he had an audience of a half thousand ticket holders within the stockade, countless other spectators perched on the rooftop of the city hall, and still others crowding the windows of a building across the way. Faces appeared in trees and at the windows of the jail cells.

First to climb the steps was Oren Coleman. Jim Pritchard followed. Next came Phil Hanna, followed by Sheriff W. T. Flannigan of Jackson County. The fifth man up was Charlie Birger. A deputy from Franklin County walked behind him. His eyes never leaving the Bible in his hand, Rabbi J. R. Mazur of East St. Louis slowly ascended the wooden steps. He was followed by another of Pritchard's deputies.

After walking to his assigned spot over the trapdoor, Birger "smartly executed a left face," acknowledged several in the audience, and waited. As one of the deputies knelt to strap the prisoner's legs, Phil Hanna stepped forward to ask forgiveness for the terrible task he was about to perform. Birger said he had forgiven everybody, thanks to the Rabbi's counseling. "You're a great old boy," he said to Hanna moments later when the big man pulled tight the straps around his chest and arms.

Looking to the sky, where tufts of clouds drifted upon the blue, Birger may have remembered that Rado Millich was also hanged on a beautiful day. That, however, didn't stop the Montenegrin from lashing out at Birger and Boswell while tearing his typed speech into shreds. This time there was to be no speech and no raving as had marked the sanity hearing—only sky above, faces below, and a man in a blue serge suit standing on a scaffold between trapdoor and infinity, and one timeless remark. "It's a beautiful world," Birger said softly.

Other things he said that morning were duly reported and quickly forgotten. But that one line, heard only by a few, would make the front pages and be repeated in sermons, on street corners, and in homes, until at last it became a part of the Birger legend, a counterweight (like the groceries left at the doors of the poor) to his many victims.

Phil Hanna had visited Birger in his cell only a few minutes earlier. Apparently, this time the procedure went as scheduled, and the appropriate narcotic was administered. When asked if he wanted a white or black hood, Birger took the opportunity to direct a faint jab at an old foe, the late S. Glenn Young. "Black," he said with a flourish, adding that he was no "Ku Klux."

Prior to pulling the hood over the victim's head, Hanna was careful to keep the well-oiled, expertly noosed rope behind his back. He always did that, out of respect. His display of good manners on such a grim occasion may have struck his fellow executioners as being a trifle, old-fashioned, if not downright absurd.

Was Birger finally at peace, now that the black hood was over his head and the clock ticked toward the appointed time of 10:00 A.M.? Tradition would have us believe so, but not so, said Sheriff Flannigan, who noticed the "withering death stare—half sneer, half grin"—that the condemned man leveled toward Jim Pritchard just before the hood was lowered.

With the end of his life only minutes away, Birger asked that they hurry it up. That wish was granted at 9:48, according to Alpheus Gustin, one of the many from Harrisburg who had driven to Benton for the occasion. Watching the drama from the top of a building, Willard St. John saw the rope "spin like a top" after the trap was sprung. The man who had set the trap did not see it function. Assuming that the execution would not occur until 10:00 A.M., Joe Schafer had heeded Judge Hartwell's request to "go out and get some of the men in here [the city hall] that I want in." Minutes later, as the last public hanging in Illinois was under way, Schafer recalled, "I looked around and the Judge was trying to get in the city hall window. I couldn't get in at all. I missed it all."

Despite the fact that Birger died owing him money, Charles V. Parker warned his employees that day in Harrisburg not to make wisecracks. He warned them not even to comment about the hanging in Benton.

Five minutes after the trapdoor crashed under his feet, Birger was pronounced dead by the doctors. Briefly, Boswell saw the body as it was carried in the wicker basket to the hearse. "I wanted to be sure, through curiosity only, that his neck was broken," Boswell recalled. A close friend of the state's attorney, Willard St. John, did not understand the reason for the hats on the wicker basket as it was carried along. No doubt this was a mark of respect for the dead.

"Speed cops" stationed near the ambulance were taunted by several men who, St. John believed, were gangsters. This was not likely, considering the number of armed guards Jim Pritchard had stationed throughout the area.

Birger's last trip to St. Louis did not begin immediately. His body was taken to a Benton undertaking parlor, where it remained while the hearse, doubling as an ambulance, was sent out to pick up an old woman who had been knocked down by a barn door on that windy morning. Meanwhile, with her head in her hands, Rachel Shamsky waited inside the mortuary. The delay gave Boswell the opportunity to inspect the corpse in the wicker basket more closely. The neck was visibly stretched, he said, and a telltale depression on the side of the neck where the knot had been, was proof that Phil Hanna had, as usual, done his job well. "No question about it, his neck was broken."

At last the hearse and its police escort began the long trip west. Maintaining a speed of about forty miles an hour, the entourage reached the Chesed Shel Emeth Cemetery in University City just before 4:00 P.M. There, about seventy-five friends and relatives had gathered. Although no rabbi was present, one of Charlie's brothers—probably Samuel—read a Hebrew prayer for the dead.

One reporter was still not satisfied that Birger had paid in full for the chaos he had brought to a region already known nationwide for its lawlessness. Elva Jones of the *Marion Evening Post* harked back to the fiery sermons in lantern-lit churches for the proper summing up of a man who had once reminded the reporter "of the western heroes of the movies."

But those kind words were written when Birger was Lord of the Manor at Shady Rest. Having heard so much about the gang leader, Jones was surprised to feel "safe" in his presence. Gun-toting thugs alert to the first hint of trouble remained on guard, and that fact may have contributed to this sense of security.

That interview had been in golden October—or more than two months before the murders of Lory and Ethel Price. Now, with the trapdoor so recently sounding for all the world like a shotgun blast enhanced by megaphone, Jones saw the need for a second opinion. Looking back over events of months past, he now recalled that all along he knew Birger "was crazy, blood crazy, man crazy, murder crazy."

Jones had been denied the privilege of hearing the gang leader that last night in his cell tell one story after another—such honor was reserved for Roy Alexander, who represented the same big city newspaper young Charlie had once hawked on the streets of St. Louis. Still, Jones wanted the last word and felt he had a right to it.

In southern Illinois, Charlie Birger had loved and entertained and murdered and died—all in a dramatic fashion. Reflecting upon such a career, the crack reporter of the *Marion Evening Post* could do no less than inject the very spirit and drama of which the region was famous into his editorial: "For his breakfast in hell we'd suggest two bowls of TNT mixed with his favorite 'soup,' for his dinner the rat-tat-tat of machine gun fire as bullets pierce his malicious body, and for supper all the torment and anguish, grief and pain . . . " In his zeal to write the last word on the enigmatic Charlie Birger, Elva Jones only added to the legend.

It was left to "Ray" to pay the burial expenses, which amounted to $430, or so she claimed three years later while trying to beg a burial allowance from the government. Her request was refused on the grounds that the deceased had served in no "war, campaign, or expedition." In the cold print of a form letter, a legend lost some of its luster. Still, her claim application preceding those dull two inches of prose must have brought an admiring chuckle from her brother's ghost. She claimed to be Charlie Birger's widow.

## 32
# A Bystander Who Had Stumbled into a Nightmare

FTER A DELAY OF SEVERAL MONTHS, THE TRIAL OF THE AC-
cused murderers of Ethel Price finally began early in the afternoon of January 7, 1929, in the Williamson County courthouse. Arlie O. Boswell, who had earlier boasted he would hang
Newman, had meanwhile suffered a defeat at the polls the preceding November. More recently, he had been indicted for conspiring
to violate the National Prohibition Act and was awaiting the
charges against him to fly, as he knew they would.

Of the ten who were indicted, only four were actually tried, the
others being either dead or still at large. The men, Art Newman,
Freddie Wooten, Riley Simmons, and one other, were tried on two
counts each of murder and two other counts of conspiracy to
commit murder.

By agreement with Boswell's successor, J. Roy Browning, Newman's attorney, Delos Duty, entered a plea of guilty on behalf of
his client, as did his fellow attorneys for their own clients. Despite
these guilty pleas, Judge Hartwell insisted on hearing the prosecution evidence before passing sentence, and that afternoon Art
Newman took the stand.

Newman said Lory Price was abducted after Boswell told Birger
the patrolman had sent a letter to the president of the Pocahontas

bank promising to name those who had committed the robbery in return for the $2,500 reward being offered at the time. When confronted with this accusation, Price was quick to call Boswell a liar, but his accusers were not completely convinced.

In the middle of January, Newman continued, Boswell again approached Birger, this time insisting that Lory Price had to be killed. The anxiety of the state's attorney was well founded, for he had not only kept $2,700 in marketable bonds taken in the robbery, Newman said, but he had also shared the split in the stolen car racket operated by the Birger gang, Price, and Boswell. The gang would steal the cars, Boswell would learn which of the stolen vehicles carried rewards, and those that did were invariably "discovered" by Price along the roadsides where the thieves had abandoned them. The three-way split of the rewards had proved very profitable for all concerned, according to Newman. Once Price started talking, his revelations, even those made unwittingly, could destroy them all. He had to be hushed up and very quickly.

To add salt to the wounds of the former state's attorney, who sat nearby chewing an unlighted cigar, Newman added some extra charges that seemed irrelevant to the Price case itself, but which, if true, would certainly indicate Boswell's involvement with the Birger gang. On the night of April 12, 1926, Boswell, the witness testified, had met the gang at the County Line roadhouse, between West Frankfort and Johnston City, and had told them to "shoot hell out of Herrin" the following day and, while doing so, to kill John Ford, one of the poll watchers and a noted Klansman. As deputy circuit clerk of Williamson County, Ford had the bad habit of checking too closely into criminal records.

A few days after the shootings, Boswell again met with the gangsters. Angry that they had killed the wrong Ford—John's brother, Harland—he gave them the "make" of the man's car and told them the approximate time he drove to work from Herrin to Marion. He also urged Ritter and Newman to visit the newly elected sheriff, Oren Coleman, in his office, for the purpose of "feeling him out" as to his stand on bootlegging. Later, when he learned they could get no answer from the taciturn ex-schoolteacher, Boswell said he would visit Coleman on his own. Apparently this effort was equally fruitless, for soon the word came down that both Coleman and Ford were to be killed.

As could be expected, the charges created a sensation. Shaken by the mounting accusations, Boswell was quick to reply: "If I've done all these things, I ought to be put away. If the officers believe one iota of it, and having known it for a long time, they have been sorely negligent in the performance of their duty in not having sworn out a warrant and had me arrested."

The sensation created by these charges tended to overshadow details of the abduction and killing of Lory and Ethel Price. What Newman revealed about this crime matched, in general, the story told later by other defendants. As usual, he presented his role as that of a bystander who had stumbled into a nightmare.

Sometime after midnight on January 17, 1927, two carloads of Birger gangsters arrived at the patrolman's home in Scotsboro, a community just north of Marion. Several men went inside. Presently Lory Price, Birger, Wooten, and Newman got into Newman's car. A short time later, Ethel Price, accompanied by Ernest Blue, Connie Ritter, Riley "Alabama" Simmons, and another man got into the second car.

According to Newman, Price was first driven to Birger's home in Harrisburg. They went there, Birger told Simmons's pal Frank Shrader, to kill Jack Crews. Both men were staying in the house at the time. Shrader ignored the order. (One of the ten originally indicted for the Price killings, Shrader could not be found at the time of the trial. The charges against his codefendant, Crews, were dropped.)

Back at Shady Rest, or what remained of it, Price and his abductors got out of the car and went into the barbecue stand. As the long-legged patrolman sat on one of the porcelain tables, defending his innocence, Birger continued his tirade. Among other things, he insisted Price had tipped off the Sheltons that the cabin was unguarded prior to the attack, that he had informed officials at the Pocahontas bank that the Birger gang had committed the robbery, and that, in general, he talked too much. Then he shot Price twice.

Although seriously but not fatally wounded, Price was still denying the allegations when the second car pulled in. Rather proud of the night's work, Connie Ritter announced on entering, "We've got rid of the woman and threw her in a pit north of Marion." The groaning patrolman was wrapped in a piece of canvas and taken to Newman's Chrysler—much to that gangster's chagrin, it should be added, for his car was paid for and the Buick was stolen. Birger sat on Price's shoulder as Newman drove the car. Those in the Buick followed.

Finding a guard at a mine shaft near DuQuoin, they drove on, arriving at last at an abandoned schoolhouse. Had it not been for a steady rain, this tumbledown relic would have served as a final and fiery resting place for their old pal Lory. Their plan was to drive to the Okaw Bottoms, but because Newman's car was running low on gasoline, they pulled off the road near DuBois, in Washington County. Still pleading for what was left of his life, Lory Price was dragged or carried into a field and shot. The man who recounted the events of the night as effortlessly as he might have described a poker game claimed he and Freddie Wooten stayed in the car while the *coup de grace* was administered to the patrolman among the rattling, frozen weeds of winter.

Listening to this gruesome tale, Arlie O. Boswell had reason to believe that Newman was lying. Another of the defendants, one he had come to trust, had given him a far different account. As Boswell recalled in my interview:

They brought him out [to the barbecue stand] and old "Slim" was sitting on the table—didn't have his puttees on, they brought him out too quick—and he was swinging his legs. They were talking to him and he was denying it, and Charlie more or less appeared to be in favor of "Slim." Just about that time, two other guys walked in and Lory said, "Where's Ethel?" They said, "Why?"

This was when the firecrackers started. Newman said, "You lying son of a bitch, you'll be where she is in a very few minutes!" Lory threw his hand up and said, "You mean something's happened to Ethel?" Newman said, "Yes, the same goddamned thing that has happened to you," and BINGO, he [Price] took it right in the guts.

Well, at that—Birger didn't have a gun—he grabbed a gun from one of the boys there, and he started for Newman. Birger was grabbed and Newman was grabbed and there was quite a little wrestle around there. And when it was over, Birger said, "Look what you've done now, you son of a bitch. I should have killed you long ago." Art said, "Yes, I know, but you were afraid to kill me. You know I had too much on you."

Well, Charlie kinda cooled off and said, "We've got to get rid of this right now. Somebody comes in here and we're in one hell of a shape." And they began to scurry around, and they put him [Price] in the car and they drove off.

One of those accompanying Mrs. Price had assumed both parties would meet at the mine. In the presence of his wife, "Slim" would be threatened, maybe slapped around a little. Perhaps even Ethel Price would be threatened to further impress upon her husband the dire consequences of "squealing" to the authorities. When they arrived at that desolate spot, this Birger gang member was surprised to discover that "Slim" and the others were nowhere to be found. When Mrs. Price complained of the cold, he put his coat around her shoulders. Still, Newman's car had not arrived.

Even Ethel Price was apparently unaware that she was to be murdered that night. The truth became apparent, however, when Ritter ordered one of the men to kill her. Rumrunner and associate of thugs though he was, the young man in question was above killing an innocent woman, and he said so in the most scathing terms. Ritter was stunned. The less squeamish Ernest Blue, along with Ritter, fired the fatal shots, dropped their victim into the darkness, then covered her with debris.

Here the informant's account differs sharply both from Newman's version and the one told by Boswell. They were driving back to Harrisburg, he says, and were about two miles east of Shady Rest when Newman's car passed them going west. Badly shaken but otherwise unharmed, "Slim" was on his way home. Both automobiles pulled to a stop. Birger got out of the car, walked over, and looked in the window of the other car. "Where's Mrs. Price?" he said.

"We killed her and threw her down a mine shaft," Ritter replied.

"You're nuts," Birger said. He thought a moment. "Turn around. "We've got to go back. We've got to get rid of 'Slim' now."

Both cars were driven back to the barbecue stand. Because he had remained in the car, the informant did not see the subsequent shooting of Price inside the building.

On the way back to Harrisburg from Washington County, Birger admitted he had made a lot of mistakes in his life but that "this is the worst." In that dark moment, he also observed, prophetically for him, at least, that Art Newman and Connie Ritter were "going to get us all hung."

On January 8, Freddie Wooten took the stand. Although, for the most part, his testimony matched Newman's, there were important differences. To his knowledge, Boswell had not informed Birger that Price had written letters to C. E. Holles, the president of the Pocahontas bank. As best he could recall, the man who had allegedly written those letters was someone named Newell—nor did he remember Boswell being at the County Line roadhouse the night of April 12, 1926, as Newman had previously stated. While admitting he was ignorant of many details to which Newman and others were privy, Wooten said he had no personal knowledge of Boswell's participation in Birger gang activities. As a matter of fact, he hardly knew the former state's attorney at all.

Following the testimony of Riley Simmons, Roy Browning recommended that the court sentence the defendants to life imprisonment for the murder of Ethel Price, fifty-seven years for conspiracy to murder Ethel Price, and fifty-seven years for conspiracy to murder Lory Price. Browning hastened to add that he was reserving the Lory Price murder case as a sort of lever to use against the defendants if they did not fully testify in clearing up the unsolved crimes remaining. He could always reinstate it and ask for the death penalty. If he had asked for the death penalty in the present case and been successful, there would be no one to use as witnesses against Ritter and Blue if ever they were apprehended. To blunt the criticism sure to come his way for not seeking the ultimate penalty, he pointed out that none of the defendants could be released from the penitentiary in less than fifty-eight years.

Although he believed the defendants deserved to hang, Judge D. T. Hartwell agreed with the recommendations of the state's attorney, but for reflection "and the good of your consciences if you have any," he ruled that on each anniversary of the Price murders, the men were to be placed in solitary confinement for five days.

Simmons was returned to Leavenworth, where he was serving a sentence for counterfeiting. Newman and Wooten were taken to Greenville, in Bond County, where they pleaded guilty to robbing the Bond County National Bank at Pocahontas. The indeterminate sentences meted out to them by the judge merited little space in most Illinois newspapers.

# 33
# The Mystery of the Destruction of Shady Rest

ANOTHER TRIAL WAS COVERED AT LENGTH BY THE PRESS. WHEN the United States District Court convened in the Federal Building in East St. Louis on January 21, 1929, those under indictment for conspiring with gangsters to violate the Volstead Act included former Williamson County Coroner George Bell, former Marion police chief Thomas Boyd, former Johnston City police chief Hezzie Byrn, and a bootlegger from Colp, one Pete Salmo. However, most of the attention was focused on the fifth defendant, former Williamson County State's Attorney Arlie O. Boswell.

Listening to the charges leveled against him, Boswell could only reflect on the irony of it all. Only a few months earlier he had been mentioned as a possible choice for district attorney of eastern Illinois. Now he chewed his cigar and listened as district attorney Harold G. Baker called witness after witness. Noting Boswell's usually buoyant mood during the proceedings, reporters took delight in such witticisms as "I'm as much at home at a hanging as at a ballroom." That little jewel got wide circulation.

Among the sixty-three testifying for the prosecution was that veteran "songbird" Art Newman. Both he and Connie Ritter were at one time or another collectors for Boswell, he said. Their predecessor had been Charles "Chink" Shaffer, who had since disappeared. (Wanted for the murder of Ezra Fowler at Halfway in July of 1923, Shaffer was finally located in Ely, Nevada, on October 3, 1929. The elusive "Chink," after being released on bond and awaiting extradition, once again vanished. He was a close friend of Judge Hartwell, who more than once urged Boswell not to prosecute "Chink," despite the murder charge lodged against him. Fastidious, personable, in all a most unlikely gunman, Shaffer avoided recapture and, presumably, remained a free man for the rest of his life.)

Meeting with gang members on April 12, 1926, at the County Line roadhouse north of Johnston City, Boswell had ordered them to "shoot hell out of Herrin" the next day, Newman said, repeating the story he had told at his own trial two weeks earlier. Again he told of the chiding Boswell gave him and the others for killing Harland Ford instead of his brother John.

Attorney Harold Baker called John Ford to the stand. The one-time Klan leader said he had warned the state's attorney the day before the riot that trouble was imminent and that he should call out the militia. Not only was no action taken, but Boswell was out of the county on Election Day, Ford said. When he returned that night, six people were dead, among them Harland Ford.

After the memory of the shooting faded away, John Ford compiled a list of 484 witnesses and turned the list over to Assistant State's Attorney C. Ray Smith. The list disappeared, he continued, but luckily he kept a carbon copy. Upon learning that this copy was in Ford's lockbox in Herrin, Judge Walter G. Lindley ordered the witness to return to Herrin, get the list, and return to East St. Louis the following morning.

Following John Ford's revelations, there was speculation that the election riots of 1926 would be investigated by a federal grand jury. But that did not occur.

No stranger to the witness stand, Harvey Dungey recalled how Boswell, Birger, and Newman had threatened him with death if he did not testify against the Sheltons at the trial in Quincy. Not one to bear a grudge, however, the witness found himself one of a joyriding threesome on the day Joe Adams was shot, the other passengers being Birger and Boswell.

Later, when questioned about the incident, Boswell said he and

Maurice Potter were having supper in the B. B. Tea Room when Birger swaggered in, bearing the intriguing information that someone had been killed in West City. Following the meal, Boswell, accompanied by Birger, went to his office to place a phone call to Sheriff Pritchard.

Oren Coleman testified that the gangsters often visited Boswell in his office and that bootleggers were customarily fined on one count while the other counts against them were dismissed. For these reasons he had failed to support Boswell in the campaign, something that rankled the man now on trial.

Perhaps the single most damaging piece of evidence was offered by a banker who said that during his four-year term of office, Boswell had deposited $87,000. In reply, the former state's attorney said that the sum consisted of fines, fees, and forfeitures he had collected, plus salary and business profits. In other words, the county's money and his own money were commingled in the same account. Because he had the receipts showing which was which, he had given the matter little thought—so little, in fact, that he forgot to inform the banker. That, he admits was a very foolish mistake.

The jury apparently thought it went farther than that, because a week later, Boswell was fined $5,000 and sentenced to two years in prison. (On April 11, 1930, while in the federal penitentiary at Alderson, West Virginia, after being moved from Leavenworth for his own protection, Boswell was disbarred.) With the exception of Boyd, all those tried were found guilty.

Four members of that jury were among those impaneled to hear similar charges lodged against other Williamson County officials a few days later, the most prominent being Herrin mayor Marshall McCormick, the man who, perhaps more than any other, was responsible for getting the Sheltons out of Herrin. Largely on the testimony of the water superintendent, who turned state's evidence, the mayor, his brother Elmer, and police chief John Stamm were found guilty on February 15 of conspiring with bootleggers to violate liquor laws; a week later, they were sentenced to Leavenworth.

The mayor, who received the stiffest sentence of two years in prison and a fine of $3,000, had not helped his cause by admitting he once gave an elaborate corkscrew to a group of salesmen attending a convention in his city, although he repeatedly denied telling the fun lovers that his town was "wide open," as the government charged. Like Boswell, McCormick was a onetime ally of S. Glenn Young, the man hired to save Williamson County from the law violators.

Despite the trials and the various sentences handed down, several mysteries remained. Some would never be solved. One of the most intriguing concerned the destruction of Shady Rest. What really happened?

At first, a story made the rounds that the Sheltons had put a tank on the back of a truck, filled the tank with gasoline, and parked the truck in the woods so that the gasoline ran down a convenient ditch toward the cabin. When the cabin's perimeter was sufficiently soaked, a tossed match made ashes of Birger's dream. Those who fled the inferno were systematically machine-gunned—their bodies tossed into the flames.

One who saw the gangsters take Price into the barbecue stand the night of the killing distinctly recalls hearing Birger say he wanted to show Lory the damage he had done. Price, of course, protested his innocence. The kidnappings and murders, coming as they did shortly after the destruction of Shady Rest, led many to believe that the patrolman did, indeed, play a role in the affair.

If he did—and there is no evidence of it—it was only at the prompting of Birger and certain of his gang. Harry Thomasson was right in believing Birger himself was responsible for the death of his brother Elmo and the others. But why and how did he do it?

With the possible exception of Mrs. George, all those killed were burdened with an excess of information about the gang and its activities. Lena George, they had reason to believe, had learned from Steve too much for her good and for their peace of mind.

The other three had either participated in or witnessed murders. According to the testimony of Eural Gowan at the Worsham trial, Steve George and Ward "Casey" Jones machine-gunned to death Lyle "Shag" Worsham. George and Harvey Dungey carried the body into the farmhouse while Birger poured the gasoline. (Testifying at the same trial, Clarence Rone said that George poured the gasoline around the house and that Birger lit the match.)

Steve George and another man were convicted of robbing Hosea Parks's store at Rudement. The case went to the Illinois Supreme

Court, but on October 28, 1926, that august body upheld the ruling of the lower court. Out on bail, compliments of Charlie Birger, this murderous fellow with the solid gold teeth would soon have to begin serving his prison term. Not particularly bright, Steve George would easily be induced to tell inquiring authorities anything they wanted to know—or so Birger felt. He did not intend to let this henchman serve one day behind bars.

According to the testimony of Rado Millich, Bert Owens witnessed the killing of Ward "Casey" Jones. Millich further testified that Owens and Jones were planning to kill him at the time, but when the shooting began, Owens fled. According to the testimony of Eural Gowan, Owens was present when Worsham was killed. (It should be pointed out that his presence was not confirmed by Clarence Rone.) It is known that Owens was afraid for his life; once in Harrisburg, the young man panicked when a relative entered his room unannounced.

For Elmo Thomasson, it was more than enough that he had helped kill Joe Adams.

The Sheltons' attempt to bomb the place from the air, clever as it was unsuccessful, would, Birger felt, draw the blame to them once the cabin was destroyed. The bodies found within would be four more casualties of the gang war, four more notches in the guns of his enemies. With the press clamoring daily for his arrest in the Adams killing, Birger thought it expedient to eliminate a few potential witnesses and let the Sheltons take the blame.

How was the deed accomplished? On that bone-chilling morning of January 9, 1927, one of Birger's men drove his car a short distance from the cabin. He fully intended to do some rabbit hunting but discovered his car wasn't running right. Despite the bitter cold, he crawled under it to see what might be the problem, and while tinkering out of sight, he heard another car pull in. Out stepped two boys carrying what appeared to be two five-gallon cans of gasoline.

From his vantage point beneath the automobile, the amateur mechanic heard Connie Ritter tell the boys to "tote" the cans to the basement. Then he heard Ritter say something that further chilled his bones. Under the pretense that Steve had been wounded in a robbery, Mrs. George was to be spirited from Harrisburg to Shady Rest that night. The rest could be figured out easily enough.

The man under the car and Steve had been good friends. In fact, his own connection with the Birger gang had evolved from associating with the accomplished gunman, dedicated dope pusher, and sometime coal miner.

Sudden death, either from the bullets of rival gangsters or at the hands of supposed friends, was a fact of life and death for men of their caliber. So said another old-timer, Charles "Blackie" Harris, during an interview at the minimum security prison at Vienna, Illinois. "Remember," said that most grandfatherly of convicts, "your best friend today can be your worst enemy tomorrow."

Inured as he was to the death of a friend, the eavesdropping gangster could not bring himself to accept the fate of Mrs. George, who, as far as he knew, had detached herself from the darker side of her husband's life. (While it is doubtful that Lena George had never visited the cabin prior to the night of her death, as reported in the *Daily Register*, it may very well be that the two were estranged and contemplating divorce, as the newspaper indicated.)

When it became safe to do so, the man crawled out from under the car and drove to West Frankfort, there to be tortured by the knowledge of what was to come. Unwilling to play the hero, he was plagued with a sense of utter helplessness.

"But what could I do?" he recalled more than a half century later, adding, "after all, I had one foot in the grave myself." So he did nothing until it was too late.

That night, something—perhaps some twinge of heroism or perhaps only morbid curiosity—drew him back to Williamson County. While checking his car at a filling station on the outskirts of Marion, he saw two familiar automobiles go past. One was Birger's; the other was Newman's.

Although it continued to give him trouble, he managed to get the car started and drove east. When he pulled into the half-moon driveway in front of the barbecue stand, he saw men down at the cabin scurrying around "like a bunch of bugs." Thinking back, he felt he must have arrived just after the killings but before the explosions and fire. By morning, Williamson County's most notorious roadhouse would be in ruins, and in those ruins would be found four charred bodies.

However, morning was a world away for the one who watched from the drive, and even then, one of the cars was coming his way.

He had been seen. He turned east at the hardroad and drove hard, soon nearing the curve just west of Shady Rest, where he turned left onto the gravel road that joins Route 45 at Stonefort. Needless to say, dawn came as a particular gift to him later that morning in his West Frankfort apartment.

Having driven his "jalopy" into an orchestrated nightmare, he had peered into the abyss that is the human heart at its worst and had fled, finally losing the headlights behind him. For the moment, danger had passed, but one foot still remained in the grave.

Sleep being impossible, he thought back. At first only a Saline County coal miner whose habit it was to stop by Birger's joint in Ledford, he had watched the friendly bootlegger evolve into a gang leader with a will of steel. This hardening of character he blamed on Birger's partnership with the Sheltons, that clever threesome with Florida connections.

Meanwhile, at the urging of fellow miner Steve George, he "hooked up" with the Birger gang, serving both as Birger's bodyguard and collector for his whorehouses and slot machines. For some reason, perhaps only his friendship with George, he soon began to realize that his boss no longer trusted him, and he began to fear for his life. Once while driving Birger to Dowell for a rendezvous with a lady friend, he managed to have a sawed-off shotgun draped across his lap. One finger was not quite on the trigger, nor were the twin barrels quite pointed at the gang leader's midsection, but the message was clear.

"Why not drive with both hands?" urged Birger, his eyes glued to the gun.

"No," came the reply, "I drive better this way."

A wiser man would have quit the gang at that point, being careful to put half a continent between himself and those who, mistakenly or otherwise, doubted his loyalty. Instead this man found himself in West Frankfort exhausted and badly shaken.

There was a knock on his door later that day. Although Connie Ritter seemed friendly enough, he asked too many questions about the night before.

"Connie," he said at last, "all I saw was some Ku Klux Klansmen pouring gasoline. That's all."

Far from satisfied with his answer, Ritter suggested that they take a drive to talk over a few things.

"No," came the suspect's weary reply, "I can read what's on your mind."

There was another onlooker that night, a man who in days or weeks following would be interviewed by a reporter from the *Marion Evening Post*. Although proof is missing, it is suspected that this man was Jack Crews, who was accused by Steve George of spying and whom George threatened to kill, according to Lory Price. Using the information from other sources as well as that of this eyewitness, the reporter was able to present a convincing account of the unfolding tragedy. (The careful reader will notice that the following account mentions the gangsters arriving at Shady Rest in one car; the version given earlier had two cars arriving at the scene, Birger's and Newman's. That point aside, the two accounts dovetail very well.)

Birger, Ritter, and Newman arrived around eleven o'clock. While the drunken Ritter waited in the car, Newman and Birger got out. They were armed. "The stranger," meanwhile, had either slipped out of the cabin after the car pulled in or just after the shooting began.

Whenever and however his exit, he watched as death unfurled her tapestry. First to fall was Steve George, who was shot down by Newman. Elmo Thomasson was shot next, as he cowered by the east wall.

Mrs. George, who had been lured to the cabin that afternoon and who was knitting when the killers arrived, was shot point blank. Either Birger or Newman then ordered Bert Owens to take the stick of dynamite that served as a memento of the bungled bombing attempt by the Sheltons and blow up the power plant. Having obliged in this, providing the "jar" noticed by Lory Price as he drank his coffee some miles away, Owens started back, only to be shot down sixty feet away from the cabin's front porch. His body was thrown through the front door of the east room.

Mercy was shown to frail Clarence Rone, who lay drunk in a corner of the west room. He was escorted to the car. Empty of weapons—guns from the place had been taken to Harrisburg earlier that afternoon—and littered with bodies, Birger's masterpiece of revelry was doused with gasoline and set afire.

While driving first toward Harrisburg, the gangsters changed their minds, turned around, and drove back toward Marion and points west. Birger, so the account goes, spent the night at Dowell in the arms of his lady friend while Newman and Ritter drove on to Belleville.

On Sunday afternoon, the Newmans, Ritter, Ollie Potts, and Clarence Rone returned to inspect the ruins and to shake their heads for the benefit of sightseers. Inspecting the damage earlier in the day, Charlie Birger had sworn vengeance on the Sheltons for doing such a deed.

Several months later in a restaurant in Bay St. Louis, Mississippi, a man struck up a conversation with a woman from Hardin County, Illinois. "Southern Illinois!" he said enthusiastically. "That's where Charlie Birger's gang was." Clearly, he was eager for news of the area and the gang. The man's name, she was surprised to learn from the proprietor, was Connie Ritter. She was even more surprised to learn that the fugitive was well known along the coast.

Too well known, as it turned out, because on October 18, 1929, the once dapper gangster was captured in nearby Gulfport, Mississippi. In his nearly two and a half years on the run, Ritter had seen much of the South. Once he had barely eluded authorities, when they raided a nightclub in San Antonio, Texas. Now it was over.

After pleading guilty before Judge Miller at Benton, he was sentenced to life imprisonment. The term was to be served at Menard, where so many of his former friends were in residence.

# 34
# "If It Hadn't Been . . ."

**M**OST OF THE GANG WERE TO SURVIVE THEIR YEARS IN PRISON. Beginning in 1941 with the release of Eural Gowan and ending with the departure of Riley Simmons in September 1953, they one by one stepped out of confinement into obscurity. However, for the one who had joined the gang with a shrug of his shoulders and a "why not" grin, fate was to exact the last drop of retribution. On January 4, 1948, Connie Ritter died at Menard.

Less than three months earlier, Carl Shelton had fallen before enemy bullets while driving a jeep on a country road in Wayne County. Mortally wounded, he staggered to a ditch, where he died after firing his .44 several times at those who had fired a machine gun, a rifle, and a revolver from a car that was half hidden by underbrush. Watching it all, first from a truck, then from a ditch, were his nephew, "Little Earl" Shelton, and Ray Walker, a Shelton ally for twenty years. It was their testimony that revealed Charles "Blackie" Harris as the prime suspect in the killing. Harris, himself a former Shelton gangster—now the unofficial leader of a group of local farmers who resented the Shelton efforts to try to strong-arm them into paying a toll on the grain they took to market—was a former inmate of Leavenworth. His underworld connections included Frank "Buster" Wortman—a onetime Shelton gangster and alumnus of Leavenworth—who in 1947 was the most powerful racket figure in and around East St. Louis. Wortman had ties with "the Syndicate" in Chicago; the syndicate was deeply interested in the Sheltons' Peoria-based gambling empire and its swath of territory extending from Peoria to fabled Cairo at the southern tip of Illinois.

Unlike his rival Birger, Carl Shelton left this planet a wealthy man, having raked in millions from gambling in East St. Louis before he was chased out of that city and out of St. Clair County by Sheriff Jerome Munie. Hardly missing a beat, he moved the operation north to Peoria, where the political climate was more hospitable. The "take" was from slot machines and jukeboxes, from a cut in the nightly haul of casinos in downtown Peoria, and from local officials up and down the state who profited from such activities. Carl, careful to keep the circle complete, doled out a percentage of the profit to other, more powerful officials in Springfield. It was a well-oiled operation, one worthy of the attention of big city gangsters. After the mob's proposal of a partnership was rejected, underworld rumor had it that sizable bounties were placed on the heads of Carl and Bernie Shelton.

On July 26, 1948, Bernie was killed by an unknown assailant outside his tavern in Peoria. Another brother, Roy, was ambushed and killed on June 7, 1950, while driving a tractor on his Wayne County farm. Earl, "number three," the one Art Newman and Freddie Wooten had such a good time trying to kill back in "the good old days," moved to Florida in the early 1950s, along with most of his family after an attempt was made on his life. He was shrewder than his brothers were. He had quit the rackets in the late 1930s, after serving a short prison term in Atlanta on a liquor violation, and had returned to Illinois, where he became a successful farmer. In Florida, he was even more successful when his real estate investments paid off handsomely.

One day in the early 1950s, Jesse Cremer was having lunch at the Dinner Bell Café in West Frankfort, when in walked Harry Thomasson—he had been released on January 23, 1951—and two fairly rough looking fellows. Not liking the looks of the strangers, Cremer slipped away as soon as possible. About a year or so later, Thomasson was killed in an automobile accident.

A very difficult quarter of a century brought some changes to the former "number two man" of the Birger gang. One story has it that Art Newman even kept a cat in his cell to sample his food lest some of it be poisoned. A pariah among former gang members because of his penchant for "spilling his guts to save his own hide," Newman was finally moved to Stateville Penitentiary in Joliet, but his reputation followed him, and the death threats continued. He became interested in horticulture and was made chief attendant of the prison's flower beds. At the time of his release in 1953, the former gangster said he intended to raise flowers commercially in California. In 1979, he was living in Arizona.

Newman's legacy lives on in Illinois. Despite the interval of a half century, Arlie O. Boswell had not forgotten or forgiven. "I don't think anybody ever heard me make the statement that I would kill him . . . [but] . . . if that guy Newman were to walk in this door right now, one or the other of us would get killed."

Concerning his own role in the Birger era, the elderly Boswell still clung to the position that he was a fearless, often shot at young prosecutor whose enemies included not only gangsters like Newman but also important political figures such as Congresswoman Ruth Hanna McCormick and Mable Walker Willebrandt, the assistant attorney general in charge of Prohibition enforcement. Another enemy was Oren Coleman, a onetime sheriff of Williamson County.

At times, Boswell's own candor was as damaging as the gangsters' bullets or the politicians' outrage. Remarks he made to that crack reporter John Rogers to the effect that Prohibition was unenforceable began, he believed, the chain of events that led to his seventeen months imprisonment.

It was unlucky for him that some of those with whom he served a part of those seventeen months were men he had prosecuted in Williamson County. Too well they remembered. Despite having his throat cut in Leavenworth by "Blackie" Armes and Riley "Alabama" Simmons—"like peas in a pod they were," said Charlie Harris—and despite a severe beating there, one that left him with broken jaws and unable to eat anything tougher than soup for a time, Boswell survived his relatively short stay behind bars. Upon his release, he moved to Michigan and there was admitted to the Bar. When he again became an Illinois resident, he was readmitted to the Illinois Bar. By this time, he was also an alcoholic. In later years, if he happened to be on a drunk prior to an important case, Boswell would instruct the Saline County sheriff to lock him up until he sobered up. He usually won the case. After much effort and agony, he finally won his battle against alcoholism but admitted that one drink would undo what years of abstinence had achieved.

White hair, a cane, a friendly smile, and the esteem of the community (Harrisburg) where he had practiced law so many years cannot erase a controversial past. When asked about questionable aspects of that past, the old lawyer had a tendency to answer with a speech, extolling his virtues and blasting his enemies—the latter a scheming lot, one was assured, but no longer a problem since most were dead. At times, however, his candor was revealing:

> I've probably bent over backwards the last few years to erase an image that I think a lot of people had of me, because I think a lot of people had the idea that I was a tough guy who would kill you at the drop of a hat. The funny thing is that I don't have to deny anything. My theory of life is you'll find out whether I'm a liar or whether I'm telling you the truth. Anybody I hate is a damn liar. I'll never forgive them for that. They can steal from me and I'll forgive them. But never a liar.

As to why Williamson County suffered more than its share of gangsters during his term there as state's attorney, Boswell placed much of the blame on Prohibition and the rest on a man brought to southern Illinois and Williamson County to make Prohibition work. "If it hadn't been for that damn Glenn Young," he said, bristling at the mention of the name, "I don't think anybody would have ever heard of Carl Shelton or Charlie Birger."

The best epitaph of Birger's career was left to W. V. Rathbone, the Harrisburg clothier from whom the gangster purchased much of his wardrobe. A small-town merchant with a taste for good literature, Rathbone was no born journalist, easily dashing off phrase after telling phrase, but it was he who covered Birger's hanging for the *Daily Register*. Part of what he wrote touched the man he and fellow businessmen had, in former days, called friend:

> As we stood in front of the bare, rough and unpainted scaffold, a symbol of its tragic purpose, we thought of the first time we had

talked with Birger. It was at his home on business of the moment, when, happening to remark about a large stein which sat on the mantle over his fireplace, such a stein as was once seen adorning the bars of the more pretentious saloons, he took it down and handed it to me and entered into a long discussion as to its beauty and worth. Painted on its sides in gorgeous colors were Arthur and Guinevere, and while he knew nothing of the gallant Arthurian knights, the bright colors and the little silver knight surmounting the lid with sword and shield held in brave attitude appealed to his ideals of beauty.

A vain, ignorant boy who never grew up, caring nothing for money but the excitement of earning it; jacketed in a steel vest and surrounded by enemies of his own making, demanding the adulation of the mob and seeking glory in the only way he knew how to gain it—a knight of another sort.

# BIBLIOGRAPHY

# INDEX

# Bibliography

## Books

Angle, Paul M. *Bloody Williamson*. New York: Alfred A. Knopf, 1952.

Galligan, George, and Jack Wilkinson. *In Bloody Williamson*. Oklahoma City: Leader Press, 1927.

Hill, E. Bishop. *Complete History of the Southern Illinois Gang War*. Harrisburg, IL: Hill Publishing Co., 1927.

*Illinois Reports*. Vols. 323, 324, 329, 332. Bloomington, IL, 1927, 1928, and 1929.

*Life and Exploits of S. Glenn Young*. Published by Mrs. S. Glenn Young, Herrin, IL, 1925.

Martin, John Bartlow. *Butcher's Dozen and Other Murders*. New York: Harper, 1950.

O'Shea, Margaret. *Oldham Paisley: A Community Editor*. Marion Daily Republican, 1974.

## Pamphlets and Broadsides

Kern, Fred J. *The Bark of the Automatics*. Belleville News Democrat, n.d.

———. *The Bright Star of Hope is Shimmering and Shining over Herrin* (Broadside). Belleville News Democrat, n.d.

*The Life Story of Charles Birger*. Marion, IL: Illinois Book Co., 1927.

Small, Curtis G. *Mean Old Jail*. Harrisburg, IL, 1970.

Trovillion, Hal K. *KKK Experiment in Journalism*. Herrin News, n.d.

———. *Persuading God Back to Herrin*. Herrin News, 1925.

## Magazine Articles

"The Birger Gang Brought to Bay." *Literary Digest*, Aug. 20, 1927.

"Bloody Herrin Again." *Literary Digest*, Sept. 13, 1924.

"Charlie Birger, Southern Illinois' Very Own Gangster" by Gary DeNeal. *Outdoor Illinois*, Aug.–Nov. 1976.

"Egypt" by W. A. S. Douglas. *American Mercury*, Nov. 1927.

"Gunfire Lays Low One More Shelton." *Life Magazine*, June 19, 1950.

"Gunplay and Sudden Death in Herrin." *Literary Digest*, Feb. 21, 1925.

"Herrin's Wet and Dry War." *Literary Digest*, Feb. 23, 1924.

"The Mystery Couple in the Ford Coupe" by Gary DeNeal. *Springhouse*, Dec. 1984.

"The Reformation of Herrin." *Literary Digest*, Aug. 1, 1925.

"Robin Hood Is Hanged" by W. A. S. Douglas. *American Mercury*, Aug. 1928.

"Terror in Southern Illinois" by Harry B. Wilson. *Esquire*, Feb. 1951.

"Terror's End" by Paul Havens. *Master Detective*, Nov. 1942.

"They All Talk to Rogers" by Richard Owen Boyer. *Plain Talk*, Sept. 1930.

"War for a Brunette" by Robert Lincoln. *Inside Detective*, Feb. 1948.

## Newspapers: Special Articles

Alexander, E. Roy. "Inside Stories of the Southern Illinois Gang War as Told by Charlie Birger's Lieutenant, 'Art' Newman." *St. Louis Post-Dispatch*, Jan. 31–Feb. 9, 1927. (Note: Much of the writing of this noteworthy series was done by Sam O'Neal and John Rogers, both reporters for the *St. Louis Post-Dispatch*.)

Butler, Homer. "Glances at Life." *Marion Daily Republican*, Dec. 3, 1977.

Forshey, Guy. "Doom Sounds for Illinois When Birger Henchman Chorus." *St. Louis Post-Dispatch*, Aug. 14, 1927.

Givens, Charles. "Herrin Area a Battleground for Feudists Since Days of Shawnees." *Sunday Star* (Washington, D.C.), Nov. 28, 1926.

Gruver, Marcia M. "The Birger Gang in Bond County." *Greenville Advocate*, Aug. 18–Sept. 29, 1977.

Kleinmann, Julius. "The Sympathetic Hangman Explains His Technique." *St. Louis Post-Dispatch*, Feb. 20, 1927.

Terry, Dickson. (Series on the Shelton Brothers). *St. Louis Post-Dispatch*, Nov. 24, 1947.

## Unpublished Sources

Hahesy, Edmund C. "The Newspaper Editor and Community Conflict: Williamson County, Illinois: 1922–1928." (Master's Thesis). Dept. of Journalism, Southern Illinois University, 1956.
McCormick, Michael R. "A Political Study of Williamson County, Illinois, in the Early Twentieth Century." (Master's Thesis). Dept. of History, Southern Illinois University, 1972.

## Diaries, Journals, and Scrapbooks

DeNeal, Gary. Personal Journal, 1975–1980.
Gustin, Alpheus. Diary, 1923–1928.
Oldham Paisley Scrapbooks. Marion Public Library, Marion, IL.

## Special Collections

The Paul M. Angle Papers. Chicago Historical Library.
Illinois State Archives.
The Gov. Len Small Papers. Illinois State Historical Library.

## Government Records

Birger, Charles. Pension Record, National Archives.
Muster Roll. 13th United States Cavalry Troop G, June 3–July 25, 1902.

## County Records

County records were researched in the following county seats in Illinois: Belleville (St. Clair County); Benton (Franklin County); Carlinville (Macoupin County); Edwardsville (Madison County); Harrisburg (Saline County); and Marion (Williamson County).

Also, useful information was found in the courthouse at Clayton, MO, county seat of St. Louis County.

## Libraries

The following libraries also proved useful in the research: Belleville Public Library; Chicago Historical Society Library; Harrisburg Public Library; Illinois State Historical Library (Springfield); Marion Public Library; Morris Library, Southern Illinois University at Carbondale; St. Louis Public Library; Shawnee Library System (Carterville); Southeastern Illinois College Library (Harrisburg).

Also helpful were the libraries of the Saline County Historical Society (Harrisburg); the West Frankfort Area Historical Society; and the Williamson County Historical Society (Marion).

## Newspapers

*Baltimore Evening Sun*
*Belleville News Advocate*
*Belleville News Democrat*
*Benton Evening News*
*Carterville Herald*
*Chicago Sun Times*
*Chicago Tribune*
*Daily American* (West Frankfort)
*Daily Register* (Harrisburg)
*Danville Commercial News*
*East St. Louis Daily Journal*
*Edwardsville Intelligencer*
*Eldorado Daily Journal*
*Evansville Press*
*Gallatin Democrat* (Shawneetown)
*Hardin County Independent*
*Herrin Daily Journal*
*Herrin Herald*
*Herrin News*
*Illinois State Journal* (Springfield)
*Marion Daily Republican*
*Marion Evening Post*
*Marion Weekly Leader* (weekly edition of *Marion Daily Republican*)
*Metropolis Herald*
*St. Louis Globe Democrat*
*St. Louis Post-Dispatch*
*St. Louis Star*
*Wayne County Press*
*Zeigler News*

# Index

**Gary DeNeal** is the publisher and editor of *Springhouse*. He has lived in southern Illinois all his life.

Shawnee Classics: A Series of Classic Regional Reprints for the Midwest